A DIRTY YEAR

A DIRTY YEAR

*SEX, SUFFRAGE, AND SCANDAL IN
GILDED AGE NEW YORK*

BILL GREER

Published by Chicago Review Press Incorporated
814 North Franklin Street
Chicago, Illinois 60610
ISBN 978-1-64160-251-8

Library of Congress Control Number:2019955655

Interior design: Nord Compo

Printed in the United States of America
5 4 3 2 1

CONTENTS

Part I: The New Year, 1872

Part II: Winter

Part III: Spring

Part IV: Summer

Part V: Autumn

Part VI: The New Year, 1873

I

THE NEW YEAR, 1872

Temptations Facing Young Men.
James D. McCabe Jr., Lights and Shadows of New York Life;
or the Sights and Sensations of The Great City, *1872*

1 | STATE OF THE CITY

AS THE NEW YEAR OPENED, a love triangle splashed across the front page of the *New York Times*. The *Times* liked to sneer down its long Republican nose at the *Herald* for advertising smut dealers and quack doctors, to berate flash rags like the *Day's Doings* for publishing little better than obscenity. But the editors recognized a juicy scandal walking through the door, and they knew scandal sold papers.

The lovers were no strangers to New Yorkers. Jim Fisk had spent the last four years stealing the Erie Railroad, cornering gold, and cavorting in licentious pleasures. In the swindle to take over the Erie, he and his partner, Jay Gould, outwitted two of Wall Street's titans, "the Great Bear" Daniel Drew and "Commodore" Cornelius Vanderbilt. They bilked other investors of millions. The collapse of their gold ring bankrupted brokers across the country and came within a hair's breadth of corrupting President Ulysses S. Grant.

Fisk reveled in his notoriety, gallivanting around town in a carriage with high-stepping horses and four liveried footmen, who unfurled a purple-and-gold carpet for him to descend on. He wore gaudy suits, a nugget of a diamond on his chest, and actresses on his arm. He didn't mind being insulted so long as he wasn't ignored. For all the business rivals and society matrons he offended, he had countless friends and admirers, people cheered by his rags-to-riches tale and the exuberant joy with which he paraded through the city.

One of the actresses on his arm was Josie Mansfield. Penniless and divorced by nineteen, Mansfield maneuvered into Fisk's path at Annie Wood's bordello wearing the only dress in her wardrobe. She possessed other assets, however: eyes deep and bright; pearly skin that flushed pink with pleasure; purple-black hair piled in massive coils; a full, dashing figure. Fisk was captivated. The voluptuous beauty now resided in the Twenty-Third Street brownstone he bought, furnished, and frescoed for her. The house was steps from his own. At the corner with Eighth Avenue sat the Grand Opera House, where Fisk had moved the Erie into opulent offices; where he staged theatricals featuring beautiful blondes, ravishing brunettes, and the Demon Can-Can; and where Mansfield entertained in her private box. Rear passageways connecting the properties allowed Fisk to move freely between business and pleasure.

One evening two years past, Fisk invited his friend Ned Stokes to dine at Mansfield's table. Stokes had grown up with all the advantages in life. But a taste for women, horses, and gambling, along with a poor head for business, drove him to hard times. He'd bankrupted the Brooklyn Refinery Company his mother funded. Fisk, generous to a fault and relying on the refinery for the Erie's oil, had bailed him out.

At that dinner two years ago, Stokes had charmed Mansfield. He was a younger man, athletic in build, outfitted in the latest fashion, and sparkling with diamonds. Their affair proceeded for several weeks before Fisk discovered it. Infatuated as Fisk was, he'd asked Stokes to step aside. Stokes scoffed. Fisk worked on Mansfield. Refusing to choose, she would have her cake and eat it too. Soon charges of libel and blackmail and embezzlement flew within the triangle, suits were filed and counterfiled, papers served, lovers indicted, arrested, and bailed out of jail.

As 1872 opened, it was old news. What warranted six columns across the *Times* was the bullet that settled the lovers' disputes out of court.

The shooting occupied another six columns the next day. A reader tiring of the coverage could flip the paper to the backside, page 8, and find the news from Washington. Twelve lines buried within announced "the grand entrée" of the season in the nation's capital, the convention of "the Woodhull and Claflin wing of the Woman Suffrage organization." Not satisfied naming the group after the two sisters who were sure to inflame passions, the editors added that when the Boston wing met in Washington earlier, Woodhull had laughed at them for being dull and promised a livelier gathering.

A feud among the liberal ladies promoting the vote had been festering for years. After the Civil War, suffragists united behind the banner of the American Equal Rights Association (AERA). But in 1869, a rift pitted black suffrage against women's. Though the AERA advocated for both, what became known as the Boston wing placed the higher priority on the black vote through the Fifteenth Amendment, which was advancing toward ratification. The New York faction, led by Elizabeth Cady Stanton and Susan B. Anthony, argued for women first. The debate devolved into a bitter exchange between Stanton and Frederick Douglass, who had escaped slavery and become the nation's most prominent black man. Stanton wondered how American statesmen could make their wives and mothers the political inferiors of unlettered and unwashed ditchdiggers and bootblacks fresh off the plantations—Patrick and Sambo, she said, didn't know the difference between a monarchy and a republic and couldn't read the Declaration of Independence or Webster's spelling book. Douglass didn't take well to being called Sambo, nor did he think white women had endured being hunted like wild beasts, torn from their homes, hanged by infuriated mobs, or forced to witness to their babies' brains dashed out against a lamppost. Let women suffer such horrors, he said. Then he would admit to an equal urgency for them.

Midway through the AERA convention in May 1869, the *Times* reported the female suffrage agitators proposed to "throw the Negro overboard and advocate only for women." By then not even the great conciliator, the Reverend Henry Ward Beecher, who for so long had fought for the rights of both groups, could heal the wounds. Two days after the meeting adjourned, Stanton and Anthony led disgruntled members out of the Equal Rights organization to establish the National Woman Suffrage Association (NWSA), labeled the New York wing despite rather muddled geography. Before 1869 ended, the AERA disintegrated and the Boston contingent formed the rival American Woman Suffrage Association (AWSA) with Beecher at its head. The rift extended into Beecher's family, for two generations one of the most prominent in American theology. Younger sister Isabella Beecher Hooker became a leading figure in the New York–based organization. Older sister Harriett Beecher Stowe sat on the fence. Eldest sister Catharine Beecher repudiated the very idea of women voting.

Despite the *Times* using their names to stir the cauldron, Victoria Woodhull and Tennessee Claflin played no role in this conflict beyond Woodhull watching the proceedings from the back benches. The sisters had been leading a nomadic life as spiritual healers and clairvoyants in 1867 when a spirit's guiding hand propelled them to New York—to seek "fatherly care and kindness," the spirit advised, as it led them to a home on Washington Square. Behind its door lived the richest man in America, Cornelius Vanderbilt.

Vanderbilt was no fool even if Jim Fisk had bested him in the Erie Railroad takeover. He was a shrewd judge of character. These ladies were sophisticated and savvy. Though he wouldn't spare a penny for a beggar, he generously helped those who helped themselves. While the suffragists warred on one another, he took the sisters under his wing. Victoria tended his spiritual needs, which included communing with his dead mother. Tennie serviced his desires of the flesh. Meanwhile, Vanderbilt tutored his new friends in the ways of Wall Street.

As the gold corner engineered by Fisk and Gould collapsed on Black Friday, September 24, 1869, Woodhull put her learning to use. Parking her carriage outside the Gold Room on Broad Street, she surveyed the frenzy. While Vanderbilt poured $1 million into stocks to confine the panic, she speculated. Others lost their wits and their shirts when gold prices plunged. Woodhull's coffers overflowed. Her year-end tally measured the gains at $700,000.

Shortly thereafter, Vanderbilt signed a check to the sisters. Though the $7,000 was a paltry investment in the new brokerage firm of Woodhull, Claflin & Company, the association with the signer was invaluable on the Street—"the open sesame to its charmed precincts," Woodhull recalled. The *Herald* was the first to remark upon the two fashionably dressed ladies mingling among brokers, buying and selling thousands of shares in the principal stocks. The paper sent a reporter to the Hoffman House, where the ladies set up shop. His feature on the new Queens of Finance was subheaded VANDERBILT'S PROTÉGÉS. After commenting on the photograph of the Commodore peering from the wall, the *Herald* man noted rumors of other leading financiers supporting the firm. How else could the ladies have acquired their reported half million in capital?

Victoria Woodhull.
Photograph by Matthew Brady, Wikimedia Commons

Tennie Claflin.
National Archives and Records Administration

Prominent brokers and bankers were soon filing into the offices the firm opened on Broad Street. Carriages released ladies at the door, the wealthiest in the city, eager to deposit moneys for trading stocks and bonds. "A thorough-bred business woman" greeted prospective clients, who were perhaps more interested in Woodhull's financial acumen than were the papers, which devoted more space to her weight, estimated at 160 pounds; shoe size, appraised at number five; hair, observed as dressed with imported ox marrow; and shoulders, admired as alabaster. Visitors were not put off by the press's airing of the sisters' antecedents as clairvoyant doctresses advising on maladies of the heart and treating more physical ailments with electricity, magnetism, and other natural forces—not to mention a history of billing irregularities and patients hauled away in hearses.

More than one editor lauded the sisters' chutzpah. Horace Greeley's *Tribune* delivered its verdict with a slap at the suffragists: "We are so deafened with the demands for the unrestricted activities of women, so pestered with claims for the ballot and for office, that it is pleasant to see a woman do an unexpected and important thing, without iteration and reiteration of her right to do it, and of the injustice, the tyranny of Society in withholding her. . . . We commend [this] philosophy to the Woman's Rights Association and the Editors of the *Revolution*."

The *Revolution* noticed. In March 1870 its proprietor Susan B. Anthony walked through Woodhull and Claflin's door. A woman firm in Wall Street marked a new era, and she would see it for herself. Her assessment in the resulting article: instead of making shirts at fifty cents each, these two ladies were using their brains, energy, and knowledge of business to earn a livelihood.

Woodhull gave the suffragists ample opportunity to pay her attention. The first week of April, she made news with a letter to the *Herald*. "While others of my sex devoted themselves to a crusade against the laws that shackle the women of the country," she declared, "I asserted my individual independence; while others prayed for the good time coming, I worked for it; while others argued the equality of woman with man, I proved it. . . . I boldly entered the arena of politics and business and exercised the rights I already possessed. I therefore claim the right to speak for the unenfranchised women of the country. . . . I now announce my candidacy for the Presidency."

A month later the sisters launched a newspaper their patron Vanderbilt was underwriting. WOODHULL & CLAFLIN'S WEEKLY blared the banner. "This journal will support Victoria C. Woodhull for president . . . and will advocate suffrage without distinction of sex," read the defining editorial.

In May the *Revolution* commended Woodhull's run for the presidency and the new journal. The suffragists were nonetheless astounded when several months later Woodhull revolutionized their movement, and they welcomed her into their organization. For the upcoming suffrage convention in Washington, she was preparing an even bolder play.

A few days after the suffragists' "Woodhull and Claflin wing" closed its January convention, the *Times* headed a story Obscene Literature—A Filthy Depot in the Heart of the City—How the Morals of Our Youth Are Corrupted. From early morning to sunset, the story stated, youth of both sexes crowded a dirty and dingy newspaper store. A case at the door displayed vulgar and indecent photographs, stereoscopic views, and books. The *Times* called it a foretaste of the temptations inside. The proprietor, William Simpson, sold the foulest and most demoralizing literature and pictures. At good prices, the *Times* noted.

If the editors wanted to titillate readers of any age, they could hardly have done a nicer job. Nor could smut ads in the *Herald* or the *Day's Doings* promote the business better. The *Times* needn't print the name and location of the store. After a dozen years in business, the Great American Book, Stationery and Novelty Head-Quarters had built a wide reputation. At 57 Centre Street, the store was conveniently near the city's court-houses and the prison known as the Tombs—facilities with which Simpson was familiar.

A dogged fellow named Anthony Comstock had raised yet another ruckus over Simpson's business. To this point hardly anyone had heard of Comstock. Raised as a Connecticut farm boy, he'd moved to New York and over the past five years worked his way up in the dry goods business. He was now a salesman at Cochrane, McLean & Company on Broadway. Despite his success, dry goods was not his calling. Policing morals was. He had started down that path at the tender age of eighteen when he broke into a local gin mill, opened the taps, and drained all the liquor onto the floor. After Gettysburg, he'd enlisted. He raised his sword, though not against the rebels. His enemies were the vices of his fellow soldiers—liquor, tobacco, swearing, lust, breaking the Sabbath, and every other temptation the devil could conjure up. He didn't let himself off the hook for his own sins either, one of which involved wasting an hour reading a novel and another admiring "the moon lavishing upon the earth its purest crystal ray" before remembering Satan might be on the other side sending silvery rays from the pit of hell. He was likely the most hated soldier in the Union army. His getting out alive was nearly miracle enough for one to swallow his claim that God's hand steered him through life.

When Comstock arrived in New York, that hand steered him toward obscenity. In the summer of 1871, he learned that his friends' children had gotten hold of some filth. He traced the material to Simpson. For a dime a week, the smut dealer loaned obscene titles such as *Fanny Hill* and *The Lustful Turk* to young men and boys. To attract youth, Simpson advertised a good stock of baseball equipment. His wife handled the lending to girls who came into the shop. Appointing himself volunteer detective, Comstock secured Simpson's arrest, only to have the judge dispose of the matter with a fifty-dollar fine.

Awakened to the realities of New York justice under Tammany Hall, Comstock bided his time. Late in 1871 he discovered a ring of boys serving as Simpson's agents to circulate obscene books and prints in schools. Fathers had caught their ten- and twelve-year-olds lusting over the smut. Working with a captain from the Sixth Precinct, Comstock had Simpson arrested again. After posting $1,000 bail, Simpson went right back to business. He didn't fear the law, he declared, not with a member of the board of education helping him through these difficulties and his Tammany-connected landlord collecting forty-five-dollar-a-month rent, double the going rate. Still, he must have gotten nervous as his January 10 trial date approached. When the Court of General Sessions called his case, Simpson forfeited the bail. Rumor had him hiding out in Maine. Meanwhile a *Times* reporter discovered the doors open on Centre Street and Simpson's wife behind the counter.

One specimen of a loathsome business infesting the city, the *Times* editorialized. Active measures were expected shortly to stop it. Such an outcome sounded far-fetched to anyone who didn't know Anthony Comstock.

A few days earlier, the *Times* commented on a crime it considered even more abominable than obscenity. Thankfully two of the deed's most notorious practitioners, Thomas Evans and Jacob Rosenzweig, were residing in Sing Sing for the next seven years, the maximum sentence allowed under the law but nowhere near the punishment deserved, according to the *Times*.

Dr. Evans had operated a lying-in asylum across from city hall. Fifteen months earlier, in July 1870, a woman from Boston named Mary Geary sought the doctor's services when caught unexpectedly in the family way. The pills the doctor dispensed didn't produce the promised miscarriage. Geary suffered convulsions for several days before dying of her botched abortion. Police discovered the body—and several more women seeking abortions—in a squalid blood-streaked den. Hundreds of letters from troubled women across the country testified to the scope of Dr. Evans's business. The press dubbed the good doctor the Ghoul of Chatham Street.

Several months later, the baggage master at the Hudson River Railroad noticed an awful stench coming from a trunk checked for Chicago. He opened it. Crammed inside was the body of a nude woman, guessed to be eighteen. Her face was lovely. Golden hair lay upon her breast. No violence marred her skin, though decomposition around her pelvis hinted at her fate. "A new victim of man's lust, and of the life-destroying arts of those abortionists," concluded the *Times*. The police traced the body to Dr. Rosenzweig. The press tagged him the Fiend of Second Avenue and his crime the Trunk Case.

The abortionists of New York, estimated to number at least a hundred, were surely glad to see 1871 close. Early that year, a jury convicted Dr. Michael Wolff of killing a patient in another abortion gone bad. Over the summer, *Times* reporter Augustus St.

Clair went undercover and produced an exposé titled "The Evil of the Age," including covert interviews with Dr. Rosenzweig, Dr. Mariceau, and Madame Van Buskirk. St. Clair couldn't secure an interview with the most infamous of all, Madame Restell, known as the Wickedest Woman in New York, but he found plenty of space to recap her career, which spanned three decades in the abortion business. Days after Rosenzweig's trunk was discovered in August 1871, Madame Van Buskirk and her colleague Dr. Perry were charged with dumping a dying woman in Brooklyn. Police hauled in Ann Burns in the death of another.

While praising the judges who sent Evans, Rosenzweig, and Wolff up the river, the *Times* lamented they could not impose stronger sanctions. The New York Medico-Legal Society had drawn up a tough bill to correct that situation. An assemblyman had introduced it into the state legislature. The *Times* urged quick action.

The abortionists had only two defenders. One, in its backhanded way, was *Woodhull & Claflin's Weekly*. The sisters had no sympathy for the practitioners. But they believed it was society that drove abortionists' victims to seek their services. "You screech at Rosenzweig today," ranted the *Weekly*. "You employed him yesterday, and will produce patients for his successor tomorrow." Only when women were released from the oppressive rules of society, when they were taught the mechanisms of their bodies, when they were not ruined by a single impropriety would childbearing cease to be a disease to be extinguished and become a beautiful office of nature, the paper argued.

The second defender was Howe & Hummel. The law firm kept offices across Centre Street from the Tombs. William F. Howe was the city's preeminent counsel to the criminal element, taking on murder, robbery, vice, and other cases of a wicked and violent nature. Abe Hummel was building a practice in civil matters without caring much whether his client was the wronged woman seeking redress or the gentleman fending her off. The firm never let anything get in the way of winning a case—not the facts, the law, the depravity of the crime, the victims' suffering, or, least of all, the lawyers' own scruples.

When detectives armed with a coroner's warrant captured the ghoul Dr. Evans at his farm on Long Island, Howe rolled his 250-plus pounds into the inquest to take charge of the defense. In case anyone missed his mass or his overbearing personality, he was no doubt wearing one of his outfits that made Jim Fisk's wardrobe look like preachers' garb: checkered pants, velvet vest, colorful tie, huge watch at the end of a heavy gold chain, diamonds on his chest and on several pudgy fingers, all topped off with his ever-present yachting cap. As the coroner was not ready to proceed, the matter was postponed until the following morning. Not wishing to waste the trip, Howe called out Dr. Shine, one of the men who examined the victim Mary Geary.

You're blackmailing my client, he charged.

Shine threatened to "put a head on" the jolly counselor were he not more discreet with his remarks.

Howe followed that opening salvo with objections to hearsay evidence, medical debates with doctors about the cause of death, cross-examination that drove Evans's other patients to tears, and testimony on abortion procedures deemed unfit for publication. All that preceded the indictment.

And when police traced the woman's nude body discovered in a trunk to the fiend Rosenzweig, Howe petitioned the New York Supreme Court for a writ of habeas corpus on behalf of the doctor. Rosenzweig was restrained in the Eighteenth Precinct Police Station on an unfounded accusation of murder and abortion, Howe charged. Nor had his client been examined or given the opportunity to confront his accusers.

Despite all the times Howe's logic, persuasion, and personality had turned hopeless cases into acquittals, juries convicted both Evans and Rosenzweig. In December 1871 Howe suffered another stinging defeat when, inside of ten minutes, a jury returned a guilty verdict against abortionist Ann Burns and the judge sent her up the river for seven years. But a jury's decision need not mark the end of a case. As his contemporaries in the bar noted, if a case had a defense, Howe would find it, and he would avail himself of every technicality the law afforded. In all three trials, the counselor laid groundwork for appeal. No matter how pleased the *Times* was that the abortionists were locked away, none of the cases had finished winding through the courts. The war waged on, and with the New Year, Howe was attacking.

Stories of love and murder, warring women and feminine financiers, smut dealers and moral crusaders, mommy mutilators and baby killers, and the year was barely two weeks old. The episodes appeared unrelated as 1872 opened. But together they symptomatized the decay in public morals the *Times* so frequently decried. On New Year's Day, the editors deplored the sharp jump in divorces as yet one more sign of the decadence infesting the city.

In the seven years since the Civil War, the social order had fallen into chaos. Cut loose from their families, young people flooded into New York City, taking up residence in boardinghouses, where the comings and goings of the housemates were replayed each evening in the dinner table gossip. A man enjoying a newfound freedom could spend his leisure in billiard rooms, "gambling hells," or concert saloons, where pretty waiter girls took a cut for each drink they poured down his throat and steered him to the keno table to lose his money. Twenty such saloons beckoned in seven blocks along Broadway. A fellow could buy sex at cigar stores, in brothels, in the third tier of Bowery theaters, or on the sidewalks of Greene Street. A dozen guides to the city helped him satisfy any desire.

Women arrived in lesser numbers and found the city harder to survive. They filled positions as shopgirls, seamstresses, clerks, and factory hands, making as little as two to four dollars a week. Unscrupulous employers stole their wages. Respectable board-inghouses turned them away as undesirables likely to miss the rent. How long before a handsome man promising comfort and security would tempt a young woman, before she accepted an opportunity to supplement her meager earnings? Many discovered a fine line separated courtship and promiscuity.

The upheaval extended beyond the boardinghouses and working-class precincts. The fashionable set endlessly chased extravagance. Sumptuous houses, furnishings, wardrobes, and other luxuries ate every cent of income. As the carriage trade returned from its afternoon shopping, the ladies wore a restless disquiet. Their wistful eyes darted at neighbors whose indulgences they were trying to surpass. The men, too, bore features strained, stern, and hard as they pondered their precarious wealth that did not quite measure up to ambition, their own or their wives'.

Within the up-and-coming family, the mother had become a butterfly, a creature of style and frivolity. She sought to keep the family small. Those children she bore she committed to hirelings. Society duties occupied her time. She and her husband would as likely seek pleasure outside their marriage vows as in. They taught their children naught but to be images of themselves—the son to enjoy the vices of father, the daughter to embrace mother's beauty and extravagance.

Such was the state of morals in the eyes of the city's chroniclers in the years after the war. Such was the state of the nation in the eyes of the Christian gentlemen of the National Reform Association gathering at the Reformed Church on Eleventh Street. Those gentlemen understood the source of the trouble. God was angry. The nation's founders had failed to enshrine the Almighty in the US Constitution, bringing His wrath upon the country. The men of the association intended to return the country to His grace through a constitutional amendment that formally recognized the existence of a Supreme Being and avowed that the United States was a Christian nation.

Could God save America? It was a tall order. The roots of decay had spread vig-orously over seven years of postwar upheaval. Those stories in the *Times*, seemingly no more than disconnected symptoms as the year opened, would intertwine in ways unimaginable. The paths of Fisk and Woodhull and Claflin and Beecher and Comstock and Howe, and others as yet unnamed, would cross and recross in a tangle not even God could unravel. Nor could He halt the bombshell that would burst, sending shock waves across the country.

II

WINTER

FRENCH BALL.

The French Ball.
George W. Walling, Recollections of a New York Chief of Police, *1887*

2 | "I'VE GOT YOU NOW"

WHEN NED STOKES AWOKE THE FIRST SATURDAY OF 1872, he was marking the end of a bad year and the beginning of an even worse day.

A year earlier found him in financial straits so severe he pawned his diamonds. With that financial strain wearing on him, Stokes had visited the Devoe Manufacturing Company to collect checks totaling $27,500 owed the Brooklyn Refinery Company, of which he was secretary. Stokes deposited the moneys in his personal account at the Fulton National Bank, and on January 4, 1871, he withdrew $20,000. He took out the remainder three days later.

Upon discovering the embezzlement, the other officers of the Brooklyn Refinery had secured a warrant for Stokes's arrest. James Fisk, Treasurer W. A. Byers, and a detective sought the culprit. Unable to find Stokes in his usual haunts, they speculated that he had sailed for Europe with the funds. But the next morning the detective spotted him jumping into a carriage outside the home of Josie Mansfield. The carriage stopped at an ill-famed house on Thirteenth Street, then proceeded to the Hoffman House, where Stokes violently resisted arrest. The detective subdued him, confiscated his revolver, and hauled him to the Tombs police court. The judge refused to accept bail on Sunday. Stokes spent a distressing night in a cell.

Stokes made bail Monday. He quickly maneuvered out of the predicament when the judge ruled that though the refinery was incorporated, all the shareholders served as trustees. Under that arrangement, the company functioned as a private partnership. Partners were entitled to appropriate funds.

Stokes made a crucial error, however. Rather than wait for the judge's ruling on a technicality, he issued a statement claiming his arrest had stemmed solely from Jim Fisk's jealousy over his longtime flame, Helen Josephine Mansfield. Despite the house, jewels, and Erie stock Fisk lavished on her, Mansfield now preferred the company of an old friend of the family—namely, Stokes. Fisk blamed Stokes for the loss of his lover and was determined to do his former friend in, the statement charged. The embezzlement accusation was merely the latest in a series of vengeful acts.

A wiser man would have realized the press could never resist a tale of such prurience. The public lapped up details of the three-way affair. No one swallowed Stokes's "friend of the family" nonsense. Denying his carriage ever stopped at the Thirteenth Street bordello of a well-known beauty didn't help his credibility.

And a wiser man would not have doubled down when he won the case. Stokes did, inviting a reporter from the *Herald* into a meeting with his lawyer, Tom Pittman. From the interview, the reporter produced a burlesque worthy of Lydia Thompson and her British Blondes, whose performances had taken the city by storm a couple of years earlier. Adopting the Trojan War as his theme, the *Herald* man introduced his cast. The gentleman with the sinewy build and expression that "takes well with the female sex" was Mr. Achilles Stokes. His companion with a head deeply intellectual and slightly bald, "like the floor of a rink," was Mr. Ulysses Pittman. Fisk was tagged as Menelaus, cuckolded husband of Helen of Troy.

Ulysses led the attack: "I wonder how the newspapers can be humbugged into believing that there is anything to this bloated fellow Fisk. . . . I've found him as thin as a sheet of ice in a tumbler that's been standing in a bachelor's chamber during a frosty night."

Achilles chimed in. Fisk had "never had anyone to give him a good square stand up fight until now. . . . Unless he keeps very quiet, I shall sue him for libel."

Ulysses extended the threat, invoking Belle Helene Mansfield: "Mrs. Mansfield should tell all she knows about that Erie business. . . . She can smash him when she likes."

The reporter next called on Mansfield, a.k.a. "Belle Hellene." Admitted to the dining room, he waxed poetic about the royal sofa in the corner where Menelaus Fisk had sobbed before the Modern Helen, succumbing to her unrelenting glances, the "most destructive and seductive of her sex." In her saloon, Fisk had met "the fiery assault of Achilles Stokes and had been vanquished by his death dealing spear."

Belle Helene hurled her own ridicule. Yes, Fisk could be insane. It was hereditary in his family. She guffawed over Fisk's galoshes, which she had tossed out with their owner. Finally, she added to the threats of Ulysses and Achilles: "I am ready for Mr. Fisk if he makes an advance against me or lays a finger on any friend."

The burlesque painted Fisk as a lovesick schoolboy. One cartoonist drew the Prince of Erie shedding enormous tears into his thrown-out galoshes. It certainly added to Mansfield's notoriety. But its instigator, Stokes, suffered far greater damage, the least of which was that he looked like a fool. Of the trio, he alone possessed any respectability to lose. Fashionable society had already banned Fisk and Mansfield. But Stokes came from good, moneyed stock, and while his behavior had often been horrid, it had usually been discreet. With the *Herald* piece, he pulled back the curtain and turned himself into a pariah.

The friends, Josie Mansfield, Ned Stokes, and Jim Fisk, during happier times.
Barclay & Co., Life Adventures, Strange Career and Assassination of Col. James Fisk, Jr., *1872*

Among the people witnessing the spectacle was Stokes's wife. Humiliated, Mrs. Stokes wanted nothing more to do with her husband. In June 1871 she packed her trunks and the couple's daughter aboard a steamer for Europe. Perhaps the mineral springs of Germany could restore her vitality, she hoped. Mother and child celebrated that Christmas in Paris, ignoring Stokes's entreaties to return home.

Despite his victory in court, the Brooklyn Refinery's river of money, flowing into Stokes's account at $90,000 a year, had dried up. On the day of his arrest that January, a hundred of Fisk's men had scaled the refinery's walls. In a pitched battle, they tossed out Stokes's crew. Negotiations began later that month, but the hot-tempered Stokes blew up at the $110,000 Fisk offered to buy out his refinery shares. Stokes believed he deserved $200,000 and that he wielded the weapons to get it.

Stokes had filed suit for malicious prosecution and libel. That attack was a feint. His big guns came from Mansfield, letters Fisk had written from early in their courtship through the breakup. Mansfield pressured Fisk for money under threat of handing the letters to the newspapers. Stokes upped the ante, floating his $200,000 target as their price and hinting the letters contained enough Erie secrets to land Fisk and Jay Gould in the penitentiary. Fisk knew better. He wasn't so stupid as to have put such business deeds in writing, even if Mansfield had witnessed him stealing Erie from under

Vanderbilt and Drew's noses. The missives were love letters to his "Dolly." Fisk hadn't gotten over his beloved, even after Stokes entered the scene. Now he couldn't bear being exposed as a bereft and spurned puppy.

Fisk could dawdle, however. Every moment built the financial strains on his rival, as he well knew after a dealer offered him the diamonds Stokes had pawned. Furthermore, the threat to hand the letters to the newspapers was idle. Once the letters were published, Stokes and Mansfield would lose their leverage. They had to come to the table.

In April 1871, they did. Stokes agreed to arbitration for the sale of his refinery shares. Fisk accepted his proposed arbitrator so long as Stokes surrendered Mansfield's letters when the proceedings began. The arbitrator valued the refinery shares at $27,500, exactly the amount Stokes had already collected via Devoe Manufacturing. He granted another $10,000 as compensation for spending a night in jail and $5,000 for attorney's fees. Stokes was furious. He still had weapons to snatch both the Erie Railroad and the Grand Opera House, he swore. Bluster, Fisk decided, and stuck to his guns. In July Stokes accepted the amount, less than a quarter of the $200,000 he sought.

The settlement stuck in Stokes's craw. He had kept a certified copy of the letters despite giving his word as a gentleman to the contrary. With the threat to publish them still hanging over him, Fisk took preemptive action. He secured affidavits from Mansfield's former servant, Richard King, and from Annie Wood, the madam who had introduced Mansfield to Fisk. After getting King out of town, Fisk released the servant's testimony describing how Mansfield and Stokes lived as man and wife and connived to blackmail Fisk with the letters.

His frustrations rising, Stokes sued to set aside the arbitration decision as fraudulent. He lost that round while Fisk secured an injunction to prevent publication of the letters until a judge examined them. Meanwhile Mansfield sued Fisk for libeling her and Stokes. Her servant Richard King's affidavit about her and Stokes cohabitating and plotting extortion? All lies fabricated by Fisk, she insisted. As that case recessed for Christmas 1871, rumors spread that Fisk was asking a grand jury to indict Stokes and Mansfield for blackmail. If this legal tangle were not peril enough, one of Stokes's lawyers threatened to sue him for $5,000 in unpaid bills. Over the year, attorney's fees had eaten almost the entire award in the arbitration of his Brooklyn Refinery holdings.

As Stokes faced a lonely holiday without his wife and daughter, the senior Mr. Stokes was worried. His son had always been dutiful and obedient. Now whenever he encouraged Ned to ignore Fisk's persecution and abandon the jumble of lawsuits, his son flew into a frenzied rage. He appeared deranged in the mind.

Such was his state when Ned Stokes awoke January 6, that first Saturday of 1872, and began what would be his worst day since the arrest for embezzlement fifty-two weeks before. Mansfield's libel trial against Fisk resumed at ten that morning. Even if troubles had addled his brain, Stokes intended to put on a good face for his appearance in court. His habit was to spend mornings in his suite at the Hoffman House, lounging in a velvet jacket while enjoying his first cigar. He ate a good, hearty breakfast, perhaps an omelet with mutton chops and a pot of tea. Afterward his hairdresser trimmed his curls and shaved him. During these ministrations, Stokes paged through the *Herald*.

On this particular morning, a story on page 3 potentially brightened his mood. William Magear Tweed, the longtime political boss who had run New York with his Tammany Hall ring until being indicted last year, was haggling over his million-dollar bail. Fisk losing the protection of his friend Boss Tweed and the corrupt judges he owned could only help Stokes in court.

Stokes may also have chuckled at the sporting news followed by men like himself. Henry Bergh of the American Society for the Prevention of Cruelty to Animals had disrupted another pigeon shoot. While the *Times* moralized against such sport, the *Herald*'s headline lampooned, DON QUIXOTE DEFENDS THE DOVECOTE.

Any humor vanished at page 11. FISK—MANSFIELD—STOKES, a headline blared. THE INJUNCTION RESTRAINING THE PUBLICATION OF FISK'S BILLET-DOUX TO HELEN JOSEPHINE SUSTAINED. In his decision, fully reprinted, the judge rambled from the literary merits of private correspondence to odious breaches of personal confidences and on to Mansfield's loose tongue. But the bottom line was clear. The judge considered the letters privileged information under the sanctity of private relations and the claims of fraud in the refinery arbitration wholly without merit. Stokes had lost again.

The valet tucked his master's pants around immaculately polished boots and assisted him into an elegant Ulster overcoat. Though fashionable as always, the outfit could not disguise the anxiety Stokes displayed when he strode into the Yorkville police court. Mansfield seemed more at ease in her black silk dress, velvet jacket, and jockey hat. She smiled slyly at spectators craning their necks for a glimpse of her charms.

Mansfield took the stand. Fisk's attorney, William Beach, began cross-examination, determined to demonstrate her blackmail scheme was real. Mansfield insisted Fisk had bought her servant Richard King's perjury to persecute her. Beach pressed her little and moved on to his next topic, Annie Wood, using the madam's damning affidavit as his script. Mansfield admitted knowing Wood but denied any conversation about Fisk.

Miss Wood did not introduce you to Mr. Fisk after describing him and his character? Beach asked.

No, Mansfield claimed, *I met him at her house by accident.*

Didn't you meet Miss Wood at 19 Brevoort Place, calling the dress you wore the last you had in the world and saying you had not the money for the week's rent?

Nothing of the kind. Mansfield denied ever encountering Wood at that address.

Did you not say you wanted to meet Mr. Fisk as you had no way of making a living?

Never, Mansfield said. *Nor did Miss Wood make an appointment for the next day to introduce Mr. Fisk.*

Did you not later tell Miss Wood that Fisk had taken a fancy to you? Did you not show her costly diamonds and elegant dresses Fisk bought you?

Never and never, Mansfield said. A quiver entered her voice. Tears formed.

Did you not say, "Annie, Annie, look at these, when I met Fisk I had but one silk dress and no money for my purse," and did not Miss Wood say, "You have been with him long enough to get more than that"? And did you not answer you didn't want to bait him too fast but you would get all the money you could and then let him go?

Mansfield's counsel, John McKeon, objected and objected until Beach decided the damage was done. He moved on to Nully Pieris, whose affidavit claimed Mansfield and Stokes had promised her a piece of the proceeds to help blackmail Fisk. By this time, Mansfield had spent an hour on the stand. When she completely broke down, the judge intervened. Beach had more—he could have revisited her prior extortion efforts, the time her stepfather walked in on her and another man clad in nothing but his shirt and pointed a pistol at the man's head and demanded he sign a check on the spot. But earlier testimony had entered that episode in the record already.

As Stokes glowered and Mansfield tried to regain her composure, her cousin Marietta Williams took the stand. She had shared Mansfield's home for two years, but during that period no conversations of the like King described had occurred, she said, nor any discussion about obtaining money from Fisk, nor even an allusion to the man. Stokes came once in a while, perhaps three or four times a week, she acknowledged when pressed, but never had he and Mansfield sat at table without Williams present.

Having established him in the house, albeit chaperoned, Beach called Stokes to the stand. Stokes testified that he had originally met Mansfield in Philadelphia when he'd visited the city on business. Fisk first took him to her home in New York. He could not recall how often he visited her after that, perhaps eight or ten times in the past half year or so. Maybe he called three or four times in one week and none in others, though he could recall none of the latter. He didn't need an appointment; rather, he knew the dinner hour. Spectators laughed.

Have you threatened Fisk that unless he settled you would pursue and crush him? Beach asked.

Only to pursue him in lawsuits, Stokes said.

To pursue and crush him, Beach repeated.

Only in a legal way, Stokes insisted, *not physically.*

Threatened again and again to make publications against him in the newspapers?

Yes, Stokes admitted, *but only to expose how he swindled me.*

The crowd twittered. The day's entertainment was better than the leg shows at Niblo's Garden. When the judge called a recess, Stokes stalked off the stand. In the witness room, he brooded over making such a fool of himself. He must have been desperate for a good belt when the court adjourned at two o'clock.

The prosecuting team of Assistant District Attorney John Fellows and Mansfield's counsel McKeon took Stokes to lunch at Delmonico's. Mansfield was worn to a frazzle and wanted only to hole up in her bedroom.

Stokes remained agitated. Fellows advised him to drop the libel case. Pursuing it would only bring more trouble, quite likely the rumored indictment for blackmail Fisk was seeking. Stokes wouldn't listen to reason.

As they guzzled beer and inhaled oysters, Judge George Barnard came in from the courts with news. The grand jury hearing Fisk's blackmail charge against Stokes and Mansfield had returned an indictment. Fellows wasn't sure Stokes heard, as he had moved down the bar. But Stokes quickly finished his lunch and flagged a hack on Chambers Street.

Jim Fisk slept late that first Saturday of 1872. He had caught a bug with the New Year. Upon awakening, he felt restored. His friend Georges Barbin joined him for breakfast. Fisk had hired the Belgian to interpret when three actresses from his homeland had performed at the Grand Opera House. His company had proved so amiable that Fisk kept him on the payroll.

The valet laid out a modest outfit for the day. Fisk dressed in brown pants with a black-and-gray coat, matching vest, and silk hat. The sole hint of color was the red lining of the cape, adding a military touch, an affectation Fisk frequently adopted. He was colonel of the National Guard's Ninth Regiment. While he had admitted to absolutely no proficiency at soldiering when the unit's officers called three years ago—hardly able to sit on a horse, he told them—he hadn't turned them away. The regiment had fallen into dismal repair and desperately needed a benefactor. Fisk, always generous, and enticed by the respectability head of a regiment endowed, accepted the position. His leadership and his money, and some said his drafting of Erie employees, rebuilt the regiment and its pride. Fisk earned the undying loyalty of the ranks, now numbering close to a thousand.

While 1871 had been tough, Fisk didn't let troubles weigh on him. The agony of his infatuation with Mansfield had ended at last. He parked the lingering lawsuits where they belonged, with his lawyers. Between the Erie Railroad takeover and the gold corner, he had long had dozens of suits pending, with groups of lawyers assigned to each sphere. If a particular area required his attention, his legal bird dog William Morgan, overseeing the lot, would keep him posted. Today, for instance, Fisk needn't bother to attend his trial for libel. Let attorney Beach torment Mansfield and Stokes on the stand.

Before the holidays, Fisk had visited his wife, Lucy, in Boston. Though they lived apart, he had long praised her as a saint. She must have been to endure his notoriety. On this visit, he confessed what she surely already knew. She forgave him his indiscretions with Mansfield.

His good works also brightened his mood. When fire had devastated Chicago in October 1871, he personally drove a wagon through New York's streets collecting contributions. The Erie speeded trains with supplies to relieve the suffering. Fisk had awarded his returning engineers gold medals for reaching the city in record time.

In November, the New York Association of German Musicians had expressed their gratitude for a contribution of $2,000, marching 150 strong to his home. Five thousand spectators had heard the band serenade him with *Der Freischütz*. The crowd cheered when he'd appeared on the porch to say he merely gave what little his meager resources allowed. On Christmas Eve, his regiment's band had performed at a holiday gala at the opera house. Though Mansfield spurned him, he could feel the love of untold thousands.

So, on that first Saturday of the new year, Fisk went about his business. By noon he was in his office on the second floor of the Grand Opera House overlooking Eighth Avenue. He tended to pressing Erie affairs, then turned to a promise he'd made the day before. In the wake of revelations on Boss Tweed's embezzlement, reformers had tied up city funds. The police department couldn't pay its force for December. Fisk had a close relationship with the cops on the beat. Through them he anonymously gave coal and food to the needy around the opera house. He refused to see the police suffer and was advancing the $250,000 the department needed to meet the payroll.

In midafternoon his friend John Chamberlain visited. Chamberlain described himself as a speculator and sought Fisk's advice on stocks. Really he was a gambler. Fisk enjoyed the camaraderie of the card table at Chamberlain's clubhouse two blocks away. Today Chamberlain found Fisk in high spirits. The favorable turns in his lawsuits elated him, and he was leaving shortly to visit his good friends the Morse family.

At half past three, Fisk headed downstairs. Chamberlain scooted out to his own carriage. As it rolled east across Eighth Avenue, he noticed Ned Stokes in a coupé traveling the opposite direction. Stokes stared at the windows of the Erie offices.

Fisk's coachman waited to carry his employer to the Grand Central Hotel, where Mrs. Morse resided at Fisk's expense. She was the widow of a close friend whose neck had been broken in a diving accident. In memory, Fisk supported the family, which included two daughters, a son, and a grandmother. The gesture typified his generosity. The Grand Central had opened on Broadway two years ago. One of New York's most elegant hotels, it was also the nation's largest, stretching from Bleecker to Amity Street and rising ten stories to the top of its mansard crown. The furnishings alone had cost half a million dollars.

The coachman turned onto Fifth Avenue, avoiding the more direct diagonal down Broadway. It added a few minutes to the trip, but still the carriage pulled up at the Grand Central before four o'clock. Fisk skirted another carriage and went through the ladies' entrance. Though this was not strictly allowed, the callboy on duty knew it was Fisk's usual door. Fisk asked if Mrs. Morse and her younger daughter were in. The callboy thought not but guessed the older daughter was with her grandmother. They started up the stairs.

When Ned Stokes climbed into a coupé outside Delmonico's, he directed the hack to the Hoffman House. He went in briefly. They then drove to Twenty-Third Street. Approaching Josie Mansfield's house, Stokes changed his mind. The hack turned around and headed for Broadway. At Fourth Street, Stokes jumped out. He dashed in and out of a liquor dealer before rushing down the sidewalk, crowded as the workday wound down. Reaching the Grand Central Hotel, he collided with a woman, bounced off, and darted through the hotel's ladies' entrance. The callboy was standing atop a ladder polishing windows as the man bounded up the stairs.

Stokes paced the hallway. He went into a parlor where he could view the carriages along Broadway. Returning to the hallway, he crouched a couple of steps down the stairs. Fisk was climbing from the bottom. Stokes mumbled to himself, "I've got you now." He pulled a pistol from his coat and leaned on the balustrade. He fired at the massive bulk of Fisk's torso. The report echoed through the hotel. The bullet slammed into Fisk's guts, knocking him down. Fisk got to his feet. A second bullet punctured his arm. He slid down the stairs crying, "Oh, oh, oh, don't."

Stokes hid the gun in his coat. A hallboy named Thomas Hart stared. Stokes said, "There's a man shot. Somebody had better go and pick him up."

Hart said, "Yes, and you are the man that shot him."

Stokes walked down the hall. He ducked into a parlor to fling his pistol between the folds of a sofa, then ducked out again. Hart followed him to the hotel's main stairs. Halfway down, Stokes called again, "There's a man shot upstairs, and somebody better seek him and pick him up."

Hart pointed and said again, "Yes, and there goes the man who shot him."

Other men trailed Stokes. He trotted through the barroom, coattails flapping. As he passed the barber's shop, Stokes could see the Mercer Street door and his escape. The men pounced. Manhandled into a chair, Stokes nearly fainted away.

Lying on the stairs, Fisk cried out, "Will anyone protect me from the assassin?"

A guest from Massachusetts heard. "Is that you, Colonel?" he asked.

"I am shot," Fisk said. He placed his hand on his hip and his heart. Other men converged. They carried the wounded man to a suite on the second floor. Blood gushed from an ugly wound in Fisk's arm. A messenger fetched the house doctor. Fisk pointed to his stomach. The doctor uncovered a large hole from the other bullet. He probed the wound, but his longest instrument couldn't reach the bullet. "Doctor," Fisk said, "if I am going to die, I want to know it. I'm not afraid to die."

"Colonel," the doctor said, "you are not going to die tonight, and not tomorrow either, I hope."

In short order, Captain Thomas Byrnes, chief of detectives, arrived with the culprit. Stokes wore a stiffly dignified air. "That's the man who shot me," Fisk said. "That's Stokes." Was it a deathbed identification?

A bevy of doctors soon surrounded the patient. A surgeon probed the wound. The bullet had entered inches above the navel and torn a gash through the stomach wall. It lodged beyond the surgeon's reach.

Within an hour of the shooting, newsboys hawked an Extra of the *Evening Telegram*. People poured into the hotel and the surrounding blocks. One gentleman cursed the shooter: "Damn it, it was a mean trick to shoot a man without giving him a chance. It was a cowardly act."

Responded another nearby, "By Jove, if things were only as they are in some of the states, it would be a just act to lynch Stokes."

After reading of Mansfield's heartless cross-examination in the evening papers, several ladies ascribed the shooting to madness. Was it any wonder that witnessing his beloved's humiliation drove a man to such an insane act?

A policeman admitted Fisk's closest associates to the suite. Boss Tweed paced. His jovial good nature had vanished. Jay Gould buried his head in both hands and sobbed. Among the Erie employees gathering in a death watch, a man poured out a string of oaths. "Let's go to the Station-house and take Stokes and hang him," he concluded. For the moment, cooler heads prevailed.

With Fisk's condition critical, the coroner arrived to take his antemortem statement. Fisk swore how, when he'd started up from the ladies' entrance, Stokes stood above with something in his hand, how a second later he'd seen the flash and heard the report and felt the ball burst into his gut, felt a second bullet pierce his arm; how when Stokes was brought before him later, he'd identified Edward S. Stokes as the person who shot him. From a man sure he was dying, an antemortem statement constituted the truth in a court of law. The coroner asked the question that was his duty: "Do you believe that you are about to die from the injuries you have received?"

"I believe that I am in very critical condition," Fisk said.

The answer was ambiguous. The coroner asked again. "Have you any hopes of recovery?"

"I hope so." Fisk was not a man to give up.

The doctors gave Fisk morphine. He slept. The police guard allowed a *Herald* reporter into the suite. Boss Tweed had plopped onto a sofa and was comforting friends. New York would mourn Fisk for the kindness of his heart and his enterprise second to none, Tweed predicted. When the reporter peeked into the bedroom, Fisk lay on a bed snoring loudly. His hair was combed, his moustache waxed. His arms lay on the covers, their muscles still displaying the physical power of the man. But his eyes drooped in their sockets. When he suddenly drew an arm across his face, a doctor rushed to the bedside.

"Keep away the pain," Fisk said. "It is all I ask."

"He is the gamest man I ever saw," the doctor said.

At 10:00 PM, Fisk whispered to another doctor, "Is there even a chance of my getting well again?"

"Keep up a good, stout moral resolution and buoyant hope, Colonel," the man said. "They often bridge us over a good many rough rivers."

The doctors conferenced an hour later. The patient was getting along nicely, they reported. The anxious faces in the anteroom brightened. Nonetheless, when Fisk awoke before midnight, he asked for one of his attorneys. He wanted to make his will.

After Fisk identified Stokes, Captain Byrnes took his prisoner downstairs. The man in charge of the hotel's front office handed Byrnes a four-chamber revolver. A woman had found it tucked between the back and seat of a sofa. Two chambers were loaded, two discharged. The front office man also gave the captain a spent bullet found on the stairs. Then Byrnes hurried Stokes toward the Fifteenth Precinct station house. The accompanying police held a crowd at bay until Stokes was ushered before the desk for arraignment. He answered the usual questions about name and residence, then invoked his right to say nothing more.

He was taken to a low, narrow cell, dark and gloomy despite ghostly whitewashed walls. A slab ran against the back for a prisoner to lie on. Stokes was repulsed and told his escort so in no uncertain terms. Shortly the officers brought him back to the captain's room. He walked nonchalantly through a gauntlet of reporters like the well-bred gentleman he was, complete with high silk hat, kid gloves, and cane. His attorneys, led by John McKeon, met with him. When the coroner came, Stokes again refused to answer questions.

Stokes was sullen returning to his cell. Hearing the iron door slam, he paced. He demanded cigars. One after another, he lit them and flung them away. At one point he stopped and asked an officer outside, "What do you think, is the man seriously injured?" The officer didn't know. Stokes resumed pacing, muttering to himself.

The officer remained beside the cell all night. The captain feared the prisoner's mental state was unstable. He didn't want a suicide on his watch.

At 7:00 PM, a reporter rang the bell at 359 West Twenty-Third Street. A servant girl opened the door. "Is Miss Mansfield home?" the man asked. Mansfield's cousin Marietta Williams came to say the mistress of the house was too ill to appear.

"Have you heard of the shooting of Fisk by Stokes?" the reporter asked.

"No, it cannot be possible. It must be a false report."

"But it is so, madame." He related the facts: Fisk lying in the Grand Central Hotel, Stokes arrested, excitement throughout the city at fever pitch. Williams ran to Mansfield's bedroom. The woman who had inspired the shooting came down the stairs. Looking pale and agitated, she asked for a truthful account of the affair.

"Had you any reason to anticipate the tragedy?" the reporter asked.

"Not the slightest." Mansfield had never heard Stokes say an unkind word of Fisk, not even when Fisk meant to harm him. She had not seen him since leaving court in the afternoon, returning home so ill that she retired to her room.

"He must have been insane," she said, "or laboring under some temporary aberration of mind, or he never would have allowed himself to run into such a rash act."

An awful headache took hold of her. She sank upon the stairs and rested her head in her hands. Slowly she regained her composure—and thought of herself. "I want it distinctly understood that I am in no way connected with the sad affair. I have only my reputation to maintain."

To the reporter's eye, she showed not a shred of sorrow over the fate of either of her lovers.

At 3:00 AM Sunday, Fisk's snoring reverberated through the Grand Central's hallways. At 4:00, he awoke. "Doing nicely," he told the doctor. Could he have a drink of water?

Two hours later, Lucy Fisk arrived from Boston. Her husband was comatose. After nine o'clock, his breathing grew labored. Lucy Fisk wrapped her arms around his neck and cried as if her heart would break. As death approached, Jim Fisk breathed in short, convulsive gasps. Yet he showed no sign of agony, no contortion of his face, no twitching of his muscles. He had always possessed a knack for setting his troubles aside when he had dealt with them as best he could. He did so now. Peacefully the life ebbed out of him.

At daybreak the halls of the Grand Central had filled for the death watch. News of the end spread quickly. By noon both sides of Broadway were jammed, the entrance to the hotel impassable. The outpouring of sympathy and affection astonished observers. Said one old man who had served Fisk, "Ah, they may well talk of him who did not know him, but to those who were about him there never lived a kinder or a better man."

A nearby gentleman took up the remark: "A really good man is loved by his servants and I have never seen so much real feeling manifested at the death of a man before."

A third added, "It is not only the personal friends but the general public who take an interest such as I have never witnessed."

It was true. The body was laid in a coffin, its color gone. Fisk's face was placid, as if he were enjoying a restful repose instead of one from which he would never awaken. The coffin was moved to the parlor and the doors opened. Hundreds passed by the corpse. Beside Fisk sat his forlorn partner, Jay Gould. Later, as the undertaker's men prepared to close the coffin, Boss Tweed entered to gaze one last time on the face of his friend. Then the lid slammed shut and the bearers carried the coffin up a private stairway, through the building, and down to the Mercer Street door through which Stokes had nearly escaped. With bowed head, Tweed followed silently, perhaps thinking of this death as a final blow to his own life being torn asunder.

During Fisk's final hours, his assassin awoke in a calmer frame of mind. Though deprived of his routine and fresh clothes, Stokes washed and dressed in his usual meticulous manner. At 9:00 AM, an officer brought him up from his cell. Captain Byrnes waited to take him to the Tombs. Chatting with Byrnes in the carriage, he indicated his stomach was out of sorts. Could he get a bottle of wine to settle it? Byrnes refused the request.

The captain steered the conversation back to Fisk, noting he was not expected to live. "I shot him in the abdomen, didn't I?" Stokes said. Byrnes described the injuries.

"I heard the Ninth Regiment fellows were going to turn Mansfield's house inside out last night," Stokes said. "Is that right? If some of those Erie fellows were to run across me they would meet their match." It was a bit of bravado. If Stokes could have seen the crowd gathered at the Grand Central, he might have considered it a premonition.

The carriage's destination was a granite monstrosity of Egyptian architecture. While the Tombs' facade might have looked like a pharaoh's palace, its cells were more like his crypt. Four tiers' worth occupied an inner courtyard. Most nights the inmates crammed the place so tightly a man could suffocate—unless his crime was brazen enough to fetch a fortune. Then he could buy all the luxury a pharaoh dreamed of, no matter how long he was imprisoned.

Encountering the chill dampness greeting visitors and inmates alike, Stokes did not hesitate. He passed over the Bridge of Sighs connecting the outer building with the cells, the route condemned criminals took on their walk to the gallows erected in the courtyard—a walk he might soon take. On the third tier of cells, faces pressed against the bars to view the man who shot Jim Fisk. Stokes recognized one. He smiled and said, "How do you do, Ed? Why you have got comfortable quarters here."

As well Edward Haggerty should. He was a city official accused of stealing $10 million in fraudulent vouchers, which could have served as evidence of Tammany Hall's corruption. For making the potentially damning vouchers disappear, Boss Tweed was ensuring Haggerty suffered no discomfort until Tweed could get him released. Stokes was not so pleased when the guard unlocked the door to number 73 and he realized he would be sharing quarters with another occupant. He protested.

For the moment, his consolation was the satchel of clothing and toilet articles a friend had delivered. He changed into clean linen, gray pantaloons, and a ruffled shirt.

The brilliant diamond solitaire nestled in the folds atop his chest announced that he could well afford to maintain his standards behind bars.

Late in the morning, the warden offered Stokes a reception room for an interview with a *Times* reporter. The reporter offered condolences for the situation Stokes found himself in.

"Have no fears for me," Stokes said. "I am no murderer. I have read the papers, and I assure you there is a tale yet untold."

"Mr. Fisk is dead," the reporter said.

"Is that so? It is a sad loss to the business community. But the papers should not prejudge me a murderer. I never wished Colonel Fisk any harm. I could say more but my counsel has sealed my lips."

The reporter asked whether he had followed Fisk down Broadway, whether his indictment for blackmail had inflamed him, whether the heartless examination of Mansfield had driven him to intercept Fisk. His attorneys' admonition notwithstanding, Stokes denied it all. He pulled out a pocketbook. "Do you see that wallet?" he said. "Well as sure as you see it, just as sure will I be acquitted by any jury."

He tapped the door for the warden, who asked if he was ready to return to his cell.

"I merely wished to trouble you for a match to light my cigar," Stokes said.

———

As Fisk lay dying, the directors and executives of the Erie mustered at its opera house offices. A great catastrophe was overtaking the railroad. Fisk had been its presiding genius. Financial shenanigans notwithstanding, he brought prodigious energy and executive capacity to the business. Few men could endure the workload he relished. Fewer still could so quickly cut to the crux of a situation, decide on an action, and send a subordinate scurrying off with instructions. Forty or fifty people often awaited with some matter requiring Fisk's attention. Through all the details, he maintained a remarkable vision of where the Erie was headed. On this morning, men crowded around Jay Gould, whose shoulders would now bear the load.

The officers of the Ninth Regiment had also gathered. Beneath the portrait of their colonel in the Erie's Presidential Room, they cast down eyes red from weeping. The loss of the main prop and stay of the unit was imminent, of the man whose riches and generosity had restored its grandeur.

In the afternoon, the hearse carrying the coffin appeared on Twenty-Third Street. The assembled multitudes wailed. The greatest grief erupted from the officers and men of the regiment. A vengeful determination settled on their faces, a look that boded ill for the instigator of this calamity if only he were within their reach.

———

A conspiracy was afoot, sources deemed reliable reported to the police in the afternoon. At the Tombs, the warden heard that members of the Ninth were forming at their armory on Twenty-Sixth Street. They intended to march to the prison, bust through its doors, and hang Stokes in the quadrangle.

The warden wasted no time. He demanded the police superintendent provide protection. The superintendent telegraphed precincts in lower Manhattan. *Send reserves as speedily as possible*, he ordered. Within minutes the nearest arrived at the concentration point, the Sixth Precinct station house. Soon three hundred armed men had assembled. The superintendent directed half to the Tombs. The rest readied for deployment where needed.

Detectives scoured the city for information. The Ninth also contemplated attacking Mansfield's home, according to the best available reports. A police officer stood guard there. Reinforcements collected at the precinct station three blocks away, ready to rush to an impending attack. Others watched the ferries. Laborers from the Erie were massing in New Jersey, eager to cross the river and lynch the assassin.

As the police fanned out around the Tombs, someone warned Stokes a mob was coming. "I can only die once," he said, "and I have never yet been afraid to die."

By half past eight that evening, 350 soldiers of the Ninth Regiment milled around its armory. The meeting was called to order. A committee drew up a resolution. The ranks approved it unanimously. Outside they formed into lines and marched toward Twenty-Third Street.

At the opera house, mourning festooned Fisk's portrait. Behind closed doors, his second in command, Lieutenant Colonel Charles Braine, presided over a meeting of the officers. When the ranks drew up outside, a deputation of privates and noncommissioned officers came in. They presented the ranks' resolution to Braine. He, too, had heard the rumors and was due shortly at police headquarters for consultations.

The soldiers outside were not a crazed mob seeking to avenge their colonel, however. They had moved beyond vengeance to honoring their fallen leader. "That as an expression of the feelings of this meeting," read the resolution, "and as a tribute of respect to the memory of our esteemed Colonel, we recommend the Board of Officers to allow the rank and file of the regiment to escort the body to its final resting place."

The soldiers were disappointed. The Fisk family desired little military display at the funeral. A few officers would accompany the body to its interment in Brattleboro, Vermont, where Fisk grew up. As consolation, the ranks could see their colonel off in a grand procession tomorrow.

The plans agreed to, Braine and two other officers met the police commissioners. They scoffed at the rumors. Yes, the regiment was worked up, but its members would not take the law into their own hands.

If the men hoped to see Stokes get his just deserts through the courts, they would need enormous patience. Sporting men were betting $50 and $100 that Stokes would never hang.

The armory of the Ninth Regiment filled the next morning. Men greeted comrades with words that died on their lips as they hid wet eyes. No longer did they demonize Stokes. As the loss of their leader settled into their minds, many viewed the assassin more with pity than hatred.

Soldiers polished their weapons. Drummers muffled their instruments. Flag bearers draped the furled regimental colors in black. Veterans reminisced of Antietam and Gettysburg while tying crape to the hilts of their swords.

Noon approached. A major marched the men down the stairs. In the street, the veterans formed two lines as the vanguard. Officers of the city's other regiments, the Sixth, the Eighth, the Twelfth, formed up behind, then the regimental band joined by the German musicians Fisk supported. The officers and ranks, six hundred strong, brought up the rear.

A black mass filled Twenty-Third Street, every grade of society represented in the crowd. Ladies in mourning mounted stoops. Street urchins climbed lampposts. Faces stared from every window, every rooftop.

The procession of the Ninth pressed through. Between Fisk's home and the opera house, the ranks formed lines and presented arms. Soldiers carried the coffin out Fisk's door. A stillness as of death took hold of the crowd. Entering the opera house, the men bore the load up the stairs to an immense hall. Black and white muslin draped the gallery running around it, broken at intervals by satin rosettes and by a portrait of the slain colonel draped with an American flag.

The coffin was placed on a velvet pall, its lid raised. Fisk lay in his uniform. His cap and sword rested on his body. White lilies were sprinkled atop it. The officers of the Ninth surrounded their leader as a guard of honor. Men of the Erie from Jay Gould down took up places nearby. The doors opened to the public. Twenty thousand people streamed past the coffin before the doors shut at one o'clock, not half the number seeking a final look at Jim Fisk.

The Ninth's chaplain read the Episcopal service. "I am the resurrection and the life, saith the Lord," he began. Lucy Fisk, accompanied by Jim's mother and sister, wept. When the chaplain ended, she tenderly kissed her husband's lips.

It was the Ninth's turn to pay homage. The soldiers filed past. The officers huddled for a final look before a group representing all the regiments carried the coffin out. The band played the "Dead March" from *Saul*. The coffin approached the hearse sitting halfway down the block. The house beside it was tightly shuttered. Its number was 359. Josie Mansfield hid inside. If for a moment she drew back the curtain, no one noticed.

At two o'clock a hundred policemen led the procession toward the New Haven depot. A thousand Erie employees followed and then the Ninth—the veterans, the officers, the ranks leading four horses drawing the hearse. A groom led Fisk's black charger, his spurred boots backward in the stirrups. Jay Gould headed a quarter-mile line of carriages in the rear. Spectators thronged the route from sidewalks to rooftops, along Twenty-Third to Fifth Avenue, up to Twenty-Sixth, and over to Madison. At the depot, the pallbearers carried the coffin to a special car. Fisk's family entered another.

Amid breathless silence the train chugged away carrying Jim Fisk to his final stop.

Funeral procession of Jim Fisk passing the Grand Opera House.
J. W. Goodspeed, The Life of James Fisk, Jr., *1872*

3 | "BRAVO! MY DEAR WOODHULL"

THE MORNING AFTER JIM FISK WAS LAID TO REST, a crowd filed into Lincoln Hall, the cultural center of Washington, DC. Sitting halfway between the White House and the Capitol, this massive pile of Victorian gaudiness seated thirteen hundred guests on its floor and in galleries along each side. As ten o'clock approached, Elizabeth Cady Stanton led a line of women onto the stage. Black silk draped her portly proportions, observed the reporter from the *Washington Patriot*. He complimented her face full of sunshine. Her partner as a leading light of the National Woman Suffrage Association, the New York wing of the movement, followed. Susan B. Anthony's silk was wine colored, and the face behind her gold spectacles was angular rather than handsome. In compensation for her lack of sunshine, the reporter noted vim and logic filled her mind and spirit.

Third in line was a woman who a year ago played no role among the suffragists. They knew of her as a financier and publisher, yes. Anthony had once interviewed her in those capacities. The other prominent figures had never set eyes on her, nor exchanged letters, nor considered her their partner in advancing the cause. Yet at the sight of her today, the audience broke into applause. She took a seat in the rear, by all appearances deferring to the others, Stanton and Anthony and Isabella Beecher Hooker and several more ladies who had been advocating for the vote so much longer than she. At thirty-three, Victoria Woodhull was younger than the leaders she had joined. Her youth showed in a childlike look, a modest and demure demeanor. But other signs suggested less innocence. Her plain suit of blue broadcloth, her booted ankles exposed beneath her skirt, and her hair with a hint of curl trimmed unfashionably short all displayed an eagerness to break convention. A discriminating eye could detect the strains life had thrust upon her and a composure that perhaps had grown out of them.

Inwardly Woodhull must have smiled as she heard the ovation from the audience she had fought for and won. "It is an error to exclude men from the hall," she had argued. "It should be in reality a call for Equal Rights." The victory in that minor skirmish was only a first step in her plans for this convention.

Her involvement with the suffragists went back to 1870. The Fifteenth Amendment, giving black men the vote, had become law. The Sixteenth, which they hoped would grant it to women, was a dead letter. Woodhull had learned that news from Massachusetts congressman Benjamin Butler, who frequented the salons she hosted at her rented mansion in Manhattan's Murray Hill. Butler wasn't an attractive man. His squat body sat on spindly legs, his bulbous brow and vulture nose bullied those he faced, and his right eyeball wandered off on some business of its own. But his large bald head reputedly contained "a good share of the brains of the House [of Representatives]." His words carried a logic and power and audacity that compelled people to listen. Those latter qualities far outweighed physical attributes on Woodhull's scale. So, in the autumn of 1870, she moved into Washington's Willard Hotel, known as the government's "third house" for the legislative lobbying within its walls, and began working with Butler on a new approach to winning the vote. She bore a price for her nocturnal visits to his home—the gossips accused her of letting him "feast his eyes upon her naked person" in exchange for his help. But she believed she was entitled to love whomever she pleased, and she was not shy about saying so.

As 1870 closed, Butler arranged for her to address the House Judiciary Committee. No committee of Congress had ever granted such a privilege to a woman. The *Patriot* announced the meeting for January 11. The notice astonished Isabella Beecher Hooker, who was in the capital to open the NWSA's 1871 convention that very day. Who was this woman who had accomplished what the suffragists had failed for years to achieve? Amid rumors that Woodhull was "a shyster from Wall Street who had nominated herself for president," Hooker's host, Senator Samuel Pomeroy, told her that men could never function in politics if they investigated their associates' antecedents. She must do the same and accept help from whatever quarter. Following the advice, Hooker and Susan B. Anthony postponed opening the convention until the afternoon so they could attend Woodhull's appearance before the House committee.

On the appointed morning, the congressmen and their guests had assembled in a conference room of the Capitol. The legislators arrayed along the left of the table, several suffragists along the right, reporters against the wall. Woodhull waited nervously in the hall. Her anxiety was less over the congressmen than the women whose thunder she was stealing. Butler reassured her. *Ignore any who slight or snub you*, he said, singling out Isabella Beecher Hooker. A congressman overhearing offered more—"It would ill become these women, especially a Beecher, to talk of antecedents or cast any smirch upon Mrs. Woodhull, for I am reliably assured that Henry Ward Beecher preaches to at least twenty of his mistresses every Sunday." Whether the remark calmed Woodhull or not, it lodged in her mind.

When Woodhull entered the room clutching her sister Tennie Claflin, the congressmen were discreet enough not to remark on their impressions beyond wearing considerable amusement on their faces. The reporters minced no words in their assessment. Woodhull's blue outfit, skimpy in the skirt, and her clipped locks beneath an alpine hat imparted a pleasant though mannish and demanding look. Claflin appeared "a frisky lad, ready for mischief of any kind," with a "jerky movement of her face and arms [that] would appear unladylike in anyone else but lends [her] a positive charm."

At the committee chairman's invitation, Hooker introduced Woodhull. Tentatively Woodhull began. Fearing the speaker was about to faint, Hooker suggested she read from her earlier submission to the committee on "Constitutional Equality." As Woodhull took the advice, her voice grew stronger. Her cheeks flushed red. For fifteen minutes, she laid out her argument. It boiled down to the position that the Sixteenth Amendment, which the suffragists had been pursuing, was not needed for women to vote. The Fourteenth clearly defined all persons born or naturalized as citizens, while the Fifteenth guaranteed *all* citizens the right to vote, regardless of race or previous indenture—or sex. While she elaborated on constitutional details, such as how passage of the Fifteenth Amendment nullified any prior state laws restricting the votes of women, the bottom line was that Congress need only pass an act declaring that the Constitution already enshrined women's suffrage.

After the committee hearing, Woodhull had entered the NWSA convention to "anthems to Woodhull," in the words of the *Times*. The *Tribune* observed how the suffrage women gracefully acknowledged the coup d'etat she had executed with her interpretation of the Constitution. Comparing her courage to Joan of Arc, the paper asserted she had risen to her rightful place as the leader of the suffrage movement.

Victoria Woodhull speaking to the House Judiciary Committee.
Frank Leslie's Illustrated Weekly, *February 4, 1871*

So much had passed since that 1871 convention, Woodhull could reflect as Elizabeth Cady Stanton opened today's; so much had been accomplished in 365 days. Early on had come the invitation to the White House, where President Grant said, "Some day you will occupy that chair," referring to the heavy oak one in which he slouched. Shortly thereafter, *Woodhull & Claflin's Weekly* headlined its front page THE COSMO-POLITICAL PARTY. The new party would hold a national convention to nominate Victoria C. Woodhull for president in the 1872 election. The story laid out a reform platform ranging from electoral processes and government finance to labor laws and criminal jurisprudence.

In February 1871, Woodhull had filled Lincoln Hall to the rafters for what the *New York Herald* called the opening of her campaign. Reprising her "Constitutional Equality" arguments, her face was again pale, her voice tremulous as she opened. She halted between each sentence as if she barely had strength to continue. As she stumbled, it dawned on her that "her guardian spirit" had prophesied such an audience would one day hear "her first discourse . . . in the capital of her country." The sudden realization that the moment was at hand infused her with emotions that propelled her forward. Her words rang through the hall with "fire and freedom."

Suffrage leaders Isabella Beecher Hooker and Paulina Kellogg Wright Davis had stood beside Woodhull on the Lincoln Hall stage. Hooker was becoming her closest friend in the movement, one who would stick by her through thick and thin. The elder Davis mentored Woodhull as she would a daughter. More than anyone, she encouraged Woodhull's ambitions to run for the presidency. Going abroad for her health, she promised, "Though I may be on the far side of the globe I shall come home to vote for you in 1872."

Stanton, who had skipped the 1871 convention and never met Woodhull, began a correspondence. In March the *Weekly* published three letters from the grande dame of suffrage. While lacking the intimacy of Hooker's and Davis's notes, they praised "the grand work inaugurated by you," commended Woodhull for "seiz[ing] the bull by the horns," and called the *Weekly* "the ablest woman's journal we have yet had discussing the great questions of national life."

Anthony, too, had embraced Woodhull's approach. She toured the Midwest with a lecture titled "The New Situation" focusing on how the Fourteenth and Fifteenth Amendments enfranchised women. Writing to Woodhull from Kansas City, she began, "Bravo! My Dear Woodhull," and ended, "Go Ahead! bright, glorious, young and strong spirit and believe in the best love and hope and faith of S. B. Anthony." The letter carried an uncharacteristic warmth, as did a follow-up calling her Lincoln Hall speech "ahead of anything, said or written—bless you dear soul." But another letter, to Hooker, perhaps expressed Anthony's truer feelings, which would govern how her relationship with Woodhull developed. Never would she turn away someone "who bring[s] brains or cash to our work for enfranchising women," Anthony wrote. The $10,000 Woodhull pledged carried weight with a woman whose share of lecture receipts on a good night totaled $100.

For Woodhull the fight for women's rights extended far beyond getting the vote. The social system oppressed her sex in every way. A girl growing up was taught to lace her corset tight, to cover herself in crinoline, to stick a thousand pins into her scalp. Those were the skills she needed to fulfill her station in life, a wife ministering to the needs and passions of her husband. Nowhere did she learn any knowledge to foster independence and self-reliance, to build ambitions, to enlarge her realm of possibilities. She learned not even the mechanisms of her body but to suppress her desires, for they were sin.

Why had Woodhull gone into Wall Street, why was she running for President of the United States? Not for wealth, not for power, but to show the world what women were capable of. "To show men that women equally with them are entitled to carry a pocket-book and manage a bank account of their own, and that they have the ability to do it successfully." "That a woman had political rights—that she had, moreover, intellectual capacity for the highest political position." That women could lead their own lives outside the protection of a man.

Give a girl an education, give her "the ability to earn money through some profession or some fine or mechanical art." Only with "the glorious freedom of self-support" could she escape the path society opened for her—for the favored girl, the path leading to "the gilded palaces of Fifth Avenue" where a husband would shelter, feed, and clothe her; she need only submit to his will and desires. For the less fortunate stained by an impropriety, seduced by a rake or so foolish as to express an opinion, to "the lowest purlieus of Greene Street," the brothels where a hundred husbands would support her in exchange for the same services.

As spring blossomed, Woodhull repeated her Lincoln Hall performance in New York, Brooklyn, Boston, and Philadelphia. Overflow crowds cheered her growing oratorical powers. The press acknowledged her as the "head and front" of the suffrage movement, the one who stirred up public enthusiasm and enlisted prominent politicians as Anthony, Stanton, and others never could. Woodhull realized it was not enough—suffrage was a means to the broader goal of opportunity for women rather than oppression. Suffragists needed allies to get there. At every stop, she cultivated support for her new Cosmo-Political Party. Her vision was a coalition covering not just suffrage but also Spiritualism, labor, temperance, human rights—"all the branches of radicalism and reform." In May a lecture before the Reform Labor League demonstrated how far she was reaching: "A party which would become successful and remain in power must be firm in the advocacy of all growth and reform. . . . All sectionalism, all favoritism, all specialism must be swallowed in the greater interests of the whole." Simultaneously, the *Weekly* announced its voice on suffrage had been heard enough. In a grand step forward, it would now concern itself with "the more radical and vital questions of Woman's Rights, of Social Reconstruction, of Universal Human Freedom."

The enthusiasm for Woodhull was far from universal, however. She pushed the limits, she knew. But how could the diseases of society be cured without speaking about them in plain language? She would never cease to lift her voice until everyone was free and nobody had the right to rule over another, even when it came to love.

Love. It was a core of her philosophy, that love was integral to the "sovereignty of the individual." Neither the law nor public opinion had any right to interfere, to dictate how or with whom it was expressed. Yet society forced women into marriages no better than servitude, into sexual relations filled with loathing. Promiscuity had nothing to do with the free love she advocated. Her free love was about freedom, about a love infused with truth and purity.

But her critics boiled all her controversial ideas down to this one, and they turned "free love" into an epithet equivalent to unbridled licentiousness. As the distortion of her free love views spread through the press, the animosity reignited between the New York suffragists and the Boston wing, which had formed the conservative American Woman Suffrage Association. Mary Livermore, editor of the Boston wing's *Woman's Journal*, called Woodhull's Fourteenth and Fifteenth Amendments argument a "short cut"—she preferred to wait for the Sixteenth Amendment than to rely on a woman whose "hands are unclean."

In May 1871, the press predicted a war to the knife when the two suffrage associations held overlapping conventions in New York. The *Tribune* drew blood early on, accusing the New York wing of paying homage to a woman who boastfully promulgated the free love abomination. What were blushing schoolgirl converts to their creed supposed to think? Woodhull's supporters fired back that *Tribune* editor Horace Greeley hid more "dirty moral linen" in his wash than the women he attacked. Meanwhile the Boston suffragists condemned any attempt to associate them with free love doctrines "as a slander upon the virtue and intelligence of American women."

Despite the odium flung at her, Woodhull had triumphed at what the *Herald* called the convention of WOODHULL'S WOMEN. As the May meeting opened, a Minneapolis delegate put forth a tribute that bordered on veneration: "We honor Victoria C. Woodhull for her fine intellectual ability, her courage and independence of character, her liberality and high moral worth. . . . We, as women, owe her a debt of gratitude which we can only repay by working with and for her with our whole hearts."

With that accolade hanging in the hall, Woodhull advanced toward the front of the platform for her afternoon speech. She spent a few minutes building up her demand for a declaratory act by Congress that the Constitution already enshrined suffrage for women, through the Fourteenth Amendment stating they were citizens and the Fifteenth giving all citizens the vote. She reviewed the sins of the Republican and Democratic Parties, then issued her ultimatum: "If Congress refuse to listen to and grant what women ask, there is but one course left. . . . We will have our rights. We say no longer by your leave. We have besought, argued, and convinced, but we have failed. And we will not fail. We will try you just once more. If the very next Congress refuse women all the legitimate rights of citizenship . . . we shall call another convention expressly to frame a new constitution and to erect a new government."

She was calling for treason, secession, revolution, Woodhull admitted. No alternative was left them. *We convened to declare exactly that*, she told the people filling Apollo Hall.

They bought it. The May meeting closed with the unanimous passage of a resolution: "Resolved, That this Convention do now adjourn to meet again . . . in Washington on Wednesday and Thursday of the second week of January next; that in case Congress refuses to pass a declaratory act [we] may proceed to organize a new political party based on the declaration of the fathers of '76, that 'governments derive their just powers from the consent of the governed.'"

Now the second Wednesday of the next January had arrived. As Woodhull listened to Elizabeth Cady Stanton open the 1872 proceedings, she was determined to make this convention stick to its resolve.

The "best class of society" filled Lincoln Hall this January morning, prominent men and women wearing "terrible earnestness on their faces." They were far more diverse that the usual crowd for a suffrage convention. Woodhull had seen to that. Over the past six months, the vilification of her had risen to fever pitch—a "free love panic," in the words of one suffragist. Even the Minneapolis delegate who had venerated her in May had turned against her. Woodhull needed reinforcements. To get them, she had packed the hall. Spiritualists who had elected her president of their association occupied row upon row, labor reformers too, and in lesser numbers temperance advocates and progressive educators.

Susan B. Anthony was not pleased. While her fellow leaders Elizabeth Cady Stanton and Isabella Beecher Hooker still fell under Woodhull's spell, Anthony had been holding her tongue. She viewed Spiritualism as little better than hocus pocus. She didn't want her cause watered down with it, or with labor, temperance, or any other kind of reform. More than one newspaper had commented how single-minded she was when it came to suffrage, getting hold of one nail after another and driving it home. Today she was as determined to thwart a shift toward broader goals as Woodhull was to achieve it.

In her opening remarks, Stanton echoed Woodhull's earlier talk of treason, secession, and revolution: "We now propose to take our rights. If we don't get them, we will organize a government outside of the bogus republic and carry on one of our own." Anthony heard betrayal in her longtime partner's words. When Stanton yielded the floor, she countered. Any party putting woman suffrage in its plank would win her support, Anthony pledged. The fault line between the two leaders was subtle: one willing to tear down the old institutions that had failed the suffragists, the other insisting the better course was to work within those institutions; one reaching for a broader vision, the other fiercely focused on the suffrage cause that had united them for so long.

Elizabeth Cady Stanton and Susan B. Anthony.
National Portrait Gallery

Woodhull was a wedge threatening to split the crack open.

It would not split now. Today was for rallying the troops and setting the lines, not for frontal attack. Woodhull addressed the Spiritualists she had drafted into her army. They had never been a politically oriented group. Now she told them their destiny was to carry the banner of reform, to throw off the names Democrat and Republican that had become a stench in the nostrils, to embrace "Equal Rights," to battle and never falter until those rights were planted in the hands of the Goddess of Liberty atop the Capitol dome.

When Hooker took the floor, she wandered from one side of the fault to the other. As a representative of the Beecher family, she didn't much sympathize with the Spiritualism creed. Still, she agreed that if the Spiritualists had brains enough to comprehend and soul enough to embrace the position Woodhull invited them to, they would rule the world. The times were auspicious for a new party, she said. Ties to the old guard were broken, politicians were losing their hold on the masses, and ideas on human rights had never been clearer in the popular mind. Suffrage remained the preeminent issue for any new political organization, however, and that's where she intended to concentrate her energies.

Other speakers addressed a range of issues. If a topic got too far afield, Anthony, as the presiding officer of the moment, steered it back to suffrage. It was contrary to the "conventionalities of red tape" for her to talk, she acknowledged, but she was doing it anyway. The crowd laughed.

When the evening session resumed at 7:30, Woodhull was the featured speaker. She wheeled out her big gun—the new constitution she proposed. The next day's *Herald* burlesqued it as "embodying the purposes and principles of the revolution," including denial of corporate privileges, progressive taxation, land redistribution, a voice in government for everyone, education for all children, and "a thousand other radicalisms." By the time Woodhull swore she wasn't waiting another sixty years and threatened to shoulder a musket so "our gracious masters" in Congress "tremble in their usurped seats," the crowd was roused, and talk of her Equal Rights Party, as she now called it, hurtled through the hall.

———————————————

The next morning the clock ticked past the opening hour. The crowd stamped its feet. Finally, Anthony led the women out. Her pique was evident. When the second speaker called existing political parties "humbugs," she interrupted the program to repeat her own stand on that topic. "It is this," she said. "If any party put a woman's suffrage plank in its platform, and nominate candidates in accordance therewith who are aboveboard in favor of woman having the ballot, that party is my party. I shall take the stump for that party at the next presidential campaign. . . . I will help to fly its kite, but I am not willing to be the last little paper knot in the tail." To laughter and applause, she tore off her shawl and hurled it across the stage.

"Laugh at me just as much as you please," she said, "for I am just as mad as I can be." She launched into a tirade about the names she had been called over twenty years. After swearing she would fly its kite if its candidate embraced suffrage, she all but cursed the Republican Party. It could already have enfranchised women with one scratch of the pen. "I set my heel on that party," she roared. "I am mad. Victoria Woodhull was mad last night, but she did not begin to be as mad as I am now."

With the crowd worked up, Anthony attacked her enemy. The "finger of scorn" had killed off untold women, she charged, but she would have none of it. She would welcome all the infamous women in New York to sit side by side with her on the platform, would take by the hand every prostitute at the mercy of men. Then she uttered the name Victoria C. Woodhull. "She is young, handsome and rich," Anthony said. "If it takes youth, beauty and money to capture Congress, Victoria is the woman we are after." Pausing for a moment of laughter, Anthony fired her deadly shot. "I was asked if I knew of Mrs. Woodhull's antecedents. I said I didn't, and I did not care any more about them than those of Congress. Her antecedents will compare favorably with any member of Congress. I will not allow any human being wearing the form of manhood to ask me to desist working with any woman."

The words pretended to carry praise. But Anthony had just tied the woman already branded a "free lover" to a streetwalker. The *Tribune* laid out Anthony's message in blunt terms: the immoral charges against Woodhull were irrelevant on the grounds that no degree of degradation should deprive a person of her political rights. It was damnation, not defense. Hearing it, the *Herald* headlined THE WOODHULL AND THE ANTHONY INTEREST AT WAR. Instantly a rumor was set afloat, reported the *Herald*'s man: "Mrs. Woodhull's voice of vengeance would be heard."

After a few more backhanded belts disguised as compliments, Anthony again laid down her marker. We "work for woman suffrage. We don't endorse any sect, breed or political power. We don't endorse temperance, labor reform or Spiritualism, but we do emphatically endorse woman suffrage. Now do you understand our platform?"

One of her stalwarts yelled, "Long live Miss Anthony."

Not everyone agreed. Before the morning session recessed, an angry Spiritualist rushed the stage. Woodhull was one of the grandest women God ever made, she declared, one she was willing to fight, bleed, and die for. When a second woman accused Anthony of injustice, Anthony declared the session closed. A general uprising took hold. Amid shouting, the meeting broke apart. Throughout the recess, men and women interrogated one another. *Which side are you on?*

Woodhull would not raise her voice in vengeance this day. When the convention resumed at two o'clock, Hooker, ever the peacemaker, proposed a song of patriotism. The audience bellowed out, "My country 'tis of thee, sweet land of liberty . . ." The lion and lamb lay down together, as the *Herald* described Woodhull meekly seating herself beside Anthony.

The first speaker picked up Anthony's theme of fallen women, arguing that in their present position, many women were inevitably driven to the wall. Poor Alice Bowlsby, she lamented; how often had she wept for that dear girl facing life as an outcast, murdered at the hands of abortionist Dr. Rosenzweig, and stuffed into a trunk. Only with the ballot could women avoid such calamities and rise to their full beauty and purity.

After two more speakers, Anthony read letters from gentlemen who declined to attend the convention. Most paid lip service to woman suffrage but wouldn't so much as give up their pet vices to help—chewing, drinking, smoking, and a few other vices Anthony declined to mention. The crowd snoozed through a half dozen letters before she jostled it awake with the name Henry Ward Beecher.

Beecher had addressed his letter to Mrs. Victoria Woodhull, for she had requested his presence. Though he doubted not of suffrage's "ultimate accomplishment," he was regrettably engaged this particular week. Nevertheless, he hoped always to be in sympathy with "every wise and Christian movement for the education and enfranchisement of woman."

Reading Beecher's words, Anthony understood their code. So did Woodhull, the other suffrage leaders, and more than a few in the crowd, even if a good number were fooled into applause. "Wise and Christian" did not encompass ideas held by some people in this hall, particularly the free lover to whom the letter was addressed.

The words certainly didn't fool Laura Cuppy Smith. Furious, Smith attacked the hypocrisy of the clergy generally and the Reverend Beecher specifically. "Ministers of the Gospel dare not investigate or take interest in progressive theories," she charged. Bishops were afraid to "love truth too dangerously, but ever prefer the interests of the Church. Country clergymen visiting our large cities hang upon the outskirts of spiritualism, take a peep at the *Black Crook* and venture to call upon Mrs. Woodhull, but would not dare indulge in these luxuries save in secret and away from the watchful gaze of their congregations."

She created a sensation. Many in the hall, certainly Anthony, Stanton, and Woodhull, understood that "luxuries" referred to illicit indulgences of a sexual nature, and they knew precisely how Beecher himself partook of them. Smith was calling him out: "Henry Ward Beecher's power and influence are limited by the extent of his courage." She drew a sharp contrast between Beecher and Victoria Woodhull, whose "popularity is founded upon her high-souled vindication of the truth as she apprehends it." Smith was no hero-worshiper, she said, but "my whole soul does homage to the principles of which I deem this grand woman to be the inspired representative."

With applause ringing in the hall, Stanton adjourned the afternoon session. Victoria Woodhull spoke not a word.

Woodhull got her blood up the next morning. The Senate Judiciary Committee at last had condescended to hear the ladies out. The suffragists delegated six women, including Stanton, Anthony, Hooker, and Woodhull, to attend the presentation scheduled for ten o'clock. They entered the Capitol with the fury of an invading force. An advance guard had swarmed the corridors. More women than would fit spilled into the committee room with the six ladies delegated to attend. When the sergeant at arms attempted to clear them out, Woodhull and another held the doorknob fast, refusing him entry. Meanwhile the committee members, led by Senator Lyman Trumbull, were nowhere to be seen. *Trumbull is taking a bath*, Hooker charged, admitting the senator needed purification. To the ears of one observer, that accusation was one of the more dignified remarks coming out of the mob.

An hour later, the committee wedged through the hallway. Trumbull accepted defeat. *Throw the doors open*, he ordered. For the next two hours, the senators heard Hooker, Anthony, and Stanton make the case for the "Woodhull Memorial" presented to their counterparts in the House a year earlier. After promising a speedy consideration of their appeal, the senators looked on with relief as the ladies departed for a complimentary lunch in the Senate dining room.

The convention opened at two that afternoon. Stanton led things off: "The signs of the times indicate the formation of a third party, in the presence of which both the old parties may well tremble. . . . We shall assemble in convention all over the country." Woodhull must have relished the call for the convention she sought, while Anthony must have fumed, though no observers remarked upon either's reaction. The tide of battle became clear when the next speaker introduced a resolution: "*Resolved*, that we rejoice in the rapidly organizing millions of Spiritualists, labor reformers, temperance and educational forces now simultaneously waking to their need of woman's help in the cause of reform."

Anthony failed to seize the floor before Stephen Pearl Andrews was introduced. Andrews was a radical's radical who had long played a role in writing and editing *Woodhull & Claflin's Weekly.* Many of the ideas that got Woodhull into heaps of trouble were his doing. Anthony could only have cringed when he addressed her: "I congratulate you on the death of the woman suffrage movement; dead because it has fulfilled its mission." Neither could his congratulations to Stanton and Hooker have pleased them, the former on her imminent election to the Senate, the latter on her appointment to the US Supreme Court. He was sure both would result from the morning's hearing before the Senate Judiciary Committee.

The crowd didn't appreciate Andrews either. He rambled on about jurisprudence and science and the forces at work in society. Hisses spread through the crowd. Stanton told the audience to hear him out, he was almost through. The hoots strengthened, cheering Anthony's heart as Woodhull's champion was hounded from the stage. But the hoots turned to chants: *Woodhull, Woodhull, Woodhull!* To a wild clamor, Hooker brought the woman forward.

Her heart was too full, Woodhull said; she could hardly speak, yet she thanked her brothers and sisters for their appreciation and encouragement. She was more determined than ever to push the Car of Progress, she promised.

One woman, a suffragist and a Spiritualist but no more than a distant acquaintance, rose from her seat. She raised her voice above the din: "Woodhull for President of the United States." She was placing the name in nomination before the convention.

Anthony burst into action. No, it was premature, she argued; and what about Stanton and Hooker and even Anthony herself? They all had claims to be considered.

She was too late. The nomination was put to the convention and seconded. In a roar of unanimity, it carried, not even Anthony able to cast a *no* amid the pandemonium.

4 | "THESE HEARTLESS AND UNSCRUPULOUS SPECIMENS OF HUMAN DEPRAVITY"

WHEN THE CLERK OF THE NEW YORK SUPREME COURT called the appeal of Ann E. Burns the third week of January 1872, the abortionist stewed in Sing Sing, sentenced to seven years for manslaughter in the second degree. Burns's patient Mary Russell had died five months earlier.

Russell had boarded at a house on East Broadway. The location was one a factory girl could afford, not the worst neighborhood but close to it. A couple of minutes' walk took her to the Bowery. Wah Kee operated his opium den off one corner. On another, McLaughlin's dog pit offered a hundred-dollar purse to the most vicious terrier of the evening, double if he killed a hundred rats within a quarter hour. Running north, the Bowery was an open market for venality of all flavors.

Across the Bowery, Russell entered the star of a street crossing that gave Five Points its name. Twenty thousand people crammed into the ward's wretched tenements and spilled into its narrow, crooked streets. The gutters overflowed with filth. Bucket shops slowly poisoned the survivors of the neighborhood's violence and poverty with vile concoctions the proprietors sold as whiskey. The stench of misery and crime hung heavy in the air.

Every day, Russell passed through this horrid side of the city to her job at an envelope factory. Still she maintained an air of innocence. She was affectionate and kind and most careful to conduct herself as a young woman should. She had a dear friend in Nellie Ryan, her roommate and coworker. Her married sister lived blocks away. At twenty-two she was bright and beautiful, with golden hair and a fine figure.

Her beauty caught the eye of a neighbor, Henry Pullen. He was a younger man, eighteen, and handsome. He worked as a compositor for Frank Leslie, publisher of *Frank Leslie's Illustrated Weekly* and the *Day's Doings*. Russell and Pullen began stepping out together. Many evenings they visited another neighbor, a Mrs. Hamblin. After months of courting, Pullen seduced Russell.

Russell found herself in the family way. With women taught next to nothing about their bodies, such pregnancies occurred often enough. Any lessons about conception most likely taught that steps to prevent it thwarted the laws of heaven, as one preacher put it.

Certainly devices were available through the mail: "French safes," rubber sheaths a man wore, or "womb veils," rubber cups a woman inserted to block his seed, or douching syringes with which she washed it away. While some dealers searched the newspapers for recent brides to market their wares to, a single woman wouldn't hear much unless she happened across a guide like *Medical Common Sense*. Contrary to proper society, its author, Dr. Edward Foote, believed amative sexual relations were vital to a person's well-being. He devoted a major part of his book to "Sexual Philosophy." He wouldn't go so far as free love advocates like *Woodhull & Claflin's Weekly*, though. His discussion on preventing babies appeared in a chapter titled "Essays for Married People Only." Still, had Russell found the book, she might have ordered one of the doctor's innovative devices, which he would send closely sealed for privacy. More likely, Pullen would have seen rubber goods advertised in flash papers catering to sporting men. Smut dealers dominated the market.

So Russell did what most women did. She told Pullen she expected to be a mother. Unfortunately, Pullen didn't want to be a father. *No affair of mine*, he told her. Four months had passed since their last intimacy, and hadn't she been on many "moonlight excursions" since? That conversation was the last he saw of her, he later said.

Pullen did, however, tell their friendly neighbor Mrs. Hamblin that Russell was pregnant. He handed the woman ten dollars to give Russell in exchange for a gold ring the girl had torn from his finger. Ten dollars matched the amount charged by the abortionist Mrs. Hamblin had heard of, Ann Burns. Hamblin took Russell to Burns's office during evening visiting hours she held for less well-to-do women. *Can you get me out of my trouble?* Russell asked. Burns said yes, she helped any woman who would take good care of herself, but otherwise she would do nothing. Russell promised she would have the best care. She agreed to return the next week.

My mind is made up, Russell told her roommate, Nellie Ryan. *Will you come with me?*

Yes, Ryan would support her friend.

The next Sunday, Ann Burns's landlady showed them in. Burns again queried who could care for Russell. Her aunt, she lied, for she had not even told her sister. Burns took her into a small room. The landlady pressed Russell against a wall while Burns injected a liquid into her womb. The procedure took a few minutes. Afterward Burns told Russell the fetus would pass in a couple of days. Tonight she should take some pills. In three or four days, she would be well.

Burns cautioned that the operation was not always successful. If for some reason Russell did not lose the baby, she should return in a week. And a woman could die from the procedure. Under no circumstances should Russell identify Burns. If anyone asked, Dr. Tully gave her the medicine. Before she left, Russell had Burns check that the way was clear. She feared running into her sister.

When Russell returned to her boardinghouse, her head ached horribly. She vomited. She suffered through a few days until the fetus passed. Exhausted, she begged the help of a washerwoman she knew through her sister and soon found herself at her sister's home being examined by the family physician. She was hemorrhaging. Yes, she told him, she had taken medicine from Dr. Tully for an abortion.

Two days later another doctor examined her. She claimed to be married six months. Ultimately, she confessed her lie and admitted to an abortion by Ann Burns of Clinton Street. Russell cried in agony. Fearing her death was near, the doctor called in the coroner to take her antemortem statement. Russell spilled out everything—her seduction by Pullen, the ten dollars he paid her, the operation by Burns, the suffering she had since endured. "I am too weak to sign my name," she said, and scrawled a mark. At two o'clock the next morning, Russell died.

After a month in Sing Sing, Ann Burns could have been cursing her luck or her lawyer for landing her there. She was lumped into an isolated building with 116 other women. Its design as a Greek temple didn't make its cells any more comfortable. The women sat around sewing summer jackets and earning twenty-two and a half cents for their day's work. Burns believed she was meant for better things.

For two decades, women in trouble had sought Burns's help. Plenty needed her, or others like her. Rakes who called themselves gentlemen got women in trouble, and a woman faced ruin when she started showing. Yes, women should take precautions. But it was a man's world. That's who sat in the New York legislature and outlawed any article or medicine preventing a pregnancy. That's who likely as not refused to sheathe himself, or ripped the rubber out of even his wife if he caught her protecting herself, so what that she already fed a half dozen kids.

So Burns had a thriving practice, a professional practice, not like the butchers the news screeched about. She didn't advertise in the *Herald* or the *Mercury* or the *Day's Doings*. She wouldn't associate her name with hacks, and her reputation brought plenty of business. Wealthy women called by appointment at the rooms she rented on Clinton Street. Those of modest means visited during evening hours she held a night or two a week. Their treatment cost just ten dollars. Sure, many were frightened. To show how safe her concoction was, Burns tasted it before injecting her patients with it. Beforehand, each patient had to arrange a safe place to recuperate and promise to return if she had problems. But most women didn't have to return, making the treatment the last Burns saw of them. She valued their unspoken gratitude.

She had prospered. Not like the lady with the mansion on Fifth Avenue, Madame Restell, who might charge a society lady thousands to rid herself of an extra child. The wealthy of the city—merchants, bankers, physicians, attorneys—flocked to her soirees, attracted by her generosity and charm and perhaps her touch of notoriety. New wealth, anyway, along with those it could buy—magistrates and legislators and others of the political class. Restell paid them handsomely to keep her out of Sing Sing.

Burns didn't aspire to that kind of society, though. She was happy with her farm on Long Island, a hundred acres with a two-story house. She was entertaining there when two detectives knocked. She was needed in the city, they told her, something to do with the "trunk affair" that had unfolded over the past nine days. An abhorrent crime, she agreed, and she "could clear her skirts" of any association with its perpetrator, Dr. Rosenzweig. She would gladly accompany the officers. As no trains ran until morning, she furnished the officers with bedrooms. If fearing a ruse neither slept a wink, that was their problem. She was as good as her word. At 8:00 AM, they arrived in the city.

At the station house, the detectives sprang the true reason for their visit. *Your patient Mary Russell died of uterine hemorrhage brought on by the abortion you performed*, they said. *Two doctors confirmed the cause of death, and Russell confessed everything.*

Damn her fortune. At any other time, Burns might have gotten off. When another woman had accused her two years earlier, the prosecutors released her after a short detention. But the trunk affair had inflamed the city. The press lumped Burns with the fiend Rosenzweig before she even knew poor Russell was dead. The *Tribune* compared Russell's fate to "the murder of Alice Bowlsby in the Rosenzweig den." The *Evening Post* reported that Russell's golden hair fell in waves over her bosom as she lay in the coffin, reminding everyone of Bowlsby the moment she was pulled from the trunk.

Judge Gunning Bedford, presiding over the Court of General Sessions, fueled the fire. He had already sent Dr. Wolff and Dr. Evans to Sing Sing and was encouraging the medical societies to push for stronger penalties. The morning of Burns's arrest, he preached to his new grand jury, the one who would be called upon to indict her, "Of late we have been living, as it were, in an atmosphere of abortion. In one word, the very air is, indeed, heavy with the dark deeds of these heartless and unscrupulous specimens of human depravity. Let the warning word this day go forth, and may it be scattered broad-cast throughout the land, that from this hour the authorities, one and all, shall put forth every effort and shall strain every nerve until these professional abortionists, these traffickers in human life, shall be exterminated."

What about the poor girls in trouble, didn't they deserve a bit of sympathy? Mary's suffering wasn't enough. Police detectives impersonated doctors at Burns's office—"quack doctors," according to the spy the *Herald* planted among them. The next day's paper named three women who had inquired of her services that evening. The shame they faced was akin to a public stoning.

When she hired William Howe as her lawyer, Burns no doubt thought she was paying for the best. His dramatic power, honed as an amateur Shakespearean, entranced jurors. He employed every tactic to sway the twelve men—dropping to his knees in overwrought emotion, violently thrashing the prosecution's table with a murder weapon, startling the woman he was defending into tears to expose her broken heart. Even his outrageous garb was a tool, growing tamer as a trial proceeded to win sympathy with the jury.

Yet as witness after witness testified at the inquest examining Russell's death, Howe sat mute. Only after the coroner read Russell's antemortem statement did he speak up. *Inadmissible*, he argued, *the deceased did not express a belief she was about to die.* The objection was a mere technicality against the word of the doctors who attested to the cause of death; the friends and family who described Russell's condition leading up to and following the abortion; and the eyewitness, Burns's landlady and assistant, who the police intimidated into testifying lest she take the fall. The coroner's jury ruled Mary Russell died of medical malpractice at the hands of Ann Burns.

The trial in December before Recorder John Hackett proved little better. The same witnesses trooped to the stand and recited the same version of events. The newspapers didn't bother to mention whatever meager cross-examination Howe conducted. They reported only that the defense produced a few character witnesses, whom the prosecution rebutted, and put Burns on the stand to deny treating Russell beyond giving her a glass of water when she sought advice for dizziness and headache. That testimony opened Burns to cross-examination. The prosecutor forced her to acknowledge that many women sought abortions from her and that she had been arrested for that crime two years ago. Still she denied ever performing one. In his summation, Howe offered no impassioned plea, no histrionics. He simply reviewed the testimony and argued the jury was illegally empaneled. Judge Bedford had called jurors for the November term and could not extend their service for a trial commencing in December. Recorder Hackett had overruled that technicality when the trial opened.

Was Burns supposed to believe Howe could get her out of Sing Sing now?

William Howe understood how to win over twelve men better than anyone in New York. He also knew how to lose them, and so he refused to mount any defense not founded on circumstances appealing to the common sense an average juror brought to the courtroom. When the trial of Ann Burns had opened the past December, the circumstances allowed no such option. Mary Russell's condition and cause of death were beyond dispute; she had given a deathbed confession, and an accessory to the crime had promised an eyewitness account of the abortion Burns performed on Russell.

Howe's recourse was either to plead to as light a crime as the district attorney would accept or to overturn the jury's verdict on a technicality.

Thus he bookended the trial with a single issue. He offered no resistance to any of the twelve men chosen to judge his client. But immediately after their selection, he objected to the lot.

By law the Court of General Sessions began a term on the first Monday or Tuesday of the month. The presiding judge empaneled jurors to hear the month's cases. Judge Bedford, the abortionists' nemesis, had done so in November. When Recorder Hackett, presiding over the December term, began the Burns trial, he ordered jury selection from the group empaneled by Bedford. *Those gentlemen are not eligible to serve in the December term*, Howe told Hackett. *The trial cannot proceed.*

A grave question, Recorder Hackett noted. He nonetheless overruled the objection and began the testimony so damning to Burns. As the jury was about to go into deliberations, Howe insisted again that it was illegally empaneled. Hackett instructed the jury anyway. The twelve returned a verdict of guilty.

As Howe entered the New York Supreme Court a month later, Ann Burns's fate hung on the jury's legitimacy. Three magistrates hearing the appeal peered from the bench. Judges Daniel Ingraham, Albert Cardozo, and George Barnard were friendly faces to Howe. Go-to friends, you might call them. If Howe lost a case in the Court of Special Sessions, which tried misdemeanors, he obtained a writ of habeas corpus from one of these judges. The writ required that Howe's imprisoned client be brought before that judge to determine whether he or she should be held or released. Over the past four years, the judges had freed 269 such prisoners, by one estimate, without bail and without cause. While all those cases were supposed to be retried, not a single one had returned to court. According to rumor, the large sums coerced from clients for this service made a very profitable business for the parties involved.

Howe repeated his argument that the jury convicting Burns was illegally empaneled. The assistant district attorney countered with another technicality. An appeal on the basis Howe chose required a special plea by the defense during the original trial, he told the court. Howe had made no such plea.

In their remarks, the supreme court judges indicated Howe was within his rights to appeal on these grounds. It was a minor victory. They reserved the decision on the appeal itself. The case was weighty, after all. Burns was hardly the only defendant convicted under these questionable arrangements. Who knew how many prisoners convicted in the December term would be released if the supreme court ruled in her favor?

Three days later the supreme court heard another case with similar implications. The Court of Special Sessions typically operated with a single judge. But the New York State Constitution required two judges to hear a case in Special Sessions, argued defense attorneys. Howe had a vested interest. Though the case of another lawyer was chosen as the test, a favorable ruling could free hundreds of his clients. Between the Burns appeal and this case, the supreme court might instigate a wholesale emptying of the jails.

Meanwhile Burns took little solace. She remained locked in the penitentiary.

Ann Burns was not the only of Howe's clients waiting on the New York Supreme Court to overturn an abortion conviction. After her lackluster defense, she would not have appreciated all the tricks Howe had pulled for the butcher Thomas Evans. Within days of Evans's arrest in the death of his patient Mary Geary, Howe secured his release on bail. The Ghoul of Chatham Street went back to his disgusting den and was tending patients. Very likely the case would never go to trial. Multiple doctors, the victim's friends and relatives, and several women lying in with Geary were prepared to testify to her deteriorating condition under Dr. Evans's care and ultimately to her death of puerperal convulsions. But the only witness to the supposed abortion, Geary herself, was dead.

At the coroner's inquest, spectators were visibly repulsed by how shabby and beaten down Evans looked. He fidgeted nervously. Hearing the testimony against him, he mumbled repeatedly to his attorney, cried out to the court. Howe told him within earshot of a reporter to keep still, his feelings and fear were damaging his chances. But when Howe cross-examined the doctors, they admitted childbirth alone could bring on the convulsions that killed Geary. The case evaporated.

Unfortunately for Evans, another woman, named Ann O'Neill, was lying near death in Bellevue Hospital. While Evans had waited for the coroner's inquest in the Geary case, which would find him guilty of nothing more than failure to properly treat Geary, O'Neill had delivered twins. Both babies died. Their mother survived. O'Neill swore an affidavit that in August 1870 Dr. Evans had performed an abortion on her. The operation failed. In September she had returned to his Chatham Street den, where she witnessed Geary's death.

Evans nearly dropped in his chair when a police officer served him a warrant for "committing an abortion with instruments on the person of Ann O'Neill." "This is worse than the other case," he cried. "The Geary girl is dead." He understood the threat of a surviving woman bearing witness.

Evans spent Christmas 1870 locked in the Tombs. But he transferred his real estate to his sister and servant so they could serve as his sureties for $75,000 bail. He walked free. The *Herald* questioned whether he would ever be deprived of his liberty again. Howe would avert trial through bribery, disappearing witnesses, or some other scheme, the paper predicted. But this time Howe's magic failed. The district attorney locked O'Neill in the House of Detention to ensure she didn't skip town with a purse full of money.

The trial opened in May 1871. Howe launched into his courtroom antics, insisting a man who had read about the case be disqualified as a juror. Judge Bedford lectured him on how that criterion would exclude every intelligent being in New York. Before the day was out, Howe had raised a ruckus about the advertising circular that brought O'Neill to Evans, a police captain's estimate of the "inmates" discovered in the doctor's den, and the pills Evans gave out, which were harmless cornmeal dyed red.

When the prosecution closed, Howe moved for dismissal. On the stand, O'Neill had admitted her true family name was Drew, invalidating the indictment. After the judge ruled the motion nonsense, Howe denied any crime had occurred, only treatment for a disease. He claimed blackmailers demanded $10,000 to drop the case. He coached the defendant into an incoherent monologue rambling from jumbled medical jargon to how to restore paradise and create heaven on earth. Then he suggested his client would plead insanity.

Howe's tricks, along with a two-hour summation, affected the judge if not the jury. Realizing the case boiled down to a she said, he said, Bedford lectured jurors on the goodness and truthfulness all had witnessed in Ann O'Neill and the shameless incredulity and brazen effrontery of Dr. Evans hiding a career of untold wickedness. Bedford also understood that Howe's machinations cast serious doubt on the original charge of manslaughter. *Your duty,* he told the jury, *is to render a verdict on assault of Ann O'Neill with intent to commit manslaughter in the second degree.* Howe had won a minor victory before jury deliberations began. "Assault with intent" carried half the maximum penalty of manslaughter itself.

An hour later, the jury foreman announced a verdict of "guilty of an attempt at abortion." Bedford said no, not allowed; the jury must either acquit the prisoner or find him guilty of assault with intent to commit manslaughter. Howe flew into a rage. The jury had every right to find his client had used an instrument with intent to produce miscarriage, a misdemeanor. Further deliberations interspersed with further instructions followed, with Howe watching every detail for the tiniest error. Finally, the judge sequestered the jury for the night.

The next morning, Bedford got his verdict, guilty of assault with intent. He sentenced Evans to the maximum three and a half years at hard labor. Spectators applauded. Evans could hardly control his agony.

Howe appealed for a new trial and an arrest of judgment. Now, in February 1872, his go-to friends on the New York Supreme Court were set to rule on his appeal.

Howe's timing could not have been worse. The Judiciary Committee of the Assembly of the State of New York was investigating the conduct of Judges Barnard and Cardozo. The Bar Association of New York had prepared charges. One asserted that Cardozo and Barnard had been in the pockets of Jim Fisk and Jay Gould. Without the judges' corrupt cooperation, Fisk and Gould could never have made millions in their gold corner. Nor could the pair have swindled the stockholders in their takeover of the

Erie Railroad. Another charge accused the judges of conspiring with Messrs. Howe & Hummel in discharging prisoners without just, legal, or any cause. The Bar Association named 179 convicted Howe & Hummel clients turned loose.

If ever judges wanted to distance themselves from an attorney, it was now. On February 10, Barnard and Cardozo did it. The New York Supreme Court denied Thomas Evans a new trial. Barnard wrote the opinion: "I find nothing in the case that calls for more than a hasty examination to show that the trial was properly conducted."

To add insult to injury, the court ruled on the Court of Special Sessions the same day. Writing the opinion, Cardozo held decisions under a single judge valid so long as the record showed the second justice to be absent. Convicted prisoners would remain behind bars.

Despite Howe's friendly judges abandoning him this day, all was not lost. In New York, the state's supreme court was not "supreme." Both cases moved upward to the New York State Court of Appeals.

5 | "THE FEMALE FORM DIVINE IN VARIOUS AND PICTURESQUE ATTITUDES"

ONE DAY EARLY IN 1872, a troubled Anthony Comstock strode uptown to the Fifth Avenue Presbyterian Church. He was a Congregationalist himself. The church where he taught Sunday school was six blocks from his home in Brooklyn. The proximity spared him from traveling by train on the Sabbath, which he considered sinful. For whatever reason, Comstock chose not to unburden himself to his local pastor. He had briefly met the young Reverend John Hall presiding over the Fifth Avenue Presbyterians and sought his advice instead.

After five years in New York, Comstock's life was going well. He had arrived in the city with five dollars in his pocket, less the train fare from Connecticut. His first job was as a porter hauling cases of dry goods for twelve dollars a week. His initiative straightening the stock earned him a promotion to shipping clerk. Before long he moved into sales. Now age twenty-seven, he was earning $1,500 a year on commission at the dry goods wholesaler Cochrane, McLean & Company.

A year ago on a beautiful January day, Comstock had wed. His bride, Maggie, was ten years older and worn down from toiling in her father's failed business. Acquaintances recalled her as a frail skeleton always dressed in black and saying hardly a word. Comstock saw only the "little wifey" of whom he had long dreamed. After taking the train to Philadelphia for their first night together, the naughty newlyweds slept until ten o'clock. They enjoyed a hearty laugh upon discovering many couples as lazy as them sharing a late breakfast.

Anthony scraped together $500 to put down on a house in Brooklyn. Maggie's invalid sister joined them there. Anthony busied himself in domestic bliss, building a birdhouse for the yard, cooking Sunday dinner for his father-in-law, sewing the bastings on a dress Maggie had underway. "So bright, so sweet," he wrote in his diary. "I cannot realize this great blessing. O let me consecrate myself to the one who has bestowed

53

all this upon me." Before Christmas 1871, a daughter further blessed the couple. They named her Lillie.

But family life brought new responsibilities, and the house put Comstock in debt. Business was poor. Comstock blamed himself for his slowing sales, noting how the prior year he had prayed more and worked harder. He rededicated himself, swearing to "go to my Father and say unto Him, Father, I have sinned." Looking to God, he would surely succeed. Still, when pursuing customers, he had lost his enthusiasm, grown "too cold."

Money worries were not the troubles bringing Comstock to the Reverend John Hall, however. "Give me a man who dares to do right and one ready at all times to discharge his duty to the community and to God," Comstock wrote in his diary. A dry goods salesman would never be such a man, and he knew it. He needed a calling.

Reverend Hall barely remembered his earlier introduction to the young man entering his study. The visitor had the body of a boxer. His legs were as thick as tree trunks and short despite his height, only two inches shy of six feet. His chest and biceps bulged with muscle. The dome of his head showed through thinning ginger hair. Thick muttonchops forested his cheeks. His piercing gaze challenged. The overall impression must have been hard to reconcile with the tears pouring from his blue-gray eyes as the man told Reverend Hall of "the hydra-headed monster" he had unearthed.

The monster was obscenity sold throughout the city—books, pamphlets, photographs, stereoscopic pictures, playing cards, newspapers. Comstock had discovered the traffic operated as an organized business. Newspapers from the *Herald* to the *Day's Doings* advertised it openly. Young men withered like autumn leaves under the blight of its touch. Yet public sentiment against the trade was dead. Officials ignored it. Laws to fight it were inadequate and corrupted.

Comstock acknowledged the daring of the highwayman who points his pistol and demands your money or your life. He admitted to the cunning of the sneak thief creeping into a house and gathering up the spoils. But he could imagine no such traits of character in the wretched scoundrels who secretly poison the minds of boys and girls with smut.

He was taking up the sword against those scoundrels, Comstock told Hall. In Comstock's face, Hall saw a fervor he would not forget this time. He befriended the young man and encouraged him in his chosen work.

––––––––––––

Early in 1872, Comstock attempted once again to arrest the smut dealer William Simpson. A patrolman tipped off Simpson's clerk while Comstock examined a price list. The clerk refused to sell him any merchandise. Unable to gather evidence, an enraged Comstock preferred charges against the patrolman. The police commissioners dismissed the man from the force.

New York's flash press, weeklies that chronicled the less savory parts of city life, berated Comstock for meddling where he did not belong. The *Sunday Mercury* taunted that if Comstock were the Christian man he professed to be, he could find plenty more such dealers on Nassau and Ann Streets. The jibes did not deter him. "Jesus never would wink at any wrong nor would he countenance it," he confided to his diary. Neither would he, Comstock promised himself. Nor would he ever let money buy him as it did judges and juries in this murderous age.

Determined to investigate the *Mercury*'s claim, Comstock invited the *Tribune* to send a reporter with him to Nassau Street. He enlisted the aid of a police officer, a Captain Ward of the Beekman Street station.

On the cold, wet morning of March 2, the trio gathered at Printing House Square, home to the city's illustrious organs of the press. The wars of the Republic were fought here. The *Tribune* and the *Times* jousted over which would carry the banner of the Republican Party, pitting the honesty of the *Tribune*'s editor Horace Greeley against the *Times*' groveling to President Grant and his corrupt administration. The *New York World* lobbed salvos at both in support of the Democratic bastion, Tammany Hall. Having no opinion of its own, the *Herald* watched like a camp follower eager to scavenge the battlefield when the partisans lay dead. The *Sun* and dozens of smaller dailies fed on whatever scraps the *Herald* left behind.

Heading south from the square, Comstock and his companions entered the netherworld of Nassau. The street's ten blocks to Wall Street were almost too narrow for a pair of hansoms to pass. So many people crowded its walks that pedestrians risked being knocked beneath their wheels. Even on a lovely day its buildings blocked the sun. The district's hive of activity drew comparisons with the casbahs of Egypt and the Tower of Babel. So many professions occupied its labyrinth of offices that even a cat could find no empty corner to crawl into.

Comstock sought one particular profession that congregated on Nassau and the surrounding blocks. Its practitioners hid behind any number of signs—BOOKSELLER, STATIONER, DEALER IN FRENCH ENGRAVINGS, IMPORTER OF FINE MANUSCRIPTS, PUBLISHER OF MEDICAL TEXTS. Rounding the corner onto Ann, he stopped before a small shop at number 19. By all appearances, it was a simple bookstore. Inside Comstock perused the stock. Two European classics caught his eye, *The Confessions of a Voluptuous Young Lady of High Rank* and *The Festival of Love; or, Revels at the Fount of Venus*. He bought the first.

Entering number 16, Comstock obtained the title *Women's Rights Convention*. The rights referred to had nothing in common with the vote suffragists sought. Back on Nassau, he passed beneath a sign reading JAMES MCDERMOTT, BOOK-SELLER. He purchased the volume *La Rose d'Amour*. With evidence in hand, the trio went to the Tombs police court. The judge agreed the materials were obscene and issued warrants.

Printing House Square looking down Nassau Street.
James D. McCabe, Jr., Lights and Shadows of New York Life;
or the Sights and Sensations of The Great City, *1872*

A blinding sleet was falling when the three men returned to Nassau with several of Captain Ward's patrolmen. "There's the man who sold me the book," Comstock cried. He pointed at a bewhiskered fellow exiting the cellar at 19 Ann. The captain seized him. Within the cellar, they found books with titles such as *Venus in the Cloister* and *The True Marriage Guide*. "Gents' and Ladies' Rubber Goods" and "French Playing Cards" were advertised on the walls. Captain Ward tore a map down to reveal a stone passageway holding more books. Another cache hid a batch of photographs, described by the next day's *Sunday Mercury* as representing "the female form divine in various and picturesque attitudes." The *Mercury*'s editors perhaps enjoyed the irony of their paper being the first to report Comstock's exploits and doing so with such salacious language. The *Times*, *Herald*, and *Tribune* described the literature collected with nothing more imaginative than "disgusting" and "bawdy."

The raid at 75 Nassau Street captured the proprietor, James McDermott; a thirteen-year-old clerk; and, in a stroke of luck, William Brooks, brother of the man seized coming out of the cellar at 19 Ann. The police confiscated five hundred stereoscopic views and photographs, one thousand circulars, thirty books, and innumerable rubber goods for preventing pregnancy. In the other shop on Ann, the police collared owner Patrick Bannon, his eleven-year old son, and an older boy. The search of the premises turned up only a few obscene circulars. But as it was going on, another man entered with Bannon's washing. Comstock identified him as the one who had sold him a book in the morning.

The haul was a good day's work: eight men and boys arrested and five bushels of obscene merchandise seized. The *Mercury* predicted the evidence would fuel a lively bonfire when the police courts finished with it. The five men and the oldest boy were locked up for the night. Comstock grudgingly accepted when the judge freed the eleven- and thirteen-year-olds. At arraignment the next morning, two others were released. But as proprietors, James McDermott and Charles and William Brooks faced prosecution. Bail was set at $500. Patrick Bannon was already facing federal charges for sending obscene materials through the mail. The $5,000 bail that got him out of the Ludlow Street jail in February was subject to forfeit.

If Comstock felt grievance over the men let off, he could take consolation in other items seized during the raids. Business records identified dealers across the country. A steel stereotype plate captured at 75 Nassau would prove an even more valuable clue.

———————————

Like so many gentlemen living in Brooklyn, William Haynes kissed his wife goodbye on a typical workday morning and caught the ferry to Manhattan.

Born in Ireland, he had trained as a surgeon in England and married a noblewoman. About 1840, he emigrated to America alone. Some said he fled when caught in the arms of another woman. He hadn't taken up medicine in his new country. He had found an American bride. Together he and Mary built a prosperous business.

From the ferry landing, Haynes walked to his office near the corner of Nassau and Ann Streets. The space was nothing lavish, not what you might expect for a man known as the pioneer in his industry. When he arrived in New York, the business had involved trade with Europe, importing "fancy" books, as they were called, bound in cloth and illustrated with fine engravings. Such books commanded two dollars or more. At those prices, they catered to well-to-do gentlemen discreetly seeking erotic pleasures.

Unfortunately, polite society did not approve of those pleasures. Neither did the US Congress. In 1842 the federal legislators banned the import of "all indecent and obscene prints, paintings, lithographs, engravings, and transparencies." Customs officials began seizing obscene contraband. Haynes saw an opportunity. He would naturalize the smut business.

His strategy involved considerable investment. He needn't write material. The popular European titles were easily pirated. Copyright protection was practically nonexistent anyway. But books had to be set on steel stereotype plates and illustrations engraved on copper. Haynes scraped up the capital for it, then began printing and binding his books in America. Over a decade he built a marketing and distribution network surpassing all other publishers of erotica. Eventually he authored books and commissioned others. He had published over three hundred titles.

One book he pirated was *The Confessions of a Voluptuous Lady of High Rank*. The lady was Tilly Touchitt. Confessing to "the curiosity which a man incited in her," Tilly enjoyed her cousin Joe thrusting his "stiff in-driven wedge" into her as yet unpenetrated "magic circle" until "it hitch[ed] suddenly against the narrowed inlet which refused him further passage toward the interior." Haynes's edition included a "print representing a woman naked and uncovered in an obscene, impudent and indecent posture," in the opinion of the district attorney who indicted Haynes over that title in 1853.

That charge was not the first against him. Seven years earlier another district attorney had sent Haynes to the Tombs for three months. Never wanting to go back, Haynes learned to hide his tracks. These days he hardly touched his product. While clinging to his most valuable assets, the steel and copper plates, he contracted out production, distribution, and sales to a network of printers, binders, express carriers, and middlemen. He shielded himself behind imprints like "Strokeall & Company," located at "Ten inches up red lane, Maidenhead, Sportsman's Square," as some title pages read. Most importantly he learned how to sprinkle greenbacks through the justice system. Money quashed his 1853 indictment over *Confessions*.

If Haynes came into the office on March 2, 1872, he might have looked out the window as a burly man walked by with a police captain and a reporter. He wouldn't have thought much about it unless he spotted the man entering the Brooks brothers' shop. Even then he couldn't have guessed the man left with a copy of *The Confessions of a Voluptuous Lady*. And with rain turning to a blinding sleet in the afternoon, he likely would have headed home to Brooklyn before the man returned with a warrant to raid the shop.

Patrick Bannon appeared in US circuit court five days after Comstock's raid. Since the trial was for prior federal charges, Comstock didn't testify. But he was surely pleased with the sentence—imprisonment for one year and a $500 fine. Judge Charles Benedict handed down an "extreme penalty," in the eyes of the *Times*. Comstock filed that information away. Benedict would become his favored magistrate when he began pursuing federal crimes.

Several days later Comstock entered the city's Court of General Sessions to testify in the cases against Charles and William Brooks and James McDermott. A large man with a prodigious belly, garish outfit, and yachting cap huddled with the defendants. William Howe was taking a break from his defense of the city's most vicious murderers, notorious abortionists, and violent gangs to represent the Brooks brothers. He was about to introduce Comstock to his version of New York justice.

As the day's proceedings were only for the indictment, Howe probably had not settled on a defense. His subsequent actions suggested he was exploring how much money would buy his clients' freedom. He definitely was not waiting to intimidate the chief witness against them. Unless Comstock stopped persecuting his clients, Howe threatened, he would sue him for false arrest and land him in Ludlow Street jail. Comstock was chastened. He had paid the costs of pursuing the smut men from his own pocket, and the time devoted cut into his dry goods sales. With a family to support, he worried over legal expenses to defend himself and the risk of a judgment against him. And if imprisoned even for a short while, would he lose his job?

Bucking up, Comstock vowed that "Tombs shyster" Howe wasn't stopping his crusade. For the next two days, he returned to Nassau Street with more warrants. Raiding three shops, he hauled the proprietors of each plus a porter into the Tombs court. The judge jailed them pending bail.

On Broadway Comstock expanded his net. Dr. Charles Manches professed to be a physician. Really, he dealt in obscene articles, Comstock claimed: rubber goods imported from France that he gave patients not wanting babies. During the arrest, Comstock learned Paturel and Company supplied the doctor with these devices. Comstock hurried down to its store and bought some. The Tombs court judge agreed the items were immoral. But before Comstock and a police officer could serve the warrant, Paturel's staff emptied the shelves. Still, they arrested the Frenchman who had sold Comstock the evidence. When he refused to give his name, the judge locked him away as "John Doe."

Six more arrests in two days. Comstock should have been pleased. But he knew his collars so far were pawns in the business, the final link in a long chain that delivered obscenity to libertines. He wanted bigger game. On Nassau Street he had caught its scent.

The smut men who congregated around Nassau were a small community. Another crusader raiding a few shops wouldn't worry them much. Their business wasn't secret, arguably not even discreet, despite not usually displaying wares in the window. Nor were their identities hidden. Three publishers had monopolized the supply for years, and dealers needed customers. How could their names not get out?

Still William Haynes could not have been happy reading about the coppers raiding shops near his office. The *Sunday Mercury* reported this fellow Comstock was disrupting the smut business like that animal cruelty nut Henry Bergh busted up pigeon shoots. Haynes would have a few choice words for the police captain helping out. The bastard should have come around with his hand open like the other bluecoats. Five bushels of smut hauled off. Haynes supplied a goodly portion most likely. McDermott on Nassau and the Brooks brothers on Ann stocked his products. McDermott had borrowed one of his steel plates too. Fortunately, there was no easy way to trace it to him, nor the books the judge issued the warrants against, *Confessions of a Voluptuous Lady* and *La Rose d'Amour*. He had published both under his Strokeall & Company imprint, based in London, the title pages read.

Haynes was confident his network provided cover as well. His binder was nearby, but he got the sheets from a printer in Brooklyn and he sent the books on to a warehouse in Jersey City. A middleman named Ed Grandin handled sales and distribution and he contracted with a photographer when necessary. Those were far-flung pieces for Comstock to put together.

Or so he thought until Grandin showed up in a state. "Get out of the way," Grandin warned him. "Comstock is after you. Damn fool won't look at money."

Approaching seventy years in age and half of those in the business, Haynes had been around long enough to take the news in stride. He didn't though. He'd been jailed once, and he'd spent the next quarter century insulating himself from the risk of going back. Maybe he thought of those three months now and the horror of the Tombs remained too vivid to bear, or maybe he feared this time might mean Sing Sing and how much worse that would be. Or his body could have been breaking down, or his mind failing, and those could be prisons as much as iron bars. Maybe he just didn't want to die in a cage of any kind. Whether from shock or age or fear, no one could say, but he died the night Grandin told him Comstock was gunning for him. Many people believed by his own hand.

Comstock had chased down his first kill, a lion in the smut business. A few months later, the *Times* would praise him for worrying Haynes to death. Comstock picked up the refrain, saying of Haynes and two other smut men, "It is charged by their friends that I worried them to death. Be that as it may, I am sure that the world is better off without them."

6 | EVERYONE ENJOYS A GOOD PARTY

AS WINTER WOUND DOWN, New Yorkers looked back on a colorful and entertaining season. At Tony Pastor's Opera House, one of the more respectable establishments on the Bowery, the impresario sang of the gulf separating the city's Upper and Lower Ten Thousands. But whether blueblood on Fifth Avenue or down-and-out in Five Points, everyone enjoyed a good party.

The Patriarchs, twenty-five gentlemen possessing the snootiest of names and the moldiest of money, held their inaugural ball in midwinter. Each was entitled to invite five men and four ladies. To thwart a Patriarch introducing an unworthy guest to the assemblage, his associates threatened to publicly upbraid him for the offense. Heaven forbid that a Schermerhorn or Astor or Van Rensselaer rub elbows with a nouveau riche like Commodore Vanderbilt. The anointed gathered at Delmonico's, where dinner was held around an immense oval table. Flowers and fountains covered it in such exquisite arrangement that neither petal nor spray hindered the beautiful from gazing upon one another. The quadrilles and waltzes of the cotillion lasted until dawn, when another magnificent repast fortified the guests for their journey home.

Not to be outdone, the aristocracy of the Fourth Ward assembled at a rat pit turned saloon for the Beggars' Banquet. The blind, the crippled, and the maimed packed tables like sardines to celebrate their decidedly artistic profession. Bringing appetites as great as the "Bohemian" whose dinner hour was always "one o'clock tomorrow," they feasted on beefsteak and onions. The ancient patriarch among them went by "Cully the Codger." He refused to unwrap the yards of woolen scarf round his throat. "They'd be sure to steal 'em," he said, eying his sticky-fingered neighbors. Awash in whiskey, a fellow named Burkey climbed atop a chair, busting to make a speech. He swore he'd visit Boss Tweed in Sing Sing and cared no more for Henry Ward Beecher than his grandmother's aunt's cat's tail did. He'd refused a toddy from Jim Fisk because he never drank beneath himself. Dublin Mag usurped his chair to declare that "as long as a woman's a woman she ought to have a woman's rights." While Mag gave a hoot about voting, she claimed her right to drink whatever she pleased. After hours more oratory, song, and liberal doses of liquor and tobacco, the beggars went straight home to bed. Not a bit of trouble, said the copper on the beat.

The great middle, whose blood was too impure for the Patriarchs or whose bodies were too washed for the beggars, attended the annual bacchanal of the French Ball. Thousands of the best men and the worst women filled the Academy of Music, *Woodhull & Claflin's Weekly* proclaimed. Things were not quite that simple. Many married couples joined the masquerade, though frequently not with each other. For this year's event, gentlemen commonly disguised their identities as French musketeers, Italian revolutionaries, and Brother Devil. Another's getup as Aladdin in black velvet and orange satin displayed more imagination, though disappointingly his genie did not emerge from the lamp. The hooded cape known as the domino was de rigueur for a woman. Its built-in mask might hide her lovely eyes, but she should shield no other features beneath anything but tights—black, red, blue, or, most daringly, flesh colored—or was that bare skin showing on a goodly number of ladies?

Masquerade notwithstanding, the *Sunday Mercury* named dozens of revelers. Businessmen and politicos who might generally exercise their peccadilloes discreetly need fear no embarrassment here. The evening benefitted charity. The madams with whom they cavorted could ask for no better advertising. Fanny Turnbull, who presided over a first-class establishment on Twelfth Street, appeared as Diana, Goddess of the Chase. Kate Woods operated the most exclusive bordello on the most exclusive block, West Twenty-Fifth, known for its Seven Sisters—seven of the best madams in the business who competed there. Woods, whose gallery of paintings alone cost $10,000, wore a blue domino befitting a vestal virgin.

At ten, the band struck up a quadrille. At midnight, the tempo turned into a gallop. Gus Thompson banged Jennie Mitch into the buxom Eva King. All went down. Eva shook her striped domino with a frown that said *I'd like to put a head on you.* Poor May Sherwood guzzled wine provided by her good-natured Charley, while Jo Thompson and Cora Lee of the house on Thirty-First Street hustled around like a pair of lovers. At one o'clock, eyes turned upward to the boxes. A sweet creature leaned far over the velvet rail clapping her jeweled hands. She revealed so many of her charms that whistles and catcalls demanded an encore. Hours later Dashing Angola, in a short tunic of purple satin and flesh-colored tights, led the Can-Can, joined by Scotch lassie Katie and lank and limber Amelia. With lights out at 5:00 AM, the *Mercury* noted this year's ball missed only the jolly face of Jim Fisk and the seductive curves of Josie Mansfield.

So much for the season's entertainment. As winter's last gasp chilled the city, the *Times* looked forward to the baseball season. While the editors disputed whether patriotism demanded every American take an interest, they acknowledged the pleasures in the perspiring art of fielding, the headlong run from base to base under a broiling sun, the pride of martyrdom in blackened eyes and broken fingernails. In a free country, every man was entitled to tire and bruise himself to his heart's content. If only those crooked gamblers and the professional players they bribed wouldn't ruin the game.

III

SPRING

Central Park Saturday Afternoon.
Matthew Hale Smith, Sunshine and Shadow in New York, 1868. Wikimedia Commons

7 | *BLACK FRIDAY*

ONE WEEK INTO SPRING, notices for the upcoming show at Niblo's Garden appeared in the New York papers. Niblo's was a venerable name in the theater business dating back to the presidency of Andrew Jackson. The finest Shakespeareans and grandest divas graced its stage. Its audiences witnessed New York debuts of Italian operas, the dancing of the polka, and the military antics of the French Zouaves. The theater's greatest triumph opened on a September evening in 1866 when the ballet corps of *The Black Crook* pranced out before an overflow crowd. For six hours, the dancers exhibited a charm, beauty, and grace never before seen in America, or so judged the critic of the *Evening Post*. The *Times* was less kind, describing dancers wearing no clothes to speak of and performing "such unembarrassed disporting of human organism [as] has never been indulged in before." Both papers concluded the show would be a tremendous success. When the initial run ended 475 performances later, no one could argue.

With *The Black Crook*, Niblo's inaugurated a new era of gaudy spectaculars. While lamented by respectable society, they proved enormously popular among the public, particularly for those enjoying "an exhibition of leg development." The *Herald* cited Niblo's as the principal sinner in spreading this baneful and demoralizing corruption of dramatic taste from one end of the Union to the other.

Niblo's upcoming drama represented a new low. *Black Friday* centered on the life of Jim Fisk. The producers promised great pains to render his Wall Street shenanigans, romantic entanglements, and tragic end, along with still-living celebrities from financiers Drew and Vanderbilt to lovers Mansfield and Stokes.

Fisk was looming as large in death as in life and proving just as profitable. His body was barely cold in the grave when an advertiser offered busts of the colonel, twenty dollars for a life-size plaster and five for a smaller cabinet model in military dress. A publisher promised to mail his *Life of James Fisk, Jr.*, "the only full truthful account of his career," to any address in the country. To boost sales, he held out "extraordinary inducements to canvassers" who would push the product. Other biographies soon joined the mania for anything Fisk, as did a traveling exhibit of wax figures and the theatrical panorama *Chicago After the Fire*, featuring Fisk driving his carriage and soliciting contributions for suffering victims.

When Fisk's horses and equipage went up for auction, a well-heeled crowd spilled out of his stables blocking all traffic. Fourteen horses sold for as much as a $1,000 a pair. Five carriages and a sleigh, gold-plated harnesses, and other equipage pushed the proceeds above $12,000. Bids for Fisk's prized canaries reached $3,000 before the hammer fell.

Black Friday opened to immense crowds, augmented the first night by a special train from Philadelphia filled with well-lubricated brokers celebrating their dead colleague's exploits. The critics hated it. Said one of the more concise, "The play degrades the actor, disgraces the author and damns the management." Infuriated by such reviews, the producers fired back, charging the "virtuous censors of the age" with hypocrisy for covering Fisk's affairs ad nauseum in their newspapers yet declaring them unfit for the theater. The competing diatribes were sure to fill seats, concluded many. But *Black Friday* proved to be the one piece of Jim Fisk the public could get enough of. While the hissing opening night did not hound the actors from the stage, the play closed after sixteen performances.

With spring blooming outside the Tombs, Ned Stokes was growing weary of his incarceration. His velvet jacket, silk stockings, and embroidered slippers allowed a pretense of enjoying his cigar as he would any morning at the Hoffman House. But a few yards of cheap carpet and an iron bed, table, and washstand couldn't turn a cell into a home. Nor could a shaving tumbler, bottles of cologne, and a rack of brushes substitute for a proper toilet. A fresh bouquet on the table only reminded him what he was missing locked inside. He had little to pass the time but a few novels and occasional visits of friends. The commissioners forbade him even the liberty of the prison corridors. He was suffering physically from a pointless confinement to a few square yards.

The speedy trial he sought seemed like it would never come. His attorneys had wasted weeks harassing witnesses and presenting excruciating arguments in a vain attempt to prove the grand jury indicting him was illegal. After that fruitless effort, they demanded until the beginning of spring to file a voluminous bill of exceptions. The district attorney insisted on more weeks to examine it. As April ended, the trial was nowhere in sight. With every appearance in court, Stokes seemed paler and older and more careless in his habits.

What really galled was his attorneys sealing his lips. Silently Stokes watched the press castigate him. His attorneys wouldn't allow him to speak a word of defense publicly on pain of withdrawing from the case—nothing about the gross misrepresentations regarding his relationship with Mansfield, his purported extortion of Fisk, or the flagrant robbery of his Brooklyn Refinery holdings when a gang of Fisk's ruffians seized the refinery in a midnight raid.

The *Black Friday* monstrosity was the last straw. To hell with his attorneys, Stokes decided, and penned a diatribe to the public. He ticked off the injustices the play perpetrated against him. Portraying him as persecuting Fisk? That man had suckered Stokes into partnership only to steal his refinery business. Charging he was in league with Mansfield to extort money? Stokes and Mansfield had shared no business interests whatsoever until Fisk's machinations compelled them to act as codefendants. Painting him as a gambler and dissolute rake? Stokes hardly knew one card from another. Inventing crimes he hadn't been accused of, even forgery? The only discreditable document Stokes had ever signed was an oil lease Fisk designed to rob the Erie Railroad. *Black Friday* was not only a gross libel of a helpless man but also a prostitution of drama by a producer who had lost all sense of decency.

No one could honestly say he had ever knowingly wronged anyone, Stokes told the public. Yet every night at Niblo's people witnessed his misrepresentation as a gambler, roué, forger, and assassin. Quite possibly many accepted it as the truth.

With great difficulty he would refrain from addressing his portrayal as an assassin. A duty to his counsel, Stokes said, noting that he'd given his attorneys no warning before the papers printed his appeal to the public.

Stokes's attorneys were neither amused nor forgiving. Three resigned. This self-inflicted wound much alarmed Stokes and his friends. As his remaining attorney searched as far as Albany for colleagues to aid in the trial, one upstate paper wondered why Stokes didn't bring on the famous Tombs lawyer William Howe. Long having won the competition for the criminal element's business, Howe possessed the "great nerve and unscrupulous boldness, and even dishonesty," required to win such a case.

Sporting men around city hall didn't think Howe's involvement was likely. Several were offering odds the assassin would hang before winter.

During the first week of April, a woman's body was fished out of the Charles River in Massachusetts. A Boston yachtsman informed the *Commercial Advertiser* that she was Josephine Mansfield. Whether she was the "Josie" notorious in the Fisk triangle or some other unfortunate, the paper couldn't say.

As a reader who preferred the *Herald*, Stokes may or may not have heard the news. He may or may not have cared, as well. He hadn't seen Mansfield since his incarceration, or so his missive would soon inform the public. His attorneys, still on the job at that point, might have been more concerned, given her anticipated role as a witness for the defense.

Fisk's widow, Lucy, on the other hand, could be forgiven if she hoped the woman was her husband's mistress. Her spring had gotten off to a trying start when Mansfield sued her. Three years back, Fisk had signed two notes for $20,786 Mansfield entrusted to him, presumably to invest on her account. Now she wanted her money back. Any hidden joy on Lucy Fisk's part would have been short-lived, however. The woman drowned in the Charles River proved a different person. Mansfield's suit would wind through the courts for two years before the judge ordered Lucy Fisk to pay up. The amount was hardly worth arguing over relative to the million-dollar estate Fisk left almost entirely to his wife. Lucy spent more on her husband's funeral monument.

She suffered another setback when a burglar broke into her Boston home and stole $1,000 in jewels and other valuables. Again, she could take comfort that the sum was paltry compared to the $11,000 in jewels retrieved from her husband's body. She had always been retiring where he was flamboyant, explaining the discrepancy.

The lawsuit and the robbery would hardly be Lucy Fisk's only annoyances as the year progressed. As executrix, she was moving forward in the settlement of Jim's affairs. Besides selling his horses and canaries, she had bought out Jay Gould's share of the Grand Opera House and twenty-four adjoining buildings. She now held sole title to the $500,000 property. But new management at the Erie Railroad would refuse to pay the rent on its opera house offices, running $55,000 a year. Nor would they turn over her husband's papers. She would have to institute proceedings against the company on both accounts, and the company would counter with claims against the estate. Combined with the pending lawsuits against Jim in which the estate, and Lucy as executrix, were substituted as defendant, she was getting caught up in as big a legal jumble as her husband.

She also endured her husband's reputation constantly attacked. The papers were bad enough calling him "a worthless and tawdry rascal" and worse. But the spectacle of the legislature dragging him through the mud while they investigated those corrupt judges Barnard and Cardozo—and talking about the nights they frolicked at that Mansfield woman's house—was outrageous. Wasn't his murder enough to satisfy their bloodlust? And from every side, people tried to turn his death to their own advantage, like that contemptible woman Tennie Claflin.

Tennie Claflin opened the spring with a lecture at the Academy of Music, on this night taking the limelight off her sister Victoria Woodhull. As the hour approached, a mob spilled into Irving Place. Upon the doors opening, it surged through with such force as to fill the hall twice over, in the *Herald*'s estimation. The advertised topic—"Behind the Scenes in Wall Street"—might have explained the almost entire "masculinity" of the crowd but for the occasional feminine face standing out "like an exotic flower in a plantation of pines." The men's behavior, however, "as somber as the first nights of a *Black Crook* performance" at Niblo's, suggested many were more interested in viewing Claflin's charms than hearing her financial insights.

Or maybe word had leaked out of the topic she would really address. "The Ethics of Sexual Equality," or as the *Herald* reported it, "Plain Talk About the Freest of Free Love and the Tyranny of Marriage." Claflin launched into a discussion of the relations of the sexes with "a biblical plainness" that left nothing for the imagination. Her exploration of the topic approached the level of literature the police deemed it "their duty to suppress when it was paraded too obtrusively before the public gaze." The audience enthusiastically endorsed her utterances with cheers to repeat her most pestilent passages and a shower of flowers when she concluded.

Though the *Herald* omitted the specifics as "unworthy of a more extended publicity," Claflin mostly repeated arguments she and her sister had long made about a woman's right to lead her own life. Those arguments were hardly titillating or encouraging of promiscuity. But they were stale at a time when Claflin yearned for something fresh. She had announced her search for a new endeavor almost a year earlier. Woodhull was chief of the Cosmo-Political Party, she told readers of *Woodhull & Claflin's Weekly*. *Weekly* contributor Stephen Pearl Andrews was chief of the Pantarchy, though not even he could define what that was, beyond some amorphous movement for a future "Universal Government." Claflin had taken it into her head to be chief of something too, and while she might seek the help of Commodore Vanderbilt or a Rothschild or whoever could spare a few hundred thousand, she would not touch a dollar on any terms that trammeled her operations. "I just want the privilege of showing what my own genius can design and realize," she wrote.

Her first idea was to host a grand salon such as the world had not yet seen. She would invite men and women of letters, great artists, and leading reformers based on their commitment to "bettering the world we live in." The germ of this gathering had already sprung up at the Murray Hill mansion she and Woodhull occupied, but the premises were strained. Claflin envisioned leasing one of the large hotels as headquarters of her court of intellect, science, taste, and excellence in all spheres.

With no Vanderbilts or Rothschilds stepping up, and the sisters' finances stretched far more than anyone realized, Claflin moved on to seeking political office. Her ambitions were not so great as her sister's to occupy the White House. Rather she stood before twelve hundred Germans to hear the president of the German-American Progressive Society nominate her to represent New York's largely German Eighth Congressional District. The gentleman praised her as one who had proven woman equal to man through practical success in affairs such as banking, publishing, and reform. Accepting in German, Claflin argued her right as a woman to hold office, promised to fight the corruption and bribery rampant in politics, and outlined a platform to protect the freedoms of all citizens. One particular freedom excited the Germans. Just as the religious

American has the privilege of going to his church, Claflin said, so must the Germans have the right to seek their recreation on Sunday, specifically "to drink your glass of lager beer in peace and quietness so long as you do not disturb the public order." Cheers filled the hall.

The *Times*, the *Evening Post*, and the usually sarcastic *Pomeroy's Democrat* reported Claflin's candidacy with a degree of seriousness. Unfortunately, the *Herald* had a better read on the mood of the electorate when it said the rank and file in the audience treated the whole matter as a joke. So Claflin remained at loose ends when Jim Fisk's murder opened a surprising opportunity: she would buy the Grand Opera House. She had entered negotiations with Fisk's estate, reported the *Commercial Advertiser*. Whether she considered it a suitable venue for the grand salon she earlier planned or simply sought to enter the theatrical business was never clear before Lucy Fisk decided to keep the property.

Claflin soon hit on another opportunity to follow in Jim Fisk's footsteps—to wear his uniform, more accurately. Early in May, in a published letter aimed at the committee searching for Fisk's replacement as colonel of the Ninth Regiment, she proposed herself. Fisk had brought wealth, youth, and brains to the regiment. His spirit and dash inspired the men to return it to its former glory. Among the prospective candidates to succeed him, she alone possessed the sort of "magnetic influence" through which he had secured the love of his soldiers. It would be a blunder to select anyone lacking that quality, Claflin asserted. As Napoleon said, a blunder was worse than a crime. To those who objected to a woman, she invoked the military prowess of Joan of Arc. She promised to demonstrate her qualifications with an exhibition of equestrian skills and swordplay at the Grand Opera House. Her tailor was sewing a colonel's uniform for the occasion.

The proposal did not amuse Lucy Fisk. She forbade Claflin the use of her opera house. Nor could the *Times* have amused Lucy when it tucked its tongue in its cheek and patronized her husband as much as the woman seeking to replace him. The editors could find no reason Claflin would not be a worthy successor. Certainly she was as expert a soldier as Jim Fisk had been. Her appearance outfitted as a colonel would be quite as martial and rather less ridiculous than a fat man whose vanity was a laughingstock. She might spend less money on uniforms and holidays for her soldiers, but she could compensate with free admission to her sister's lectures and subscriptions to *Woodhull & Claflin's Weekly*. Moreover, with their leader's sister running for the White House, the regiment might be transformed into a presidential guard entitled to four years of feasting in the nation's capital.

Regrettably the search committee did not accept the *Times'* arguments. It elected Jim Fisk's second-in-command to take over. The clever Claflin had a backup plan, however. The Eighty-Fifth Regiment, known alternatively as the Colored Regiment, was facing even harder times than the Ninth had when it recruited Fisk. The Eighty-Fifth could neither pay its armory's $45 bill from the gas company nor furnish uniforms to a majority of its soldiers. Claflin offered her aid. She, too, had been the victim of despotism. She, too, had been refused lodgings in a hotel. She, too, had been victimized by greedy landlords who pocketed the year's rent, then returned with their hands out for more. Now she would lead these troops when despots oppressed them.

As spring waned, the officers convened a meeting of the ranks at their armory, dimly lit by lamps not requiring gas flowing through the pipes. Several drummers assembled in the top-floor drill room. At half past eight, they welcomed the candidate for their leadership, feeling prone to endorse her if she would only outfit them in uniforms.

Claflin sat in an armchair centered on the stage. Sister Woodhull, lending support but not stealing the limelight, stood in a darkened corner. With eyes beaming, Claflin took in the men she aimed to command. The sparse crew included the drummers, a musketeer, a couple of soldiers, three captains, and a major. At ninety-two, the major had fought in the War of 1812. Claflin assuming command would result in everlasting good for the regiment, he told a reporter, who sized up most of the others as more likely to ridicule than endorse. The evening appeared headed toward humiliation.

E Company parading in put off that moment. The men saluted their prospective commander. Other companies followed until over two hundred troops lined up beneath the stage. Captain Griffin called the meeting to order. He asked his fellow captains to speak. The first two stated that they and their men were at Claflin's disposal. Then a Captain Warfield launched into a long harangue detailing how through five battles he had fought and bled for his country and the "colored" race. He had seen how the black soldiers fought nobly at Forts Pillow and Wagner. He would stand by them or give up his commission. But he wouldn't be led by a woman. More companies marched in and voiced opinion. Hisses and groans filled the hall. A riot appeared imminent. Claflin looked about to cry.

But Captain Griffin had learned a trick or two about leading troops. He manhandled the ayes to one side and the nays to the other. When he counted 193 in favor and 50 opposed, cheers erupted. And when Captain Warfield tendered his resignation rather than serve under a woman, a goodly number threatened to throw him out the window. Gracefully the newly elected Colonel Claflin bowed to Captain Warfield and said she could not accept without unanimous support. Not to lose the moment, Captain Griffin accepted his fellow captain's resignation, announced there were now no dissenting voices, and moved that Miss Tennie C. Claflin be elected by acclamation colonel of the Eighty-Fifth. Amid a deafening roar, she accepted the honor.

The *Times* generously acknowledged that Claflin's military ambition had at last been crowned, and the paper pondered what it considered her greatest challenge. What sort of rig would the colonel wear? Was she prepared to discard all pretenses of skirt? Or if wearing an abbreviated one, what would she do with her sword? When mounted would she embrace the riding habit and sidesaddle appropriate to her "former" sex or put on trousers and sit astride the horse? As for color, the *Times* recommended red and yellow since the "colored" race had a tropical fondness for brilliant hues. The more difficult question was Claflin's face. Doubtless the men would realize no one could consider the regiment in uniform when its colonel's white face contrasted with the dark countenances of the rank and file. Would Colonel Claflin exchange the cosmetics of the Caucasian woman for burned cork blackface? Unless she was so prepared, the *Times* advised she not incur the expense of several hundred uniforms.

Colonel Claflin had already fashioned her uniform and ignored the *Times*' advice. She immediately began to put her regiment on a footing second to none. She would show what a woman could do when she tried.

8 | "IN DUE TIME YE SHALL REAP IF YE FAINT NOT"

WILLIAM HAYNES'S WIDOW, Mary, was aggrieved. She had enjoyed a good long marriage to her husband. The business they had shared built a comfortable life. So what if not everybody approved of the books they published? They satisfied a human desire no less than the baker or dressmaker. Countless people relied on publishers like them for a livelihood. William and Mary and a few others were the first link in a chain that led to six thousand employed, when you added up everyone involved in manufacturing, distribution, and sales across the country, or so one critic estimated with no appreciation for the families who would suffer if they were shut down. And that number didn't count the coppers and politicians whose hands their money greased.

The grease was one reason Mary was aggrieved. Sure, the business was lucrative, but heavy bribes ate up a hefty portion of the profits. Her husband didn't leave much behind to live on—not ready cash, anyway. The assets of the business were something, the steel plates for printing plus the books warehoused or in production. Their sale would bring Mary enough to get by for a while. Grandin, her husband's associate, had already offered twelve grand for the lot.

That money wouldn't relieve her grief, though. Her husband was buried now, but the senselessness of it still outraged her. Some faceless bastard named Comstock was responsible, Grandin told her. He'd threatened William the very night he dropped dead.

Days after the funeral, Mary was home nursing her grief when a caller pounded at the door. She didn't recognize him. When he introduced himself as Anthony Comstock, she just about snapped. "You killed my husband," she blurted out.

Comstock claimed he never saw William face to face. But he didn't deny being too self-righteous to take a bribe, like Grandin had told her, or that he'd been gunning for William. No, he stood right there on her doorstep demanding the books and the plates.

Mary got ahold of herself enough to say she couldn't hand them over for nothing. She was a poor widow with children. Blackmail had already stolen the money she needed to raise her family. Besides, she had a good offer on the table, thousands of dollars. When Comstock heard that, he started negotiating. He thought he could walk away with everything for a few hundred. She let him think it.

Four hundred fifty dollars, she agreed. *Get the money.*

Mary was only buying time. The most urgent task was to find a safe place for the plates. She sent for Haynes's express company to pick up the several tons of them packed into twenty-four cases. Grandin had the finished books in Jersey. Figuring his identity was compromised, they shipped them onward to Philadelphia. And the binder was stitching together a couple hundred thousand pages already printed. Mary couldn't let Comstock get his hands on them.

Damn him. Couldn't she grieve in peace?

Early in the spring, Robert McBurney climbed the steps of the French Renaissance headquarters of New York's Young Men's Christian Association. The building stretched 175 feet along Twenty-Third Street just off Madison Square. The facade of New Jersey brownstone ornamented with white Ohio freestone rose five stories, plus a sixth in the mansard-topped tower over the entrance. "One of the few buildings of which New-York has the right to feel proud," praised the *Times* when it opened in 1869.

McBurney had a special right to feel proud. He had introduced the resolution for the building's construction to the board. By then he was the YMCA's secretary and a director himself. The position was a far cry from three years earlier, 1862, when he had taken the job of librarian, earning five dollars a week. It was farther still from his flight from the Irish potato famine, when he had landed in New York, aged seventeen, and spent his first night in a room at the YMCA.

With cash donations to the organization running $7,000 a year, raising the $250,000 required for the building must have seemed an insurmountable challenge. Had the gentlemen on the board anticipated the cost would balloon to $437,000, they might have voted McBurney's motion down. But they ventured forth, hats in hand, and with names like J. P. Morgan and Abner Colgate, they cobbled together the money. Funds pledged, they relied on McBurney to build their "home, bright and cheerful," for young men. "There is not a room or corner of it but he designed," said William Dodge, the YMCA's president during construction.

Reaching the second floor, McBurney surveyed his domain. The secretary's desk sat against a wall of the large reception hall. Doors led into the reading room, the game room, parlors for socializing, and a lecture room. A second stairway descended to the gymnasium, bowling alley, and baths. Across a hallway, an auditorium seated sixteen hundred. Visitors passed within sight of McBurney perched at his desk, allowing him to watch over the young men in whom he would instill a "true Christian manhood."

He had his work cut out for him. As the YMCA contemplated a new home, McBurney and another director had chronicled the temptations facing the city's young men. The 1860 census had counted 111,021 between ages fifteen and thirty. After the war, the number boomed. No longer did they have the guidance of an employer, who in prior times would take a clerk or apprentice under his wing, often providing a place in his home and a seat in his church pew. With that practice abandoned, warned the report McBurney and his colleague prepared, men herded into boardinghouses, the virtuous and the vicious thrown together. Earning meager wages, strangers shared rooms and beds. Many could not afford a fire to warm themselves on winter nights. Was it any wonder these men found substitutes for home in the cheery rooms where vices beckoned?

Billiards led the report's list of temptations. New York's saloons contained 653 tables, with another 11,739 in private homes. Porter houses served 600 barrels of spirits a day, not excepting Sundays. The city's 223 concert saloons employed 1,191 pretty waiter girls, nearly every one a prostitute. In case that wasn't enough, 730 brothels offered another 3,417 women for the asking. The YMCA regretted such exactitude was not possible for the number and staff of other establishments preying on young men, like those spotted on a single street selling vile newspapers for ten cents and fifty filthy books at sixty cents or less.

Envisioned as an alternative to these "agencies of evil," the YMCA's new building now gave McBurney a place to carry out his vision. Sermons, bible classes, and religious sing-alongs uplifted young men's spiritual devotion. The library combined with a literary society to support their intellectual development. Classes ranged from languages and music to writing and bookkeeping. Open from eight in the morning to ten in the evening, the building offered a haven where men could socialize with like-minded friends, where they could find help securing good jobs and housing. With many men barely able to subsist, the YMCA offered the services "without charge or upon terms so liberal as to make them practically a gratuity." The strategy was working. Over the past year, membership had tripled to forty-seven hundred.

But it wasn't enough to win the war for young men's souls. Simultaneous with the decision to build, the YMCA opened a second front. Buttressed with statistics, members of the board journeyed to Albany to confer with state legislators on two items. First were concert saloons. With their dazzling lights and music drifting into the street, these establishments opened the door to the ruin of so many. Pretty waiter girls hovered through the doorways flaunting their wares in short skirts and skimpy bodices. These places must be shut, the visitors insisted. Next were dealers in obscene literature. "Feeders of brothels," the YMCA men warned. They had drafted a bill aimed at destroying the traffic in smut.

During the 1866 session, the New York legislators gave them half of what they wanted. A new law placed the licensing of concert saloons under the Board of

Health. An earlier law already banned much of what they did—selling spirits after midnight and on Sundays, hiring women to deliver drinks, and performing entertainments such as music and comedy on premises where alcohol was served. But proprietors chuckled with jolly satisfaction at the unmolested mode in which they operated, reported the *Times*. With the Board of Health now authorized to clamp down, the paper predicted the "early disappearance of the concert and pretty-waiter girl saloons," along with a sharp rise in advertisements for the sale of second-hand barroom fixtures as they shut.

Uncooperative lawmakers pigeonholed the other half of the YMCA board's request, a new antiobscenity law. But the YMCA gentlemen persisted for two more years, finally securing a ban on the sale, advertisement, and manufacture of obscene materials, illustrations, and advertisements and any article of indecent and immoral use. In case "indecent and immoral use" was insufficiently clear, the act specifically prohibited devices or medicines preventing conception or inducing abortion.

Both laws proved Pyrrhic victories, neither shuttering the saloons nor disrupting the traffic in smut. Morris K. Jesup, the incoming president of the YMCA as 1871 closed, acknowledged as much when he convened a meeting to discuss how to reinvigorate the fight. He embraced McBurney's proposal for a committee to devise a plan and appointed two directors to lead it. The group became known as the Committee on Obscene Literature.

So, when McBurney reached his desk that spring morning of 1872, he could not have been surprised to find a letter on the topic of smut. The sender wasn't much of a writer. A gentleman like McBurney was used to receiving his correspondence on fine stationery, the words eloquently scripted. This was the gibberish of a country bumpkin scratched out in pencil. Still, he caught the gist. The writer was battling the obscene books and pictures sold on Nassau Street and the hellish rubber goods sold with them. Already he had secured arrests of several dealers and seized massive amounts of contraband. He had even identified the owner of the plates for printing the infernal books and negotiated their purchase. But between the expenses he bore and the family he supported, he had no resources. To top it off, the "Tombs shyster" William Howe threatened a civil suit, a legal jeopardy he could not afford. Could the YMCA provide $450 so he could close his deal for the plates?

McBurney sympathized with the man's plight. He guessed the Committee on Obscene Literature might honor the request. But the letter was an embarrassment. He could never pass it along in its current form. *Rewrite out the whole matter fully and plainly*, he would ask the fellow. Then he would present it to his colleagues.

While the letter lay on his desk, Jesup happened upon it. The YMCA president perused it with interest. *I shall pay this man a call*, he said.

Four hundred fifty dollars? Unable to conceive how he could raise such a sum, Anthony Comstock was frustrated. So much was going right with his life. He had a lovely Christian wife, a comfortable home, a budding sales career. After church, he taught Sunday school to boys from a mission. Feeling that wasn't Christian duty enough, he carried his religious instruction to the hospital and the jail. He didn't grow discouraged when the "poor degraded souls" took poorly to his lessons. God's grace was recompense enough. And whenever he returned home, he gazed upon his beautiful daughter. A child's face always melted away his troubles.

His love of children also drove his fury at the obscenity all around. No pen could describe how that deadly poison polluted the family, desecrated the home, imprinted itself on the minds of youth. Their imaginations kept the hated visions there, wearing deeper and deeper until the innocent victims plunged into practices they loathed. Like a cankerworm, the smut silently ate away the moral purity of a generation.

Now he had tracked down the most loathsome practitioners of the horrid business. Three publishers issued virtually every title. Comstock had counted the books, 165 in all, sent from a few blocks around Nassau Street to four thousand dealers across the country. He had chased the granddaddy of the trade into his grave. He had discovered the steel plates with which the man produced the awful stuff, unearthed the books his middleman Grandin kept in New Jersey, identified his binder, too, and the carter who hauled the stuff from place to place. With one wholesale stroke he could roll up the network and the other publishers too. The prospect fired him with zeal. Yet he was impotent to do it. He had not the money even to close the deal he negotiated with the dead man's wife.

Comstock felt like a man floundering in a turbulent sea, water surging around him. The thinnest of threads anchored him to the pier. It would surely break. The water would suck him into the depths. But as he felt the thread snap, a voice called out. "Fear thou not, for I am with thee; be not dismayed for I am thy God." He laid hold of a strong cable thrown within his reach. Though his hands grew numb and he feared his grip would fail, the cable wrapped around his arm and his body and he did not sink.

That's how Comstock described God testing a man in his darkest hour. A man had but to trust in Him and he would be cared for. His faith restored, Comstock turned to prayer, asking God for a way to buy the steel plates from Mary Haynes. But now he would not rely on God alone. He reminded himself how his family taught that a man must take his own steps to bring an answer to his prayer. So Comstock scratched out a letter to the YMCA, to its secretary Robert McBurney, begging for help.

When the doorman at his employer, Cochrane, McLean & Company, announced a visitor calling, Comstock could not have expected God's answer walking through the door. The visitor had the noble face and airs of a wealthy gentleman. He introduced himself as Morris Jesup and offered a hearty handshake. *I am president of the Young Men's Christian Association*, he told the startled salesman coming out to meet him.

The Connecticut farm boy, whose father each Sunday had hitched up his four-seated wagon to drive his family and farmhands to the Congregational Church, was staring at his own kind. Jesup had spent his early years in Connecticut ten miles from the Comstock farm. His family, too, had instilled in him stern New England Congregationalism. He had carried it to New York at age seven, two years before Comstock was born. After making a fortune in railroads and finance, Jesup was devoting much of his money to philanthropy and evangelizing.

One of Jesup's causes would instantly fill Comstock with admiration. Early in the Civil War, Jesup helped found the United States Christian Commission, an organization to minister to Union troops. The USCC sent five thousand delegates throughout the army to promote the soldiers' spiritual and temporal well-being. They held religious services and distributed Bibles and religious tracts. They tended the wounded and buried the dead. Their kitchens fed the soldiers. Their libraries handed out books to entertain them—books of a respectable nature to combat the salacious obscenities inundating the encampments.

Learning of Jesup's role with the Christian Commission, Comstock could recall his service in the Seventeenth Connecticut Regiment, the sickening, sinking sensation when he came under fire in the swamps of South Carolina, the minutes dragging on as men lay wounded on every side. Harder than bearing the fusillade was having no chaplain, no services to attend, no Christian brothers with whom to share his faith. He took it upon himself to gather men for prayer meetings. In Florida they cleared a clump of wild-plum trees to pray in. The Christian Commission brought a chaplain. The visitors recruited Comstock to tend the sick and destitute, to distribute religious tracts. He served as a postmaster, forwarding keepsakes families sent their sons. Though much abused, he chastised those who drank and gambled. He dumped his own whiskey ration on the ground rather than let another drink it down, but when he found veterans too exhausted from drink to continue the march, he carried their rifles.

Comstock played a tiny role in the Christian Commission. Before him now stood a founder of the movement. And not just any founder. This man had led the USCC's charge against Comstock's obsession. The mail delivered to the troops obscene titles long associated with publishers like William Haynes. A soldier could order *Fanny Hill*, *The Lustful Turk*, *Venus in the Cloister*, and more of their ilk for fifty cents. Three dollars would bring a dozen cartes de visite of London and Paris voluptuaries portraying the mysteries of naked female beauty. So great was his haul of obscene materials that the provost marshal of the Army of the Potomac kept a bonfire in the rear of his tent to destroy it. Jesup was outraged. In the war's final year, he proposed a resolution against selling secular reading matter in the army. The resolution soon made its way into the 1865 omnibus post office bill as a provision that "no obscene book, pamphlet, picture, print or other publication of a vulgar and indecent character, shall be admitted into the mails of the United States." Though as passed the bill lacked the teeth for effective enforcement, it for the first time banned obscenity from the US mail.

At their introductory meeting, Jesup promised nothing. But he invited Comstock to his home, where he introduced Robert McBurney, secretary of the YMCA. McBurney, too, was interested in what Comstock was doing. Comstock regaled the men with his exploits on Nassau Street. Already he had driven one of the key publishers, William Haynes, to his death, he told them. Lest the man's business continue, Comstock needed money to destroy the steel plates that were its lifeblood. His ambitions were not so limited, however. George Ackerman, in the business over twenty years, published as many titles. A relative newcomer named Jeremiah Farrell issued over a hundred. Without illustrations, his books sold at lower prices common men could afford. *With the support of men like you*, Comstock promised, *I can run them out of business.*

Jesup was impressed. Here was a man who did not wait for others to do things. Neither the difficult straits of his life, nor his strained finances, nor threats and vitriol from the likes of Howe & Hummel deterred him. He sniffed out trouble and attacked. The next day Jesup sent $650. *Use $500 to acquire the plates from Mary Haynes*, his instructions read. The remainder was to reimburse Comstock. "It is not fair that you should be at any expense in this matter."

God had answered Comstock's prayer in a way he could hardly have dreamed of.

––––––––––––

The first week of April, Comstock joined the president of Brooklyn Collegiate and Polytechnic Institute at the school's laboratories, where 170 steel and copper plates waited beside a vat of acid. Mary Haynes had almost secreted them away. But another call from God told Comstock to hurry to her house. He arrived just in time to spy the express wagon on which they were loaded. The farm boy knew how to handle a team of horses well enough. He leaped into the driver's seat and made off with the prize. He had seized Haynes's book inventory from Ed Grandin, too, and tracked a couple hundred thousand loose pages to a fifth-floor tenement hideout. On the Bowery he seized the negative plates of Grandin's photographer. One image particularly enraged him, and he singled it out in the man's indictment: "The Church Tithe" depicted a clergyman bedding a comely parishioner. In Jersey City, he chased the carter who hauled Haynes's books out of business. When the man died shortly thereafter, Comstock notched another victim in his log of accomplishments: "Expressman dead . . . 1."

A wholesale stroke he had promised his new mentor Jesup. He had delivered. Still, he was taking no chances at the Polytechnic Institute. He watched for several hours as acid dissolved Haynes's plates piece by piece.

––––––––––––

Late one spring evening, a burly man stumbled along Fourth Street in the Williamsburg section of Brooklyn. The day being Saturday, he had likely headed for the nearest saloon when his workday ended. An afternoon bellied up to a bar swilling beer would explain the meandering path he followed. The man lived blocks away from the spot, but no street urchin would have identified him as one of the neighborhood drunks. Quite the opposite, in fact. Any boy recognizing the face would have been startled to see Anthony Comstock staggeringly soused. The locals knew him as the jerk who shut down their corner saloons for serving on Sundays. Under his pressure, one proprietor had dropped dead on his bar. Another threatened to break the bastard's neck. Comstock started carrying a pistol to defend himself.

Across the street, another man moved furtively. Every little while he glanced around. Whatever he was up to, he didn't want some fellow shadowing him. He darted down a side street and into a house. He hadn't taken much notice of the drunk, who in his liquored-up state kept close enough to jot down the address.

Comstock had been digging for the whereabouts of the next publisher on his list, George Ackerman. He had mostly come up empty but for the titles the man sold. Finally, he got wind of a fellow named McDowell who used to work for Ackerman. According to Comstock's tipster, McDowell was on the lam for selling stolen bonds and was living in Williamsburg with a woman going by Irish Mary. Dogged detective work and a good impersonation of a drunk had just tracked him down.

Sunday being a day of rest, Comstock waited until Monday to bang on the door. Irish Mary answered. "Is Mac in?" Comstock asked like he was McDowell's best friend.

"He's not up."

Spotting his target dressing, Comstock shoved the lady aside. *Are you McDowell?* he asked. *I'm looking for George Ackerman.*

McDowell denied knowing any such person.

Comstock said, *You do, and I know all about the stolen bonds you deal.*

Growing hysterical, Irish Mary told her lover to fess up and tell where Ackerman was. All McDowell would admit to was knowing another fellow who might be able to track down Ackerman. The fellow operated a news agency on Nassau Street. He was a respectable man, a trustee of a church in the Bronx. And the bonds weren't stolen; they came from that man as payment for books. McDowell discounted them for the publisher.

Comstock had heard enough. He didn't care about this small-time crook. But a churchman enmeshed in the smut business? That was inexcusable. Comstock tore off for Nassau Street before McDowell could send warning. The news dealer's name was Timpson. Comstock surprised him in his office. He, too, denied knowing any Ackerman. Hogwash, Comstock said; he knew all about the bonds Timpson exchanged for obscene books, and if Timpson didn't help Comstock find the publisher, he would expose him for what he was. The threat struck fear in the churchman's heart. He pressured Ackerman into meeting Comstock, and maybe the same pressure or some larger threat forced Ackerman to relent. Early in May, a covered wagon pulled up to 150 Nassau Street, home of the American Tract Society. The carter unloaded $16,000 worth of steel plates, copper engravings, thousands of vile playing cards, and cases of unbound pages, the entirety of Ackerman's business. In an irony Comstock did not likely appreciate, the obscene materials would await destruction inside the offices of the largest distributor of Bibles in the country, offices located in the heart of the smut business.

For his trouble, Ackerman got not a dime. He escaped arrest, but when he died within the year, Comstock chalked up his second smut man "worried to death."

In mid-May, Comstock again rang the bell at Jesup's home. He had followed up Ackerman with the third publisher, Jeremiah Farrell. Warned about the warrant Comstock had secured for his arrest, Farrell had fled town. But Comstock had a bead on his business associates and was preparing to take them down. He had run a fourth publisher out of business as well, one responsible for only two books but in Comstock's eyes incorrigible for introducing a certain French product to America. The man advertised his "dildoes" manufactured of white rubber as "a wonderful facsimile of the natural penis of a man," perfect "for reserved females . . . [and] a happy and harmless substitute for the natural 'Champion of Woman's Rights.'"

Comstock's convictions were piling up. The threats of the "shyster" attorney William Howe to land him in jail had proven bluster. Howe told his clients Charles and William Brooks to plead guilty, expecting no more than a slap on the wrist. Instead the judge sentenced Charles to a year in jail and a $500 fine. William got three months. Howe tried the same strategy with the photographer Comstock arrested for the picture of the parson and his parishioner. That guilty plea earned his client six months.

Jesup's invitation tonight aimed beyond congratulations. These were achievements he wanted his friends to hear about. As he and Comstock finished dinner, a distinguished company assembled in the parlor—prosecutors and lawyers, businessmen, the clergy. Comstock regaled them with the righteousness of his cause, the fiends he had outwitted, the evils he had confiscated. He saved a special umbrage for the charlatans occupying high positions within the church who made fortunes backing the smut business, though if he singled out the news dealer Timpson, the *Times* reporter discreetly omitted the name from the next day's story. Around the room lay plates, books, and rubber goods he had seized. The *Times* did not report whether any of the gentlemen blushed with embarrassment as they examined the collection or shied away in horror or suppressed their own lust, only that one after another they praised the young man and promised to wield their money and influence in support of his crusade.

In the following days, Comstock reveled in more rewards, psychic and tangible. The publisher Farrell dropped dead, one more "worried to death." Then the YMCA reconstituted its obscenity fighting under a new Committee for the Suppression of Vice, with Jesup joining the group. The committee awarded Comstock $500 as a token of its appreciation.

Comstock felt the hand of God upon him. "Let me glory only in Him," he confided in his diary. "I knew His promise would come true: 'In due time ye shall reap if ye faint not.'"

9 | "TIT FOR TAT"

EARLY IN THE SPRING, Victoria Woodhull closed the door at 15 East Thirty-Eighth Street for the last time. The Murray Hill mansion she rented two years ago reigned over its aristocratic neighbors like the lord of the block. A double staircase climbed a massive granite base. Above rose heights of Corinthian columns and plate glass. The most prominent men of the country had passed through the black walnut entryway to pay homage to the Queens of Finance.

Inside, the sisters had created an Aladdin's palace. Venetian chandeliers hung from frescoed ceilings. Carpets from the finest looms of Europe swept across the floor. A dome over the grand staircase flooded light through glass painted with the loves of Venus. Countless mirrors reflected marble, gilt, statuary, all the extravagances their new-found wealth could buy. Incense infused the air as birds sang in a greenhouse off the reception rooms. The effect was as if a magician had transported the Orient to Murray Hill.

As she left the mansion now, Woodhull could muse fondly on Congressman Ben Butler plotting her infiltration of the House Judiciary Committee as his stray eye wandered around her parlor. Or Horace Greeley arguing politics in the days before the *Tribune* scorned her. Or leaders from every reform movement in a back room plotting to upend the coming election.

One evening President Grant's father recited poetry of the fate awaiting her.

> Vic, Tennie and Utie—
> Wit, genius and beauty—
> All three born in the Buckeye State
> With your marvelous ambition
> You will rise to position,
> And vie with Ulysses the Great.
>
> Ulysses the Tanner,
> Whose name's on the banner—
> Vic, your name is destined to be there.

To Woodhull's delight, the *New York Sun* printed Mr. Grant's prophesy of her presidency. She enjoyed shocking the reporters who called on her. On another occasion, she appeared in MASCULINE COSTUME OF REVOLUTIONARY THEME, the *Sun's* headline read—stockings, breeches, blouse, collar, and cravat, all in startling hues of blue. The reporter said she would be arrested if she wore the outfit in the street. *No,* she retorted, *the police will not dare touch me.* Perhaps she still believed it.

The house represented much more than the soirees Woodhull hosted. It had mid-wifed her baby, her voice to the world. *Woodhull & Claflin's Weekly* had been birthed upon the roof, where she joined with her husband, Colonel James Blood, on beautiful nights. There she communed with the spirits, receiving the pronouncements that guided all her actions. In her trance, the voices of the spirits emerged between her lips. Blood recorded the words, changing not a one before publishing the ghostly messages that the *Weekly* carried to the world.

Not everything had been joyous, of course. When Victoria moved into the house with her disabled son and beautiful daughter, along with Tennie and James, an unruly brood quickly followed—Woodhull's dissolute first husband and father of her children; her mother, one bend away from the nuthouse; her father, one step ahead of the sheriff; a host of siblings, in-laws, nephews, and nieces bound for the poorhouse but for Woodhull's generous heart; and various unrelated hangers-on spouting heresies of Free Thought and Free Love. Twenty-five in all, Tennie counted, feeding off their Wall Street riches.

Open warfare broke out within a year. On a day Woodhull would rather forget, her sister Utica walloped Colonel Blood with a chair. Red blood streamed down his face as he staggered into the street. Woodhull's mother, Annie, followed, screaming what a hellhound the man was. A reporter descended like a fly to dung.

Through wicked magic, James Blood had alienated Victoria and Tennie from their dear mother, Annie told the judge when she filed charges. Blood had threatened to lock her in the lunatic asylum, she said. Once he had sworn he'd wash his hands in her blood before the evening was out.

"My daughters were good daughters and affectionate children before they got in with this man," she said. "He is one of those who have no bottoms to their pockets. You can keep stuffing in all the money in New York; they never get full up. . . . If God had not saved me, Blood would have taken my life long ago."

Annie didn't stop with Blood. "S'help me god . . . I call Heaven to witness that there was the worst gang of free lovers in that house—Stephen Perlando and Dr. Woodhull and lots more of such trash."

Another sister, Mary Sparr, described a night Victoria hooked her irate husband around the neck and dragged him away from her mother.

It didn't matter that the worst Blood had threatened was that he'd turn Annie over his knee if she weren't his mother-in-law. Or that Victoria had testified Blood never treated her mother other than kindly, that her mother was the violent one to the point she seemed insane. Or that Mary's husband, Benjamin Sparr, incited the trouble in the house, that he used her mother to blackmail people.

No, it didn't matter, because the damage was done when the revelation splashed across the newspapers that two of Woodhull's husbands lived under the roof and none of the parties could tell a coherent story of when one marriage ended and the other began. Woodhull protested in a letter to the *Times*, saying her first husband, whose name she still bore, was ailing and incapable of caring for himself. Taking him in was not only her duty but "one of the most virtuous acts of my life." Who heard when the headlines blared Free Love?

So the departure was bittersweet as Woodhull turned her mansion's keys over to the landlord. The man had ordered the family out a year ago when the Annie storm hit the papers. Woodhull had refused. But now she said the house no longer suited her needs. Really, she could no longer afford it.

She was going broke.

On one hand, the deteriorating finances were simple math. Maintaining the household at Thirty-Eighth Street ran $2,500 a month. Every issue of the *Weekly* cost $300 more than it brought in. Outlays to support suffrage over the past year approached $100,000. With the press vilifying Woodhull over "free love," revenues at the brokerage had plummeted. Numbers aside, in the years ahead Woodhull would puzzle over the underlying causes, from the life she led to the causes she espoused to the treachery of friends.

One thing was certain. Woodhull and Claflin could no longer count on their patron Cornelius Vanderbilt to bail them out. The man who had helped the sisters to their first big killing on Black Friday, whose barely veiled support of their brokerage brought in countless clients, who once proposed marriage to Tennie and promised to make her a queen, was no longer a friend. As recently as the past August, a reporter quoted Vanderbilt as saying he trusted "the presidency of the United States . . . would fall upon his brave, brilliant and cosmopolitical friend Mrs. Victoria C. Woodhull." But that was either a journalistic distortion or an old man momentarily remembering a fond relationship gone bad. The sisters' mother, Annie, truly had engaged in blackmail with her son-in-law Benjamin Sparr. One letter had gone to Vanderbilt, mentioning his sexual indiscretions. Tennie's account to the *Brooklyn Eagle* described Vanderbilt only as "a prominent gentleman worth millions of dollars" and suggested the affair had been patched over. But shortly thereafter, Vanderbilt told another reporter that Woodhull and Claflin "h'aint no friends of mine. From what I hear, you shouldn't be associating with such folks." The message sounded like a death knell for their brokerage business, though the doors stayed open on Broad Street.

Woodhull hit back hard in a lecture at the Academy of Music. Her topic, "The Impending Revolution," reflected the political left turn she had taken late last year.

Section 12, an American branch of Karl Marx's International Workingmen's Association, had elected her honorary president. The Paris Commune had just collapsed, and the French government had executed its leaders. Woodhull and Claflin joined a funeral march to HONOR THE MARTYRS OF THE UNIVERSAL REPUBLIC, as one banner read. Tens of thousands watched what could have been a rehearsal for Jim Fisk's send-off less than a month away. Days later *Woodhull & Claflin's Weekly* had published the first American version of Marx's *Communist Manifesto*. While the *Weekly* did not endorse the ideology, it did agree with Marx that the European powers should stop treating communism like a "frightful hobgoblin." It was high time Marx's principles were laid before the public in opposition to "the silly fables about the bugbear of communism."

The night of the lecture, a crowd packed the Academy of Music "like herrings in a barrel," observed the *Herald*. An equal crush filled the streets outside, bidding tickets to twelve dollars and still none were available. Bald-headed men and stately ladies occupied the boxes and dress circle. Woodhull lifted her eyes to the tiers of eager faces above, the working people the impending revolution aimed to free.

She pulled no punches in calling for the oppressed working classes to throw off their yoke: "Six hundred millions people constantly toil all their lives long, while about ten millions sit quietly by gathering and luxuriating in the results." Those few were stealing the many blind. She named the chief culprits. Topping the list was the patron who had turned on her: "Vanderbilt may sit in his office and manipulate stocks, or make dividends, by which, in a few years, he amasses fifty millions dollars from the industries of the country, and he is one of the remarkable men of the age. But if a poor, half-starved child were to take a loaf of bread from his cupboard, to prevent starvation, she would be sent first to the Tombs, and thence to Blackwell's Island."

Woodhull chastised real estate magnate William Astor, for relaxing in his sumptuous apartments while he threw starving tenants into the street; retailer Alexander Stewart, for never producing a thing his store sold, only stealing the production of others; and railroader Thomas Scott, for monopolizing the public thoroughfares. She moved on to succeeding generations, who inherited millions without a day's labor, before impeaching the entire clergy for supporting a system that would condemn Jesus as a vagrant and jail him for stealing corn. *If Christ appeared today, he would be a Communist*, she cried.

She strode off the stage to thundering applause and a rain of bouquets.

But titillating an audience with outrageous views on sex was one thing; advocating to undermine the capitalistic foundations of the country was altogether different. What should have been a triumph before "the largest mass of people ever called out to inquire into political affairs" was met by ridicule. The press did not deign to address her ideas, the *Weekly* charged. The *Tribune* offered nothing more intelligent than to call her "an intolerable bore." The *Herald* succeeded admirably in saying nothing. The *Sun*, the *World*, and the *Star* belittled the crowd that so enthusiastically applauded her words.

The *Times* ignored the speech for a day, then served up cheap shots about two husbands: "Mrs. Victoria C. Woodhull has been married rather more extensively than most American matrons, and hence it might be deemed inappropriate to style her a foolish virgin." The editors compared her to the foolish virgins of scripture who saw no need to fill lamps with oil to illuminate. Woodhull fancied she could illuminate the dark places of politics and society without the light of reason. Saying her speech equated property with crime, the *Times* advised she ignite her silk dresses, sealskin jackets, and diamond rings in a giant bonfire in Union Square. Workingmen could then see she would enjoy no luxuries not earned by her manual labor. Defending herself, Woodhull sent a letter for publication. The *Times* replied it could not possibly afford space for it.

With her home lost, her finances depleted, and the press heaping scorn, howls of persecution rang in Woodhull's ears. For years she had devoted her life to affirming the right of people to choose how to live, to fighting oppression of suffering women and starving children and workingmen struggling to support their families. For that she was hounded like a stag fleeing wolves? She knew her revolutionary beliefs invited a bashing. Her methods were to shock, even in her appearance, with her short skirts and short hair and none of the frippery that circled most women like chains. It was how she got men to listen and the press to broadcast her message. So what that they denounced her as utterly bad; she could withstand the abuse. But the hypocrisy, the slanderous and foul-mouthed accusations by those nearest to her in their convictions, whose private lives embodied the very practices she claimed was their right—that drove her to a boiling rage. Especially from the women. No longer could she endure the slime they vomited at her.

Lucy Stone and Mary Livermore, enemies in the rival Boston wing of the suffrage movement, had been assaulting her all year. How many times had their *Woman's Journal* proclaimed Woodhull was ruining the cause, that her ideas on free love and easy divorce drove untold numbers away? They practically blamed Woodhull single-handedly for women not already having the vote. Heaven forbid that a woman trapped in a loveless marriage should want to escape her husband's abuse, his philandering, and maybe even seek a little companionship and affection elsewhere. Stone and Livermore not only knew that was the free love Woodhull advocated; they also practiced it. The carnal intimacies in their lives were hardly well-kept secrets. And other enemies, too, like Phebe Hanaford—a reverend, no less—who whispered that Woodhull was an unrepentant Magdalen, that she gloried in shame. And Anna Dickinson and Laura Bullard—both of them indulged their passions. And hundreds more Woodhull could name, women railing against her, decrying free love while they reveled in amorous pleasures behind closed doors, hiding not just their own secrets but protecting with their silence some of the most famous men in America.

Woodhull never condemned these women for practicing what she preached. Nay, she celebrated it. She told them to declare it before the world. That's how the social revolution would be won. But their hypocrisy, stabbing her in the back again and again for behavior they secretly embraced, portraying her as a fiend incarnate? Ironically the pencil of a man drew that image for the world to see. Thomas Nast's cartoons of Boss Tweed and his Tammany Ring had done as much as anything to bring about their downfall now playing out in the papers. Over the winter, Nast had sketched Woodhull as a horned demon with the wings of a bat and cloven hooves. He gave her a sign to hold—BE SAVED BY FREE LOVE—a sign pointed at a destitute mother cowering with her two children and bearing the weight of her drunken husband emptying another bottle into his mouth. The mother said in the caption, "Get thee behind me, Mrs. Satan. I would rather travel the hardest path of matrimony than follow your footsteps."

Woodhull looked at her portrayal as Mrs. Satan—"a fit companion of devils"—and decided *enough*. Her rebuke to Nast in the *Weekly* was mild—if his moral lesson aimed at persons tempted to accept the pernicious doctrine of free love, she could name several examples his pen might target. For the women who had driven Nast to the depiction, she vowed no more. The *Weekly* had warned them with every cliché, from the pot calling the kettle black to those living in glass houses casting the first stone. Now she would sever their tongues.

Victoria Woodhull as Mrs. Satan by Thomas Nast.
Library of Congress

Recognizing the challenges ahead, Woodhull set her grievances aside for later. She moved into the modest house her sister Maggie Miles rented. Her children, Tennie, and both husbands came with her. Woodhull still earned up to $500 a night lecturing, and her reputation—some would say her notoriety—filled her schedule. Those fees kept what really mattered alive, *Woodhull & Claflin's Weekly*. It was her seed corn, which she sowed far and wide and which bore fruit a hundred-fold broadcasting her views on the vital issues of the day—social freedom, labor and capital, constitutional reforms. She would exert every effort, endure any privation, to preserve that voice.

Woodhull turned to her political agenda. She had a party to build, a presidential nomination to win, and a campaign to run. For anyone doubting her seriousness, she acknowledged that her original announcement to run had aimed at agitating for suffrage and other reforms and rallying support for the cause. But with the astonishing progress since that time, she wrote in the *Weekly*, the right woman could arouse a tempest of popularity such as the country had never seen and ride it all the way to the White House. Adding to her assurance of victory was the prophetic name her parents had conferred on her, a name that forbade the very thought of failure.

Woodhull launched a lecture tour ranging from Massachusetts to Washington, DC, and west to Detroit and Chicago. In these travels, she reached the diverse reformers she aimed to corral into a consolidated convention. Despite the backlash in the New York papers, her "Impending Revolution" speech drew enthusiastic crowds. Workingmen loved her. At a mass rally in Manhattan, they chanted, "Vic, oh where is Vic?" as Woodhull listened from her carriage. Hers was the voice they demanded to hear. Her influence spread further through "Victoria Leagues," supposedly grassroots political clubs whose formation she instigated months before.

To counter personal attacks, the *Weekly* published letters of praise from leading Spiritualists, reformers, and suffragists. In one, Elizabeth Cady Stanton wrote how proud she was that Woodhull—maligned, denounced, and wickedly persecuted—would "ever find a warm and welcome place in my heart." Whatever coldness and ingratitude some of her sex wounded her with, Woodhull could count on such noble women as Susan B. Anthony, Isabella Beecher Hooker, Martha Joslyn Gage, and several others Stanton named to be her "sincere friends."

Beginning in February, Woodhull planted stories in the *Weekly* about reformers coming together in convention. Beyond listing the month as May and the place as New York, the *Weekly* provided no details nor tied the efforts to Woodhull. Despite or perhaps because of the vagueness, letters poured in. With excitement reaching fever pitch, at least in the descriptions in the *Weekly*, Woodhull made it official. The *Weekly*'s first issue of April ran two adjacent articles.

The first, issued at the invitation of the National Woman Suffrage Association, called for a "People's Convention" to form a new political party representing equal rights for all. It would meet May 9 and 10 at Steinway Hall in New York. Four leading suffragists signed the call: Elizabeth Cady Stanton, Isabella B. Hooker, Susan B. Anthony, and Matilda Joslyn Gage.

The second called for a "Party of the People" to secure and maintain human rights. It, too, would meet May 9 and 10 in New York, and while Steinway Hall was not mentioned, it would inaugurate the great and good work of reform "in concert with the National Woman Suffrage Association." Woodhull and twenty-six others representing all movements of reform signed this call.

The dual, or dueling, calls likely sowed confusion among the *Weekly*'s more innocent readers. The better informed or more cynical could see a sleight of Woodhull's hand. A third article clarified matters little. "The May Convention," scheduled for May 9 and 10 at Steinway Hall, would be a "spontaneous uprising" of people representing all areas of reform. "Every individual who believes in humanity . . . should send names to be added to either of the two calls" announced elsewhere on the page.

The same issue of the *Weekly* ran another article ostensibly unrelated to Woodhull's presidential plans. A young woman named Emma Couch inspired the piece. Earlier in the year Couch had hurried along Bleecker Street on a mission. Bleecker was the city's most bohemian thoroughfare. Stately mansions testified to the wealth and fashion formerly inhabiting its blocks. Now signs on their facades offered cheap lodgings and cheap meals. Despite its aging, the street lacked the weariness of Greene and Mercer running south, nor did it suffer the degeneracy of the Bowery, at which it ended. Rather, Bleecker had emerged from its fall from grace with the vibrancy of Paris. On Bleecker, perversions became peccadilloes, decadence became indulgence. The artist met no reproach when he descended from his garret with face unshaven and clothes askew. The butterfly in the ballet bore no stain for pirouetting in her tutu. A young woman gazing out her window could meet the glance of an admiring gentleman, inviting him to ring the bell. While its former aristocrats might cringe with horror that they had once called it home, Bleecker asked no questions.

Couch wanted no questions asked about her mission. Her preacher, the Reverend Abraham Carter of the Church of the Holy Savior, had directed her here. She had met Carter two years before when she moved to the city from Connecticut. She boarded at Mrs. Frost's Young Ladies School. She was smart and attractive, a perfect blonde with charming features and a demeanor marked by modesty and grace. Mrs. Frost hired her to tend infants at four dollars a week. She taught them the alphabet.

On Sundays Couch attended Reverend Carter's services. One day he invited her into the vestry to procure religious books. In the privacy of that chamber, he seduced her. Their affair moved to various houses of assignation. Eventually Couch became pregnant. Upon hearing that news, Carter decided the children his wife was raising proved his manliness enough. He gave Couch $700, promised another $100 on the first of every month, and sent her to a physician.

On Bleecker, Couch hurried to meet her abortionist. Unfortunately, the doctor was not so kind and competent as Ann Burns, whose residency in Sing Sing was now under appeal. Carter's man was a quack, of which there were plenty in the neighborhood. One was known to hook his pregnant patients to a galvanic battery and turn on the electricity. Couch wouldn't let some such nut humbug her. She fled.

Friends who could overlook Couch's disgrace offered refuge. Two were doctors whose wives and daughters cared for her, she wrote Carter near the end of February. She was not reassuring Carter about her safety, however. *You promised me a hundred dollars the first of the month,* her letter said. *I want the payment you missed in February and the one due in March, or else.* As sure as there was a hell, if Carter preached another Sabbath in the church he'd defiled, she'd expose his sins to every member of his congregation and show his wife and children what he'd turned her into.

A week into March the *Herald* reported a stir in the Tombs police court when Couch, looking demure in a velvet cloak and pearl-colored veil, appeared. The reporter peppered her with questions as she clung to the burly arm of criminal lawyer William Howe. Opposite her sat Reverend Carter, who was charging Couch with blackmail by threat of exposure. Every allegation in her letter, included in his affidavit to the court, was a lie. Carter knew the lady no more than any attendant at his church. If she knew the inside of his vestry, it was only because she called there to procure religious books.

The drama played out in the press through the first half of spring. A grand jury indicted Couch on fifteen counts. The *Times* convicted her without so much as an arraignment, claiming she admitted her accusations were false. Meanwhile other papers reported her great confidence that she could prove Carter's guilt. She stewed weeks in jail while lawyers argued over her arraignment and bail. As her case bounced from court to court, prominent parties grew anxious simply to get her out of the way. When bail was set in May, they got their wish. Couch posted $5,000 and disappeared from the city's press.

Victoria Woodhull watched the case unfold. In the *Weekly*'s first issue of April, she weighed in under the headline MAGNIFICENT BEATS vs. MAGNIFICENT HUSSIES. Her story cast Reverend Carter as the Magnificent Beat, an animal who preys upon women. A Beat might be a dandified scion of wealth, living at the best hotels and driving fast horses. Or a husband and father with a name recognized as a success in business who pursues his after-hours revels incognito. Or a churchman piously preaching to his congregation as his eye alights on a pretty face.

The dandy might kiss the cheek of a blushing damsel dreaming of a future filled with the love and tenderness of a faithful mate, then steal her maidenhead. The businessman might barter for the services of a desperate woman escaping starvation through a life of degradation, only to cheat her of the proffered reward. The churchman might lead a supplicant into temptation and cast her aside in sin. As a worm turns when tread upon, the scorned women turn into Magnificent Hussies, the opposite pole of the Beats, resorting to blackmail when their base treatment converts their love to hate. Society does not condemn the man; the law does not convict him. But the woman suffers public shame; the law offers no leniency. She has no choice but the crude justice of blackmail.

Woodhull was not condoning blackmail. Too many times the perpetrator of a fraud had tried to buy her silence, and when she refused, accused her of extortion and slandered her as an immoral woman. She had stood her ground. Never had she wielded secrets for money, and she swore she never would.

Nor had she exposed personalities. As others blackened her name, she had decried their hypocrisy in tolerating in others the practices they denounced her for preaching. She had gone so far as to insinuate scandals they would surely recognize, such as the "awful and herculean efforts to suppress the most terrific scandal in a neighboring city." The city was Brooklyn and few in the Heights overlooking Manhattan mistook her reference to their community's most precious asset, the Reverend Henry Ward Beecher, who practiced exactly what they denounced her for preaching.

But naming a name and the sins that name practiced, that she had resisted. She would resist no longer with the Magnificent Beats. Away with the nonsense of protecting personalities, she wrote. Strip away the masks of these night prowlers who cry blackmail to cover their own scoundrelism. "Have you been deceived, maltreated, abandoned?" she asked those of her sex. Send her the scoundrels and their black deeds so *Woodhull & Claflin's Weekly* could broadcast them throughout the land. Like Cain, let a Beat's infamy follow wherever he goes, that his shame might deter others from like acts.

Perhaps Beats took some warning, perhaps they cared little. Woodhull could shrug over that matter. Another article set into type named the real targets of her warning, women like Mary Livermore and Lucy Stone, Phebe Hanaford and Elizabeth Phelps, Anna Dickinson and Laura Curtis Bullard. "Tit for Tat," read its title, and the pages laid out the secrets and sins in their lives.

When the *Weekly* went to press, the run omitted this story. It was printed separately, each piece slipped into an envelope for delivery to one of the women it named. Whatever the words on the personal note included, the message was clear: *vomit your slime at me one more time and I will publish, Tit for Tat.*

10 | HOWE'S MAGIC

MARIA ULZAN'S STORY WAS nothing special. She had emigrated from Germany three years earlier and worked as the servant for a janitor's family on lower Broadway. A cigar maker spotted the young and timid blonde as easy prey. With spring approaching, she was three months pregnant with a child she didn't want. Somehow she cobbled together forty dollars to get rid of it. Maybe the cigar maker cared enough to help with the money.

She made two trips to the home of Madame Julia Grindle and her husband, Dr. Henry Grindle. Madame Grindle took twenty dollars and gave Ulzan medicine to produce miscarriage. With no relief after three days, Ulzan paid another twenty dollars for more. For the next eleven days, her womb hemorrhaged. Despite her mistress's ministrations, she stood on the brink of the grave. Learning she was an immigrant, Bellevue Hospital refused her admission. *Apply to the Commissioners of Emigration,* the staff told her. *They care for girls like you.*

Ulzan was lucky. The commissioners sent a doctor. He discovered placenta decomposing in her womb, enough to poison her life away even without the hemorrhaging. Without doubt, an abortion had created the condition. In a delicate operation, the doctor and a colleague cleaned the womb. Ulzan recovered enough to swear an oath in the Tombs police court. Armed with a warrant, a police sergeant rang the bell at the Grindles' home.

The Grindles had been caring for expectant mothers for years. Their home served as a well-kept lying-in hospital. Hundreds of unwed women had borne children there. The Grindles' noble mission was to help them through their trials. But for friendly hands like theirs, "how many blasted homes, scandalized churches and disorganized social circles there would be," Madame Grindle told clients. And not just poor women but also the better classes brought by senators and congressmen. For women not wishing to raise a child, the Grindles adopted it out. And if a client stammered she did not wish to bear her baby? With a nod of her head and a finger to her lips, Madame Grindle assured that "we understand every branch of our business." So far as anyone knew, seven years had passed since the last serious mishap. Though that woman's death had attracted the police, it resulted from peritonitis following a natural miscarriage. Or at least the coroner's jury could not find enough evidence to rule otherwise.

Madame Grindle answered the sergeant's ring and ushered him into the parlor. A woman of forty, she carried herself with an aristocratic air, her voice fluttering like a hummingbird. When the sergeant delivered the warrant for her arrest, she calmly protested her innocence, as did Dr. Grindle when he joined them. *Save it for the judge*, the sergeant said.

Dr. Grindle called the coachman and sent for their attorney. Not wishing to appear unfashionable, Madame Grindle changed into a dress of black silk, accented with a camel-hair shawl, green velvet hat, and kid gloves. Gold circled her wrists and dangled from her ears. She invited the sergeant to join her and her husband in their landau drawn by high-mettled bays. They proceeded to the Tombs.

If Madame Grindle hoped to make a commanding entrance, the *Herald* man covering the Tombs had a different impression: "This alleged female infant slayer resembles not a little the notorious Josephine Mansfield, of whom the public have unfortunately heard so much."

Madame Grindle seated herself beside her attorney, William Howe. Howe informed the judge that his client denied the charge against her in toto. Upon seeing Dr. Grindle, the victim Maria Ulzan changed her story. The doctor had joined his wife. He poured the medicine. He handed it to her. Madame Grindle accepted the money.

The accused received the money under coercion by her husband, Howe claimed. The court must discharge her. An argument ensued between Howe and the judge whether the crime was murder in the first or the second degree.

Neither, Howe insisted, *there was no murder at all. Discharge the prisoner.*

The judge relented but announced he would hold Dr. Grindle without bail. That was success enough for Howe that day. He understood the evidence allowed no case against either Grindle. After overnight in the Tombs, Dr. Grindle walked free.

Despite their brush with the law, the Grindles didn't bother to cancel their advertisements in the *Herald* or the *Sunday Mercury*. Dr. Grindle consistently occupied the top slot in the medical classifieds, Madame Grindle the spot below. Had Emma Couch sought an abortionist for herself rather than rely on her seducer Reverend Carter, she could have found a dozen well-known names in those papers. Madame Restell was both the most expensive and infamous. But Doctors Maxwell, Franklin, and Selden had all made news within the past year, and Harrison, Bott, and Manches had long built reputations. Madame Van Buskirk, released in January after a jury couldn't agree on her guilt in an abortion death, lured patients with her "25 years' successful practice" as a physician and midwife.

Headlines of women butchered did not deter business. Beautiful heiress Ida van Steenburg and young Maria Shea died in March. In April, Eliza Kothe died in Brooklyn. May brought two more deaths, and all these were New York alone. The papers reported more from Philadelphia to Omaha and on to San Francisco. While the victims were tragic, their numbers seemed mild considering the rampant demand for terminating pregnancies. For mothers, if not their babies, an abortion was probably safer than most trips to the hospital.

Stirred up by the barbarities of Dr. Evans and Dr. Rosenzweig, the New York legislature was determined to fix things. An assemblyman had introduced a bill to raise the prison time of convicted abortionists to at least four years and as much as twenty. All winter the bill had bounced between the state assembly and senate. On March 20, the two chambers agreed and sent "An Act for the Better Prevention of the Procurement of Abortion and Other Like Offenses" to the governor. Three days later they asked for it back. Over the next ten days, the legislators struck a few phrases at the beginning and stuck in a hereafter, all to assure themselves that abortion would be recognized as a high felony. On April 6, three days after Dr. Grindle walked, the governor signed the bill into law.

The legislature's dawdling was another lucky break for Maria Ulzan. Sending abortionists up the river for four to twenty didn't satisfy the legislators' hunger for retribution. The shameful mothers must suffer too. Section 2 of the bill stated any pregnant woman who took medicine, drug, substance, or thing whatever, or who employed or let another employ any instrument or other means whatever, with intent to produce miscarriage, was guilty of a felony. Had the governor signed the bill one month earlier, the law could have sent Ulzan to the penitentiary for four to ten years.

Halloween 1868 was three days before the election. The officers of the Young Men's Christian Association hoped for good weather to lay the cornerstone of their new building. So did the park commissioners, who had scheduled the last music of the season in Central Park featuring Wagner, Beethoven, and Strauss. The forecast was for clouds with an easterly wind and unseasonably cool temperatures. Luckily the storm held off until late in the evening, or at least that's how William Howe remembered it. He had no time for either the cornerstone ceremony or the concert.

Elections weren't something to worry over in Tammany-run New York. The Republican Ulysses Grant would take the presidency no matter what, but Boss Tweed's people would ensure the Democrats won locally. On East Broadway, several men were making repeated trips to and from a house to register under aliases at the election districts in the Seventh and Tenth Wards. Surprisingly the local cops weren't in on the fix. Under orders from Inspector George Walling, they raided the place and hauled eight men to police headquarters.

Someone called at the office of Howe & Hummel to report prisoners arrested on suspicion of illegally registering to vote. Howe hurried to police headquarters to learn no specific charge had been entered. The inspector supposed the men were forming a society for illegal registration, so he intended to hold them. That didn't sit well with Howe. Either he or Hummel—they couldn't remember which four years later—went to city hall to get Judge George Barnard to sign a writ of habeas corpus. The writ ordered the men delivered by 7:00 PM to Barnard's chambers, which he was keeping that evening at his house on Twenty-First Street.

WM. F. HOWE.

William F. Howe.
Charles Sutton, The New York Tombs, *1874*

Superintendent John Kennedy and Inspector Walling did not take well to the writ. When 7:00 PM passed, Howe returned for a lengthy debate. Finally, after nine o'clock, when registration closed for the upcoming election, Kennedy and Walling agreed that the prisoners could do no more harm. They assigned two policemen to take them to Judge Barnard. From upstairs, Barnard asked the policemen to wait with the prisoners on the sidewalk, worrying about them soiling his carpets or stealing his spoons. Howe wrote out a discharge order and sent it up with a servant for Barnard's signature. With the prisoners freed, Howe treated them to drinks at a bar belonging to their gang leader, Reddy the Blacksmith, a longstanding client of Howe's. Wrapping up the evening, they sent round to the Fourteenth Precinct for officers to fetch the men a stage home.

The first week of the current spring, Howe relived that evening. The Judiciary Committee of the State Assembly investigating Judges Cardozo and Barnard was holding hearings at the Fifth Avenue Hotel. Howe prowled the corridors, waiting to support his go-to friends on the bench. This day was his third of testimony. By now, hundreds of Howe & Hummel's writs of habeas corpus had been entered in the record. Howe had denied his criminal practice was the largest in the city, but yes, he had earned the sobriquet Habeas Corpus Howe. Still, he testified to the Judiciary Committee that, in every instance that he had petitioned for a writ of habeas corpus, he had believed the Court of Special Sessions was illegally constituted with only one judge. He believed it to this day, and he expected the New York State Court of Appeals to believe it.

Whether Howe's argument had anything to do with years-old writs was doubtful. It hardly mattered. Howe admitted to just about everything earlier witnesses said about the Halloween writs for Reddy the Blacksmith's gang. The Judiciary Committee investigators could protest violations of police procedure, debunk the discharge papers as written in Howe's own hand, or inflame feelings throwing Reddy the Blacksmith's name around. Where was the crime?

The investigators got a little closer with two other cases. They found one witness who swore a madam paid Howe & Hummel $1,500 to free her on a writ Judge Cardozo signed. A father testified Hummel asked for $300 to free his son, then held the release up because the papers needed to go before "a particular judge." Cardozo discharged the boy when he returned from vacation. The investigators called in bankers to trace these payments. But Howe & Hummel insisted on cash from clients. The partners divvied up the receipts at the end of each day. Any share siphoned off to their friends was surely cash too.

Howe didn't like his friends threatened, and he would offer whatever testimony possible to help them. Nor did he like himself raked over the coals. But he wasn't at risk. The public airing of his antics only enhanced his reputation. And what if the investigators were right, that the habeas corpus business was about extortion and bribery, that the Court of Special Sessions argument was thought up years later? The court of appeals ended that discussion on April 2 and did Howe one better.

The Appeals Court ruling had nothing to do with whether one judge or two or fifteen sat in the Court of Special Sessions. In 1870 the state legislature had reorganized the Court of Special Sessions in a bill titled "An Act to Make Further Provision for the Government of the City of New York," commonly known as the City Tax Levy. The state constitution prohibited combining in a single bill a court action and the funding of city government. The Appeals judges declared the Court of Special Sessions void and vacated all convictions in it. Regrettably many prisoners who deserved punishment might be discharged, the judges noted. But abrogating a plain constitutional requirement was a greater evil.

The Appeals Court gave Howe another piece of good news the same day. Judge Gunning Bedford had erred in his instructions to the jury that convicted Dr. Evans. In his zeal to lock up the abortionist, he had ordered the twelve not to consider whether the fetus had "quickened," meaning moved in the womb for the mother to feel. Under the 1869 abortion law in force when Evans acted, abortion before quickening was not a crime. The ruling entitled Evans to a new trial. Though the district attorney promised to search for witnesses of Evans's crime, they had scattered to the winds. The Ghoul of Chatham Street walked free.

As for Barnard and Cardozo, they found one final opportunity to show their appreciation for Howe's support in the Judiciary Committee hearing. The second week of April, they agreed with their third-wheel Judge Daniel Ingraham on the appeal of abortionist Ann Burns, originally convicted in the December term of the Court of General Sessions under Recorder John Hackett. Ingraham, whom the Judiciary Committee let off the hook only because he was scheduled to retire, wrote the opinion. Yes, Howe had correctly called Burns's jury illegal since it was chosen from the pool Judge Bedford had empaneled for November. A jury so chosen could not serve at trial in the December term. But the opinion went further. Because Judge Bedford had not ended his November term until March the following year, the December term technically had not started until March. Not only was Ann Burns entitled to a new trial, so was every other prisoner convicted in the December term.

The *Evening Post* headlined ANOTHER WORTHLESS COURT. Other papers speculated the ruling could render null and void proceedings against the Tammany Ring thieves. The district attorney assured the public the decision did not extend beyond Burns, nor would she benefit when the court of appeals reversed it. When the court had not done so by late May, he appeared with Howe before Judge Ingraham to acknowledge that in the absence of the principal witness, a new trial had no chance of conviction. After five months in Sing Sing, the abortionist Ann Burns returned to her Long Island farm, a free woman.

One had to wonder what magic Howe would work to free Dr. Rosenzweig, the Fiend of Second Avenue.

11 | "FROM THIS CONVENTION WILL GO FORTH A TIDE OF REVOLUTION"

WITH SPRING COMING, Susan B. Anthony was tired, and frankly, depressed. After the January suffrage convention, she visited her home in Rochester before heading to the Midwest. In February she lectured through Illinois, then ventured on to Iowa, Nebraska, Kansas, and Missouri. The travel was grueling and the cost draining. Supporters dropping a needed dollar into her purse drove her to tears.

Her birthday brought a respite with friends at a reception for the Women's Hospital Medical College in Chicago. She was fifty-two and feeling fit to carry the suffrage banner for years to come. Yet papers mocked her like she was a washed-up hag. One acknowledged she really wasn't a million years old. Others disputed the legend that she had planted a thousand-year-old rosebush growing up a German cathedral. An editor commended her situation as an old maid—her refusal to marry had saved another man from ruination by a strong-willed wife. She could ignore the ridicule, but the stories claiming she "defended" Victoria Woodhull at the suffrage convention were too much. Were the editors too stupid to distinguish between praise and reproach?

Anthony felt utterly disheartened over Woodhull, and she wrote Elizabeth Cady Stanton and Isabella Beecher Hooker telling them as much. Any efforts to create a new political party were wasted. No man would vote a woman suffrage ticket. Yet Woodhull, with her newspaper and her money, was strong-arming the suffragists into supporting her—"run[ning] our craft into her port" is how Anthony put it. She wasn't about to hoist sails for that woman when it was "men's spirits" giving Woodhull the words that poured from her mouth.

As Anthony returned east, her train stopped in a small Illinois town. She picked up a *Woodhull & Claflin's Weekly* dated April 6. A headline drew her eye, PEOPLE'S CONVENTION. "The undersigned citizens, responding to the invitation of the National Woman Suffrage Association, propose to hold a Convention," the story began. It was outrageous, that woman using the organization Anthony embodied to support her new political party! Anthony read through to find worse. Seeing "Susan B. Anthony" as one of the undersigned, right below Stanton and Hooker, drove her into a frenzy. She fired off protests by telegraph and letter, demanding her name be retracted. She would have no part of a People's Convention. May's NWSA convention in New York would focus solely on woman suffrage. A new political party was not on the agenda.

With Anthony a thousand miles away, her words were impotent. No matter how much ink she wasted, Stanton failed to understand what was best not only for suffrage but also for herself personally, for her moral standing. Anthony had told her so a year ago, yet the foolishness had just gotten worse. And Hooker was like every new convert, like each apostle joining Christ thinking he could improve on Jesus's methods. How could Stanton be relying on Hooker to sail their ship in these stormy seas? It was suicidal.

If only Anthony could rush back to seize the helm. But the Liberal Republicans, a breakaway faction who could not stomach another four years of President Grant, were convening in Cincinnati. She had sworn she would support whichever of the existing parties adopted a woman suffrage plank. With the Republicans split, she had three shots, and she couldn't miss this first one.

Accompanied by fellow suffragist Laura de Force Gordon from California, Anthony set up shop in Cincinnati's Burnet House. "This Liberal Republican movement professes to be a liberal party," she told reporters. "I want to see how liberal they are." She intended to submit a plank for the platform that stated if women were taxed to support the government, they were entitled with their fellow citizens to elect who would govern them. The prospects for the plank's adoption were forbidding, she admitted. Three years out of four, suffrage had plenty of friends. But every fourth year with a president to be elected, the cause dropped from sight. Politicians happily filled seats with women waving handkerchiefs and clapping at the smart things they said, but heaven forbid women choose rulers.

Senator Carl Schurz of Missouri, an uncompromising foe of women voting, chaired the proceedings. He ignored Anthony's request to appeal directly to the delegates. When invited to sit upon the convention's stage, she and Gordon heard as many hisses as cheers. Meanwhile the band reflected the delegates' view of women by playing "I Dreamt I Dwelt in Marble Halls," about a young lady dreaming of nothing more ambitious than living in such a home. Gordon's claim to be seated as a member of the California delegation went to the Credentials Committee amid laughter and insults. Still, Anthony persisted, lobbying delegates on the floor, pigeonholing the new chair when Schurz was pushed aside. She worked the hotels too. In a final condescending blow, the police cleared the lobby of Burnet House when she and Gordon tried to address a crowd. By the time delegates nominated Horace Greeley for president, the convention had descended into chaos.

And not a word for women or their rights in the party platform.

Anthony left Cincinnati, her body as "ragged & torn" as the threadbare dresses she had worn during a year of travels, her spirit forlorn and disgusted with Horace Greeley and the stooges fawning over him.

———————————

Anthony arrived in New York a few days before the suffrage convention opened in Steinway Hall. She looked forward to a morning with friends at the Women's Bureau, a clubhouse for ladies. Its proprietress, Elizabeth Phelps, hosted receptions where reformers could meet one another, sponsored talks where suffragists honed their speaking skills, and rented facilities for women's businesses. Anthony had launched her former journal the *Revolution* there.

Married to a millionaire, Phelps enjoyed a reputation for charitable works. But two years past, a scandal had engulfed her when a Macy's salesgirl accused her of shoplifting twenty-two cents worth of candy. Hauled into court, she endured step-by-step testimony of how she secreted the candy on her person, followed by the embarrassment of defending herself under oath. Fortunately, the judge could not believe a lady of her character and benevolence would commit such a crime. Though the publicity in the papers was humiliating, Mr. Rowland Hussey Macy suffered greater damage through exposure of how he spied on customers.

Anthony found her friends unable to meet that morning and Phelps agitated by a brewing scandal of another sort. Victoria Woodhull had dropped into the Women's Bureau the prior week, Phelps told her. The visit was not their first acquaintance. Phelps had attended Woodhull's soirees in Murray Hill. During the shoplifting incident, *Woodhull & Claflin's Weekly* had exonerated Phelps while berating Macy for paying his clerks so little that they stole themselves and blamed the thefts on customers. Over time, however, as others vilified Woodhull and her free love views, Phelps had turned into a bitter critic. During her recent visit Woodhull had produced an article describing "the sexual liaisons and free love practices of some of the best-known women in the reformatory movement," Phelps said. Woodhull accused not only her but also Laura Curtis Bullard, Mary Livermore, Phebe Hanaford, and others. She demanded $500 or the story would include Phelps.

Phelps didn't have the money and could hardly ask her husband for it. She didn't pay. Woodhull would later acknowledge printing the "Tit for Tat" proof sheets to silence her enemies, but she denied ever mentioning money. Not enough money existed to stop her fighting hypocrisy and the slander against her, she said. Phelps would deny publicly any incident occurred, as would others whose names spread in the gossip about Woodhull. Nor did Woodhull ever publish the story. None of that mattered now; Anthony believed Phelps. "Called on Mrs. Phelps. Heard Woodhull's move to blackmail the women," she wrote in her diary.

The news confirmed to Anthony how right she had been in insisting the suffragists repudiate Woodhull. Anthony rushed off to Elizabeth Cady Stanton's home in Tenafly, New Jersey. Surely her friend finally would see the light. So many times Stanton had told women criticizing women to stop: *We need not all be as chaste as Diana; we need not persecute and ridicule and crucify one another with hypocritical prattle about purity. If women be crucified, let men drive the spikes and plait the crown of thorns.* Now Woodhull was blackening characters and demanding money, and she would crucify women if they did not pay. Stanton must disown her.

Stanton closed her ears. She would not relent in her staunch support for Woodhull. *You are narrow, bigoted, headstrong,* she told Anthony. *The major political parties have abandoned suffrage while, free lover or not, Woodhull has advanced the cause when it was floundering. She is our path.*

Somehow the friendship did not crack apart. Anthony and Stanton returned to New York. The bitterness grew the next morning when, by arrangement with Stanton, Woodhull and several labor radicals showed up for an NWSA business committee meeting. When they proposed to join the suffrage meeting and the organizing convention for an Equal Rights Party, Anthony exploded. The Steinway Hall meeting was for woman suffrage alone. She had rented Steinway in her name. She forbade its use for anything else. She elbowed aside a set of resolutions Woodhull laid before the committee. Ultimately, she emerged victorious. The Woodhull forces withdrew, resigned to hold their party convention at Apollo Hall.

For another day Anthony and Stanton patched over their wounds. Together they wrote resolutions and a platform to present to the suffragists. Isabella Beecher Hooker joined them that evening. She sided with Stanton. Woodhull had brought money and brains and unceasing energy to suffrage, and her Memorial to Congress had revitalized the movement. Hooker would not abandon her. The wounds opened afresh. By the time the suffrage meeting began the next day, Stanton was so angry she resigned as president of the NWSA. Anthony blamed her for the foolish muddle, all the result of conceding to Woodhull and agreeing to a People's instead of a Suffrage convention.

The next morning ladies in brilliant spring dress and fashionable men of the professional class streamed along Fourteenth Street to Steinway Hall. A showroom exhibiting over a hundred pianos occupied the ground floor. A concert hall above seated twenty-five hundred before a stage designed for a hundred-piece orchestra. The New York Philharmonic made it home. That combination showed Mr. Steinway putting his business philosophy into practice: a concert Saturday night sells pianos Monday morning. Rental fees for meetings like the suffragists' stuffed whatever space was left in his pockets after his musical profits.

The suffragists charging twenty-five cents surprised people that day. Many turned away, having heard it would be levied only for the evening session. Perhaps the smaller crowd was a blessing. With a full house and several hundred gaslights blaring, the atmosphere inside could grow intolerably hot and suffocating. The *Times* noted temperatures could rise thirty degrees during performances and called for the city's auditoriums to upgrade their ventilation. The editors expected few owners to listen.

When the ladies walked onstage, Elizabeth Cady Stanton plopped into a green cushioned chair, bouncing the snowy ringlets shadowing her forehead. The *Herald* and the *Times* men interpreted her perch as belonging to the presiding officer of the convention. Observing Susan B. Anthony running things, the *Evening Post* identified her as chairing the session. Was the confusion an early sign that tensions might erupt before the day was out?

After Stanton's keynote speech, Isabella Beecher Hooker read a proposed platform. Anthony followed with resolutions for the delegates to consider. The platform ranged from equality for all, regardless of birth, race, religion, or sex, to civil service reform to introduction of a national currency and graduated taxation. It culminated in calling for the establishment of a political party to promote its vital principles. The resolutions confined themselves to woman suffrage, berating Greeley, exhorting the Democrats and mainstream Republicans to recognize the political equality of women, and committing suffragists to work for whichever party did.

Confused, the audience spoke out. One gentleman said he had come four hundred miles to attend a human rights meeting. A woman said she had bowed and begged in vain before the current parties for twenty years. She expected to consider a new party, and if the suffragists weren't addressing it today, tomorrow she'd go to Apollo Hall, where the People's Convention would. A judge from Ohio avowed himself a Democrat for twenty-five years, a Republican for twenty, and a suffragist for four, but right now he wanted equal justice for all humanity.

Stanton tried to restrain the growing rebellion. Mr. Steinway had rented the hall only for a suffrage meeting. *We must limit ourselves to that topic,* she cried.

We paid for the hall, a man called. *We won't let the Steinways gag us.*

Let's go to another place where we can have free speech, yelled another.

A labor reformer called out, *Meet tomorrow at Apollo Hall, where we can discuss human rights.* The audience clamored in support.

The session adjourning saved the situation from spinning out of control.

When the evening session opened, a truce held through two speeches. But when Anthony put the platform to a vote, one man protested. He insisted on a broad discussion of social life. As suffragists hissed, he launched a bitter tirade against the entire proceedings. The advocates of Woodhull cheered him on. Sensing danger, Anthony tried to adjourn the meeting. With her partisans shouting Anthony down, Woodhull glided onstage.

"The eyes of the world are upon this convention," she declared. "Its enemies have sneered and laughed at the idea of combining reformers for any organized action. They say that women don't know enough to organize and therefore are not to be feared as political opponents. . . . Some confessed reformers say they don't want anything to do with those who don't belong to their 'clique' . . . but I hope all friends of humanitarian reform will clasp hands with each other."

Woodhull moved that the meeting adjourn to Apollo Hall to nominate candidates for president and vice president. Someone seconded. *Out of order*, Anthony shouted. She refused to put the motion.

Overrule the chair, another screamed from the floor. When Woodhull demanded an immediate vote, the yeas and nays were called out. The motion passed by acclamation.

Out of order, Anthony ruled again. *The motions are invalid; the people voting, the vast majority of them, are not entitled—they are not members of the NWSA. Adjourn the meeting.* Pandemonium set in. Anthony grew desperate. She left the stage in search of the janitor. *Turn off the gas*, she ordered him. Hundreds of gaslights shutting down plunged the auditorium into darkness. Several hundred people groped to the doors. Many fewer would return the next day.

"The fiasco perfect," Anthony concluded. She was hurt, demoralized, near to losing any knowledge of herself. All was a failure.

The coup d'etat at the suffragists' meeting and the next day's apotheosis by the Equal Rights Party were remarkable displays of Woodhull's political acumen and the fruits of her labor. If the coalition she brought together held, her candidacy for the presidency would carry formidable force. With the suffragists meeting a second day, Stanton and Hooker did not leave Anthony to twist in the wind. But their sympathies were clear, and many longtime suffragists joined Woodhull on the stage at Apollo Hall, rented with her dwindling money.

Luminaries throughout reform had lined up behind Woodhull: sex educator and birth control advocate Dr. Edward Foote, financial reformers Ezra Heywood and Angela Tilton Heywood, labor radicals Theodore Banks and William West, educator Belva Lockwood, Spiritualists Horace Dresser and Caroline Hinckley Spear, freethinkers Moses Hull and Robert Dale Owen. These people were iconoclasts battling the established social order. Though few yet knew of Anthony Comstock, he would turn his wrath upon them in the years ahead. Some would spend fortunes fending him off and endure years in jail when their efforts failed.

Victoria Woodhull accepting her nomination for president.
M. F. Darwin, One Moral Standard for All: Extracts from the Lives of Victoria Claflin Woodhull and Tennessee Claflin, *undated*

In the evening, Woodhull appeared onstage in plain black but for a blue necktie. Her face flushed, her hair was disheveled, her eyes gleamed. The spirits had possessed her. Yes, she was a practical woman and she used the spirits as a weapon. Nonetheless they were real, and when they came it truly was as if something supernatural inhabited her body, the way it floated upon the platform, calm amid the storm, her gaze mesmerizing. She began softly, each syllable ringing clear, her passion building, finally words pouring from her lips in reckless torrents that swept through the souls before her and incited an uproarious outburst of enthusiasm.

"From this Convention will go forth a tide of revolution that will sweep over the world," she proclaimed. "Go where we may in the land, there we see despotism, inequality and injustice installed where freedom, equality and justice should be instead."

Opportunity is a fundamental right, Woodhull said. *Yet one in ten cannot read—sufficient in itself to condemn to everlasting infamy the principles on which our civilization is based. So what that opponents of reform decry it means revolution? Shall we be slaves to escape revolution?*

"I say never! I say, away with such weak stupidity. . . . I say, let us have justice, though the heavens fall."

The audience sprang to their feet a thousand strong, waved hats and handkerchiefs, rattled umbrellas, screamed until all wind was exhausted, cheered with a frenzy to startle promenaders on Broadway, to bring crowds rushing in from the street.

One man raised his voice above the din. The moment had come to select a standard bearer, he said, and who better fit than the person who so nobly embodied their cause? "I propose the name of Victoria C. Woodhull to be nominated president of the United States, and I call upon you to carry the motion by acclamation."

Another outburst drowned his final words. A torrent of ayes flew forth, not a nay to the contrary. The frenzy refused to die as the man led a flushed Woodhull forward. Her bosom heaved, her voice trembled as she thanked them for the great honor.

After a final piece of business, the nomination of Frederick Douglass for vice president, the crowd swarmed around their nominee. Woodhull stood in ecstasy beside her beloved Tennie as ladies kissed her, kissed each other, kissed her again. Men shook her hands and passed their arms around women. Around women not their wives, noted a slightly scandalized Isabella Beecher Hooker, who showed up late in the evening to congratulate her friend. Never had she seen so much kissing and hugging in public—or in private, for that matter.

As congratulatory telegrams poured in from around the country, the party turned to business. Woodhull's husband, Colonel Blood, headed its executive committee. To raise funds, they would issue bonds bearing the Goddess of Liberty with the words "Equal Rights," which the convention adopted as the party's symbol. The bonds would be redeemable when the party came to power or the system of government was changed. With denominations ranging from $5 to $1,000, attendees pledged $3,000. The committee anticipated $100,000 within days.

They would need the money. The committee agreed to rent a house for up to $1,000 a month, appropriate as the home of the prospective president and the party headquarters. The brokerage and publishing businesses would relocate there from Broad Street. Arrangements began to make *Woodhull & Claflin's Weekly* the official organ of the campaign.

Woodhull announced that capitalists with humanitarian instincts would recognize the benefits of a more equitable distribution of income and fill the party's coffers. Her campaign clubs, the Victoria Leagues, would soon count membership in the millions. The party was engaging speakers to spread her doctrines throughout the country. She would stump from Maine to California, with Tennie beside her.

The campaign was off in a sprint.

Following the NWSA convention, Susan B. Anthony returned home to Rochester. Her heart and soul ached too much to work. She fretted over what the next *Woodhull &*

Claflin's Weekly would say about her suffragists and the schism in the movement, the schism that was tearing away her partner in her life's work, and not just Stanton but other friends as well. The *Weekly* said nothing, really, no "denunciating" of the suffragists' work. But Woodhull's trumpeting of her "glorious triumph," the way she subsumed everything into her service, repelled Anthony. She was feeling vindictive.

Several days later, a friend, Mary Hallowell, invited Anthony to join others coming to dinner. Anthony needed a convivial evening, an opportunity to let down her guard. She confessed her vehement feelings, how Woodhull would stoop to anything to succeed. She knew firsthand that Woodhull blackmailed Elizabeth Phelps and Mary Livermore and Phebe Hanaford. The woman had printed slips alleging indiscretions and demanded $500 to cover them up. Her sister Tennie Claflin was perhaps worse, if one believed the stories of how she cavorted.

Anthony repeated her story to Ezra Heywood as well, a reformer who supported the Equal Rights Party. He passed the story on, noting Anthony as its source, and Hallowell or her friends mentioned it to others. The gossip spread.

Anthony got an earful when she visited her friend Anna Dickinson in Philadelphia. Expecting a warm greeting from the younger woman she called *my darling*, she felt only ice. *You betrayed me,* Dickinson accused, *spreading what I told you about Livermore and Hanaford. And what terrible charges you fabricated against Tennie Claflin.*

Another friend heard them too, and though she refused to believe Anthony would have said such things, she warned her. *Be careful, a charge of unchastity is an indictable offense.*

Learning that a Rochester neighbor had written Woodhull about the charges against her sister, Anthony took the warning to heart. In a flurry of letters, she denied any accusations of adultery against Claflin. The neighbor had fabricated them entirely, she insisted. Stanton, too, had received a letter from the neighbor and a denial from Anthony. Anthony spiraled into a dark place. Whatever indiscretions she vented to her diary she ripped away in her blackest moments.

Anthony's mood did not improve upon leaving Philadelphia. She had attended the Republican convention there. The Republicans wouldn't allow a woman on the floor of their conclave, nor would they call for suffrage in their platform. They acquiesced only to saying the "party is mindful of its obligations to the loyal women of America for their noble devotion to the cause of freedom. Their admission to wider fields of usefulness is viewed with satisfaction, and the honest demand of any class of citizens for additional rights should be treated with respectful consideration."

Anthony did not reject that Republican bone outright. She called upon the Democrats to do better. When they embraced Greeley, "swallowing Cincinnati hoofs, horns and all," as she lamented in her diary, she accepted the Republicans' pathetic mention of women as her only option. She would "clutch it as the drowning man the floating straw." In this bitter election season, she would stump for Grant.

12 | AN AFTERNOON IN THE PARK

IF VISITORS TO NEW YORK wanted to see the patricians who cornered all the elegance, wealth, and condescension of the city rub elbows with the vermin who scraped crumbs out of the sewers, they headed for the Bowery. Silver spoons and filthy fingers alike dipped into its fleshpots. But for those with no taste for the ptomaine served there, afternoons in Central Park brewed an equally democratic concoction of the city's high and low.

With spring in full swing, forty thousand people visited the park daily, estimated the *Herald*. Crowds greeted the carriage parade that rolled through the Fifth Avenue gate at four o'clock. It often began with a collection of stout, ponderous horseflesh dragging a stodgy black brougham, its coachman and footmen bent double with age. The dowager tucked inside was as august and obsolete as her equipage. With a revered name like Livingston or Stuyvesant, she had little interest in any acquaintance with the hordes outside.

A simpler rig with unadorned horses and unliveried coachman followed in the line behind. No diamonds sparkled through its windows, for inside was the next generation of old money. The occupants needed no affectations attesting to their place in society.

A landau farther along more likely caught a visitor's eye. Its open design showed off the gaudy colors and fancy fashions of its inhabitants, "shoddies" whose new money came from finance or trade.

More exciting was the debutante relaxing in a victoria, her feminine wares fully displayed but for the parasol she hid behind to tease her beaux.

Her more daring rival snapped the reins of a swift phaeton, risking a reputation as a member of the fast set.

Suddenly a two-wheeled curricle darted by, an old man clinging to the reins of his pair of trotters. *Could that be . . . Commodore Vanderbilt?* a visitor might speculate. *Yes,* a native might respond. The richest man in the country worked briefly each morning. On any fine afternoon he indulged his passion: horses, not money. This year he was driving Mountain Boy and Mountain Girl, a pair well mated and fast.

Missing this year was the twelve-horse train of Jim Fisk, three pairs snow-white, three coal-black, with uniformed postilions astride the front two. Nor had the papers spied Miss Mansfield.

Still, the parade offered a strong dose of notoriety. Madame Restell kept her team in the stables behind her house on Fifth Avenue. The grooms hitched her Cubans to her brougham with silver harnesses. Her coachman climbed into his plum-trimmed livery and Madame into the carriage for the seven-block ride to the park. She turned sixty this spring, an elegant matron with two grandchildren underfoot. Few watching the parade would guess here was the infamous abortionist known as the wickedest woman in New York.

A madam of a different sort often joined the line. The most aristocratic gentlemen frequented her home near Washington Square Park. Josephine Woods rigorously inspected each client before admitting him to her parlors, as sumptuously decorated as Victoria Woodhull's former palace in Murray Hill. There a gentleman ordered champagne at eight dollars a bottle while he waited for two or three of Josephine's girls to join him. The price of his chosen would prove more extravagant than the champagne, but if a gentleman expected the best, he found it at Josephine's. She herself was a raven-haired beauty whose fine silks, sparkling diamonds, and magnificent carriage set tongues wagging along the parade route.

But wait, a visitor might say, *you promised a democratic concoction. Is not this a parade of the city's most wealthy and distinguished and notorious?* Indeed, but it was also the finest theater to the masses assembled along the carriageway—shopgirls dreaming of satin and jewels, clerks who toiled for rent money, rakes eager to seduce a belle and steal her papa's gold, bummers too lazy to labor, beggars too downtrodden. As swells slumming on the Bowery indulged their sin, so did the masses in Central Park relieve the drudgery of their lives mingling close to the rich and famous and infamous.

In prior years Vanderbilt would have dashed his horses through the park, ignoring the seven-mile-per-hour limit imposed on speed and heading for Harlem Lane. The lane ran for a mile northwesterly from the top of the park. Before a well-heeled crowd enjoying the competition from the piazza of Harry Berthold's hotel, the Commodore tested his horses and his mettle racing other trotting enthusiasts. The Reverend Henry Ward Beecher frequently drove two exceptional trotters bought with his eloquent sermons at Plymouth Church. Robert Bonner, publisher of the *New York Ledger*, ran the famous Dexter, who had clocked the world's fastest mile. Vanderbilt tried every trick to buy the horse, but his rival refused to sell.

Earlier this year the driving community lost the treasured Harlem Lane. Widened and filled with gravel, it became impassable. Eighth Avenue above 125th Street was the only trotting ground left in upper Manhattan, and a rail line was about to ruin it. To hell with the "spirit of improvement," the *Herald* argued, why not clean up Harlem Lane so the trotters could stretch their legs as in days of yore? Vanderbilt no doubt agreed.

The closing of Harlem Lane was not the only blow the horse-loving Commodore would suffer this spring. Bonner's young stallion Startle clocked the fastest half-mile this season in Brooklyn's Prospect Park. Days later Startle matched the record mile of Dexter. Despite the outstanding reputation Mountain Boy and Mountain Girl held, his horses playing second fiddle drove Vanderbilt up the walls of his stables. Why couldn't his millions bring the best?

A third blow fell when a fracas broke out at his stables sitting behind Vanderbilt's Washington Square home. Late one night, a liquored-up tailoress going by Carrie Love stumbled by on her way home. Vanderbilt's coachman James Ames, a stalwart black man, seized her round the throat. Terrified by her assailant's infuriated face and brutal intentions, this diminutive white woman shrieked, her screams so horror-laden that witnesses across the street stood paralyzed as Ames dragged her inside and barred the stable doors. As her terrified yells continued, they rushed to the local precinct.

Ames launched a foul and insulting torrent when the arriving officers demanded entrance. Vanderbilt poked his head through his bedroom window. *Do you consent that your stables be made a house of assignation?* an officer asked.

Certainly not. Vanderbilt rushed down in his dressing gown to open the stables himself. Ames rushed from behind a carriage and belted the officer. Fists, bottles, and batons flew until the police subdued the coachman and freed a piteously weeping Carrie Love from the room in which he had locked her.

The night was just getting started. As the sergeant at the Mercer Street station house arraigned Ames, Vanderbilt's brother-in-law Robert Crawford rushed in. *How dare you lock up Commodore Vanderbilt's coachman,* he raged. His anger stirred up the prisoner, who pulled a pocketknife and stabbed at the nearest officer. After another beating, police threw Ames into a cell as Crawford screamed at them: "You dirty sucker, you, I'm going to shoot you. . . . I'll kill you!" The cops wrestled him out the door. Crawford drew his pistol. In the ensuing struggle, the gun went off twice. One bullet punctured an officer's thigh. The second broke the leg of a passerby. Crawford escaped through the stable yard. The police surrounded the Commodore's house and discovered Crawford hiding upstairs.

Or at least that's how the *Herald* and the *Times* reported it. By the time the case reached trial the first week of June, William Howe had taken charge of the defense. Vanderbilt testified he never saw his coachman strike an officer. And when he had knocked on the room where Ames slept, Carrie Love had opened the door, saying, *I'm all right.* And to the officers: *You have no business with me, I have no complaint to make.*

She was "as drunk as the n——," the Commodore said.

That was all Howe needed. Going any further was a waste of time as the prosecution demonstrated the officers were the aggressors, he told the judge, who happened to be Bedford, the abortionists' nemesis. Neither Howe nor the prosecution bothered with summations. The jury acquitted with hardly a moment's deliberation.

When the judge discharged the defendant, Howe asked, "May Ames take his Love with him?" With spectators howling, Bedford guessed Ames had enough of the woman already.

Even the Commodore seemed amused. He would rely on his influence or his money to secure his brother-in-law's release.

And so ended the spring. No one could yet envision how brutal the summer would be. Not the public, who would wither under record heat. Not Ned Stokes in the Tombs, who hoped his trial in June would free him. Not Victoria Woodhull, who anticipated a horse race if not a victory for the White House. Not Anthony Comstock, who promised a pile of convictions to his YMCA benefactors.

Meanwhile Vanderbilt prepared for his annual sojourn to Saratoga. Money had its privileges.

IV

SUMMER

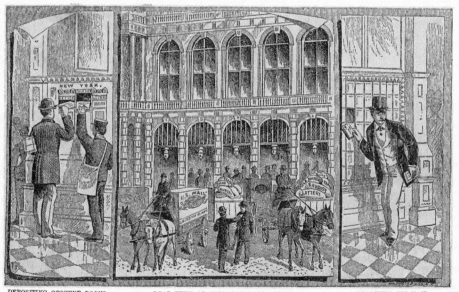

DEPOSITING OBSCENE BOOKS,
LOTTERY CIRCULARS, ETC. REAR VIEW OF NEW YORK POST OFFICE. RECEIVING HIS MAIL.

Anthony Comstock's view of obscenity in the US mail.
Anthony Comstock, Frauds Exposed, *1880*

13 | "A PIEBALD PRESIDENCY"

NOTWITHSTANDING HER FURY at the women who spewed venom, Victoria Woodhull always liked reading her name in the papers. From the moment the *Herald* admired her alabaster shoulders when reporting on the bewitching brokers, she built a cult in the press. Certainly she preferred praise. But ridicule, too, raised the platform she preached from, like the caricatures in the *Day's Doings*, Frank Leslie's naughty companion to his family-oriented *Illustrated Weekly*. This flash rag portrayed her and Tennie as brazen hussies horning in on a man's world. Whether the scene was trading securities, lecturing Congress, or parading with communists, the artists added liberal doses of sexual innuendo. The touch was good for Leslie's sales and spurred her cult in the bargain.

In June, the *Day's Doings* got around to drawing Woodhull's nomination at "the Free-Lovers' convention," featuring short-haired women, long-haired men, and mayhem no respectable member of the gentler sex would find herself in. Ironically, the *Times*, which considered the *Day's Doings* contemptible, adopted a similar theme for its coverage of the convention: ladies wearing eyeglasses and short hair demanded a complete restructure of the government and the Constitution, followed by a disturbing and boisterous discussion, including ideas on marriage unfit for publication. The *Herald* added that delegates were as homely in the face as nutmeg graters and the nominee was a young and painted creature in petticoats.

Woodhull read a lot of such claptrap in the weeks leading into summer. A South Carolina paper summed up her platform as "Women's Rights, Free Love and the total depravity of men." Philadelphia charged that her party attracted "semi-lunatics" operating on the principle that "whatever ought to be is." Most amusing were editorials calling on Horace Greeley to step aside. "Mr. Greeley now has the opportunity to be as gallant as he is wise," wrote a Rochester paper urging his withdrawal. "It is an obvious fact that Mrs. Woodhull is a more popular candidate."

One new theme appeared early on in the *Herald*. Its headline A PIEBALD PRESIDENCY referred to Frederick Douglass, the country's most prominent black man, as Woodhull's

115

running mate. The paper noted the Equal Rights ticket mingled the "fair sex" at the top with "a male brunette" playing second fiddle. Though this first reference to race was rather tame, the press focused on the mix of black and white as far more dangerous than the most radical of reforms. The *Philadelphia Inquirer* commented on the "strange combination of a white woman and a black man." An Oregon paper wondered, "Is Woodhull degraded to the level of a negro, or is Fred. Douglas sunk to that of a common prostitute"? The *New York Evening Telegram* upped the ante: "Here is a ticket which beats the most radical conception ever entertained. Free love in front and amalgamation in the rear." Amalgamation—sex between a white woman and a black man—generated hysteria throughout the country. In the South, it instigated lynchings. *Pomeroy's Democrat* took the idea beyond the pale, calling Douglass's nomination "an outrage by women." Though the paper made no specific accusation, readers recognized the euphemism that meant rape, in this case with the white woman the aggressor. The *Day's Doings* deployed the word against Vanderbilt's coachman: A FRENZIED NEGRO COACHMAN ATTEMPTS AN OUTRAGE; no matter that Carrie Love had been more than willing.

Woodhull had long invited such vulgarities or, as her friend Stanton said, "dared men to call her the names that make women shudder while she chucked medicine down their throats." The Douglass nomination was one more dose, intended to instruct her fellow citizens in the full meaning of human rights. Woodhull countered attacks on the ticket with praise for Douglass in *Woodhull & Claflin's Weekly*. Douglass had learned how to assert the liberties of the people. Like she, he embodied his own version of reform. Who better to partner with to knock down the sexual and racial barriers society erected? Together they demonstrated that the Equal Rights Party defended the rights of all mankind.

So let the papers jeer, Woodhull could tell herself. Let San Francisco call her a "brazen adventuress" with vile doctrines and worse practices. Let Washington decry her ideas as "maggots which vexed the brains." Let others condemn the great and nasty Woodhull, the "free-love high priestess." Every word of sex and painted creatures gave her a foil for unmasking the hypocrisy and injustice that ruled the country.

In that spirit, Woodhull prepared for the party's ratification rally at the Grand Opera House. She planned to introduce Douglass and for the party to confirm their nominations. Unfortunately, Lucy Fisk was no more enthusiastic about the event than the equestrian exhibition Tennie had proposed. Canceling the booking, her manager said not for $10,000 could the class of people forming the Equal Rights Party hold a meeting there. Fortunately, the Cooper Institute was less discriminating and had an opening June 6.

Red banners welcomed a boisterous crowd. NATIONALIZE LAND AND LABOR, GOVERNMENT PROVISION FROM CRADLE TO GRAVE, PUBLIC EMPLOYMENT, they proclaimed. A girl wearing red, white, and blue opened with a song to the tune of "Comin' Thro' the Rye":

> Yes, Victoria we select as our chosen head,
> With Fred Douglass on the ticket we shall raise the dead,
> Then round them let us rally, without fear or dread,
> And next March we'll put the Grundys in their little bed.

The singer earned three cheers. But hisses greeting the speakers hinted the audience was not altogether friendly. Woodhull had heard rumors that Greeley supporters might pack the hall. Police were on hand in case hecklers got out of hand. Her sister's new regiment paraded in as well. Colonel Tennie Claflin stepped through a lane formed by her Colored Regiment and took another three cheers. She lauded the bravery of her troops and promised to be more useful than generals during the war who wallowed in luxury while their men died on the front lines. When Claflin turned the stage over to her sister, Woodhull launched into a brief speech about the trials and sorrows and insults she'd endured breaking into Wall Street, checking into hotels, and speaking her mind. She and Frederick Douglass were determined to tear down those barriers and usher in a new society. Upholding "a platform which strikes directly at the heart of the system under which we live," she gratefully accepted her nomination and pledged to win the presidency by every honorable means.

The evening ended early. The papers that bothered to report the meeting described the crowd as confused, jeering, riotous, and disorderly. The *Tribune* considered the headline-worthy news the three cheers the hecklers gave Horace Greeley twice. The *Commercial Advertiser* considered the most interesting occurrence a black cook in the audience breaking her umbrella over a pale-faced, long-haired free lover taking unwanted liberties. Somehow the papers ignored the elephant not in the room: Frederick Douglass failed to appear for his ratification.

Soon Woodhull would wish for such effusive coverage.

Following the rally, Woodhull returned to the Gilsey House. Opened a year before, the Gilsey was one of the mammoth hotels going up around Madison Square. Armies of "workmen with hammers, axes, picks, grappling-irons and chains" were bringing all "the dust, dirt, heat, noise, confusion and rattle-te-bang of city life," *Pomeroy's Democrat* complained as the weather warmed. To some, the Gilsey was a magnificent monument of cast iron and opulence, with a grand staircase winding eight dizzying stories to its crowning dome. Residents enjoyed every modern convenience, from on-site saloons, restaurants, and billiard rooms to a steam elevator carrying them up and speaking tubes for calling down. With water pipes and hoses supplying miniature fire departments on every floor and a fireproof elevator shaft, no one need worry about escaping if flames engulfed the building. After fire turned Niblo's Garden into a pile of ash shortly after *Black Friday* closed, the Gilsey's residents appreciated these precautions.

Others were less sanguine about what the Gilsey represented. Though it aspired to replace the Fifth Avenue Hotel as venue of the city's most exclusive society, the verdict was in—old bluebloods couldn't abide the new-money shoddies moving into its flats. People of that class were doomed to lifelong toil and premature old age from chasing after riches. The aristocracy was fleeing their presence.

To Woodhull, the Gilsey was a waystation. In April, her first husband, Dr. Canning Woodhull, died. As she mourned and buried him, the story broke that addiction to morphine had killed him. With another scandal hitting the press, another landlord ordered Woodhull out. She put him off. But weeks of searching for a house to double as party headquarters found no agent who would rent to her. *We don't personally object to you,* they said, *but really, with the prejudice against you we just can't do it.* A dozen hotels refused her as well before she sneaked into the Gilsey when the proprietor was away.

When the Gilsey's owner, Peter Gardner, returned, he claimed that even the shoddies' noses turned up when they passed Woodhull in the building. She must go or his family boarders would desert the place. What act had she committed that she would be insulted so, Woodhull demanded to know. She had published a paper and made speeches advocating free love, Gardner said. That answer incensed her. She could live there as the mistress of any man, fine, but heaven forbid she talk loudly in the halls or parlors about social reform, or call the legal prostitution of unhappy unions under the marriage law no different than common whoredom on the street. For that she must vacate? No, she swore, Gardner would not expel her. She had rights as a citizen. Let him prove some misdemeanor if he wanted her out.

On the verge of losing her third home in as many months, she felt like a cornered animal. The Equal Rights Party bonds intended to ease her strained finances had not sold. After a month of jeers coming in from around the country, the newspapers abandoned all mention of her and her party. Even Karl Marx repudiated Woodhull, expelling her Section 12 from his International Workingmen's Association when other members protested her advocacy of women's suffrage and free love.

Woodhull had maintained the fiction as long as she could. The ratification rally had been an act. Frederick Douglass not only failed to appear; he hadn't so much as acknowledged his nomination. A sense of fatality had already set in when she stood upon the Cooper Institute's stage. The spirits failed to inspire the mesmerizing oratory that enchanted her audience. No matter how much she pretended, her words fell flat. Her supporters drifted indifferently into the night.

Several nights later Woodhull and her husband, Colonel Blood, returned to the Gilsey after a day in the Broad Street office. A guard blocked the door. Porters had removed their possessions. Woodhull's children waited beside a pile of baggage, the bright and beautiful eleven-year-old daughter Zulu Maude and her elder brother Byron, whose innocent mind could no more comprehend being thrust from his home than a half-formed butterfly torn from the cocoon. Who could be so cruel?

The family searched through the night for shelter. Every hotel rejected them. In the early morning, they returned to Broad Street. They slept on the office floor as best they could, that night and for weeks after. The financial district was a dark, dreary place when the hordes fled in the evening rush. Its gloom crept up on them, bringing sickness to Woodhull and one of her children, and later to the others.

They pulled together the strength to turn out the next issue of *Woodhull & Claflin's Weekly*. Still, Woodhull could mock the critics who mocked her. When brainless editors asked whether she and her reformers were perpetrating a large joke, she accused them of never possessing the capacity to grasp an idea or entertain a principle. Come November they would expose their foolishness. Woodhull and Douglass would sweep the election just as the "stone at first refused by the builders afterwards became the head of the corner."

Alas, few saw the issue. For weeks subscribers had complained they didn't receive their copies of the *Weekly*. Postmen stopped delivering. News dealers accepted bribes to keep it off their stands. Everyone with whom the *Weekly* transacted business pulled away, their minds poisoned by the insidious slander spread against the two sisters. Worn out in body and mind, Woodhull and Claflin could no long minister to the publication. It closed. Their enemies had torn the voices from their throats.

Night after night, Woodhull lay in the darkness of Broad Street puzzling over her downfall. Could some crime be laid at her door? Had she debauched herself in some manner to offend the public? No! She simply insisted every person was entitled to personal freedom—that each individual possessed the right to regulate his or her life and own personal matters, that no one else had a right to do it for them.

At times she blamed her support of the Communists for turning the capitalists against her. At others she blamed her success, that while she merely talked and wrote, people tolerated her. But the moment she progressed in a practical way, every opposer rose up in arms to stifle her. At the lowest moments, she wondered if she would be hunted down by persecutors determined not to let her live.

And then they hurled brickbats at her daughter. *Zulu Maude taints the other children*, the headmistress said upon expelling the girl from her school. The school could not have all the students withdraw. How could mothers be so heartless that they would disgrace an innocent child for the sins her mother committed?

Bill collectors demanded a public stoning. They hauled Woodhull into court, forced her to confess she had no property, no claim against anyone. The *Weekly* lay in its grave. She had sold leftover copies of books at auction. Furniture in the office was borrowed. She owned not even the clothes on her back.

But it is not fever or brickbats or pauperism that tears one's heart out. It is one's friends. Many Woodhull had counted among her dearest now vomited forth the bitterest gall. The gossip spread like a germ, from Susan B. Anthony to Mary Hallowell to Anna Dickinson and others. Woodhull was resorting to intentional blackmail, they whispered. S. S. Jones and his *Religio-Philosophical Journal* spread it to the Spiritualists, though he knew it to be a lie. He knew he would have been among the first if she had taken up extorting philanderers. Lucy Stone and Mary Livermore published the rumor in their *Woman's Journal*: "The secret of the final rupture of friendship between Mrs. Hooker, Miss Anthony, Mrs. Stanton," and Woodhull was "an attempt at certain black mailing operations upon some friends of the ladies first named." Stanton and Hooker and Paulina Davis, true friends—surely they would never swallow such lies. Yet the chill that came in their letters hurt even more.

So night after night upon the Broad Street floor, Woodhull spiraled into despair, friendless, voiceless, sinking so low that she contemplated committing the blackmail of which she was accused.

Her thoughts turned to Brooklyn, to Plymouth Church and its pastor, the Reverend Henry Ward Beecher. He could save her.

14 | "TOO INDECENT TO BE HEREIN SET FORTH"

AS THE CALENDAR TURNED TO JUNE, Anthony Comstock was on a roll. In the Court of General Sessions, Recorder Hackett scheduled to try eight of his arrests for obscene literature the first week. Comstock had rounded up three of the men during his March raids. The others were cronies of Jeremiah Farrell, the publisher who'd dropped dead in mid-May while on the run. The man's death hadn't closed his shop. The clerks Comstock cornered there fingered his network of printers, binders, and lithographers. Evidence confiscated during arrests of those men included six tons of steel plates and another ton of books and printed sheets. Comstock also freed forty women from working in the binder's abominable business.

On June 6, the court postponed all the cases until June 11. Comstock and the recorder might be ready, but the district attorney was not. The eleventh came and went, then a rescheduling on the twenty-first. Comstock's patience grew increasingly strained. In the case of John Meeker, dealer of obscene literature on Nassau Street, three months had passed since his arrest. Comstock despaired whether Meeker's or the other cases would ever come to trial.

The situation at home stressed Comstock as well. The women living under his roof, his wife, Maggie, and her sister, Jennie, were invalids. In his diary he expressed delight with domesticity, with the joys of family visits and birthday dinners. But he craved more. Maggie was fragile and withdrawn. As early as their honeymoon, she could not share his enthusiasm for touring the sights of Philadelphia and Washington. Nor could she share his earnest approach to life, his desire to accomplish, which he admired a neighboring couple fulfilling together. Within months of their wedding, Maggie had so provoked him, worrying over what others said, that he fled the house to avoid chastising her. Though he always expressed affection for "little wifey," over time the quarrels would grow to the point that a neighbor wondered how Maggie suffered through it.

Still, every night he came home to the joy of his life, his daughter, Lillie. Despite her weakened state, Maggie had delivered a wonderful baby weighing nine pounds.

The child's sweet face sent her father's troubles fleeing. Four days into June, the family celebrated the six-month anniversary of her young life.

Then Lillie grew ill. A nurse took over her care. Unable or unwilling to abandon the fight he had taken on, Comstock left his daughter in the nurse's hands on the last Friday of June. His cases were once again on the docket of the Court of General Sessions. After so many disappointments, he found Assistant District Attorney John Fellows ready to deliver his opening statement in the trial of John Meeker.

Young ladies' seminaries are flooded with books and pictures of the most indecent kind, Fellows told the jury. *Men such as the prisoner at the bar surreptitiously introduce them hidden in bouquets of flowers and parcels of candy.*

As the primary prosecution witness, Comstock spent the day on the stand. A clerk named Pickford had tipped him off about the merchandise he sold working in Meeker's shop. Pickford was determined to "get square" with his former employer, who had treated him meanly, then fired him. Hearing the story, Comstock rounded up two police officers. They seized glass negatives and fancy photographs, all obscene, Comstock testified. The DA entered the confiscated pieces as evidence. The gentlemen of the jury "scrutinized the filthy things with great particularity," the *Herald* reported. When the prosecution closed its case, Recorder Hackett adjourned until Monday.

Comstock headed home. The sweet face of Lillie was not to greet him this day. His daughter lay dead. His wife wept with a broken heart. Whatever tears he shed, whatever pain he suffered, he knew where to turn. "The Lord's will be done," he confided to his diary. "Oh for the grace to say it and live it!" He pulled himself together to secure a plot in Evergreens Cemetery near his home in Brooklyn, a plot with room enough for him and his wife to someday lay beside their child. A tombstone carved with a lily marked the grave of his "own precious Lillie, now gone Home, now evermore pure, waiting for her parents."

Monday morning, duty called. Comstock returned to court. Perhaps today he could take small comfort in the conviction of one of the wretched scoundrels who poisoned the minds of children such as the daughter he just buried.

The scoundrel Meeker took the stand. Yes, he had purchased twenty-five hundred negatives from a man who was going out of business, he admitted, four years ago now. He made five hundred prints. But then the business disgusted him, and he never sold a one. He locked the negatives in an Ann Street walkup until Comstock seized them.

Furthermore, nothing about them was obscene. Look at the prints he was entering into evidence. They were works by Hogarth, the English artist from a century ago, with names like "Eve" and "Greek Slave" and "White Captive," and others of a classical nature. The fun they poked at polite society and its morals might offend some, but they were not considered obscene. The stuff Comstock seized was no worse.

District Attorney Fellows argued the reference to Hogarth was no testament to respectability. *You've heard of Byron, no doubt,* he told the defendant. *But there are passages in his "Don Juan" you wouldn't send your wife and daughter.*

Yes, Meeker acknowledged, and there were passages in the Bible he would never read to them. But in fact, he had a wife and a little boy, and he had no compunction displaying his pictures to them.

As for Pickford claiming he had charge of the "obscene department" under the direction of Meeker, the defense introduced several witnesses. Yes, Pickford had sold them obscene pictures, they testified, but he insisted he was selling on his own account. Meeker was to know nothing about it, the clerk admonished with each sale.

The defense was as convincing as it needed to be. After the jury deliberated an hour, the foreman reported ten supported conviction. But with two holdouts, the panel could not reach a verdict. This trial had taken two days, Recorder Hackett objected, too long to release the jurors. He instructed them to try again. Still at an impasse hours later, he locked the jury up for the night. Ten against two, the foreman repeated the next morning. The recorder saw no choice but to discharge the jury and the defendant. As Meeker walked free and Comstock fumed, Hackett lamented how rapidly crime was rising in the city.

The *Times* found some comfort in the trial's outcome. Meeker had been feeding the appetites of foul-minded men for years. He ought to be held to account. Still, ten out of twelve for conviction was a respectable showing. If it represented the sentiment of the community, the editors trusted other panderers of the rubbish would be dealt justice. And since only a fraction of the public knew their whereabouts and what filth they sold, their danger was limited. The worse culprit was Frank Leslie. The publisher thrust his nasty *Day's Doings* under the noses of the whole community. The newsstands reeked of his rag, so conspicuously displayed no passerby could fail to notice. Meanwhile Leslie shoveled money into his pockets from advertising wicked and disgusting wares in its pages. The authorities should indict him at once, the *Times* advised.

The editorializing did not console Comstock. The hung jury in Meeker's trial was the best outcome in his pending cases. Police blackmailed dealers or pocketed bribes or tipped off offenders when warrants were issued, stifling arrests. Cases ready for trial were fixed in the district attorney's office, or pigeonholed, never to see the inside of a courtroom. The list of culprits who would never see justice, recorded in Comstock's ledger book, approached a dozen. He had secured convictions in less than half his arrests since he began his run on Nassau Street.

Why bother? his friends asked. *You are foolish and vain to think you can accomplish anything when the authorities do nothing.* The friends saw how the effort jeopardized his dry goods sales, how it would bring ruin to his family. Maggie's father said as much in a letter to his son-in-law's employer, Cochrane, McLean & Company, begging the firm to force Comstock to desist. When his superior approached him, Comstock said well and good if the firm no longer required his services, but he wasn't stopping. He kept his job, but his sales spiraled downward.

His friends warned of danger. He had made a name for himself in the press, had bragged publicly with each arrest. Over the summer, papers from the *Times* to the *Christian Weekly* praised him for the men he had driven to the grave, Haynes and Farrell and the expressman Snowden, and others. Their associates were threatening his life.

"What Folly!" Comstock cried. Could not God turn away death from whosoever he willed? Could not He halt the man whose arm was raised with a deadly weapon and ready to strike? All the evil men in New York could not harm a hair on his head were it not the will of God. "Oh, to live, to feel, to be—Thy will be done!"

No, Comstock would take no solace from a hung jury, were it only a single member dissenting. He would not shy from the futility of fighting a rigged system, from the risks to his family, the danger to his life. He would find a better way and redouble his efforts.

Smarting from his failures, Comstock perused the *Day's Doings*. An advertisement from H. Cameron & Company caught his eye. "Beautiful and rare photographs," it offered, available on Bleecker Street. The American Publishing Agency advertised "racy books that speak right out at less than half price." A Professor Rogers supplied rare photographs and illustrated books, plus rubber goods for ladies and gents, on Broadway. The name Edward Grandin jumped out, the culprit who had warned William Haynes that Comstock was after him. Comstock already had visited his Liberty Street office, a twenty-minute walk from where he worked at Cochrane, McLean. The other places were even closer. He could collect evidence, secure warrants, and round up all four dealers before the day was over. But what was the point if police refused to arrest, the district attorney's office refused to prosecute, and juries refused to convict?

H. Cameron & Company offered to send a catalog with a sample of its wares for twenty cents. Grandin promised his complete and comprehensive catalog for free, while the American Publishing Agency wanted only a five-cent stamp to cover its postage. Rogers encouraged orders by mail. Up to now, Comstock had surreptitiously purchased his evidence over the counter, then relished subsequent raids with warrants in hand. But he had learned that a huge portion of the business went through the mail. He also had learned something about the law. While local authorities and courts might hold sway over obscenity sales within their jurisdictions, shipment through the US mail was a federal crime, originally outlawed in 1865 and recodified this year. With postmasters forbidden to open first-class mail, barely half a dozen prosecutions had resulted in seven years. Comstock saw an opportunity.

Dealers made no secret of using the mail. "Recollect, none of the above can be had at our office in New York," warned one dealer who considered the post safer than a storefront. Another promised to pack items "in such a manner as to defy detection." Though first class did not permit packages, others assured they could squeeze rubber goods and sex toys into thin envelopes. A folding stereoscope with twenty-four pictures packaged first class sold for fifteen dollars. A "French tickler; or, ladies' delight, . . . giving the most exquisite pleasure to both sexes," fit both around the penis and into an envelope, its advertisement read.

This subterfuge within the mail, "the great thoroughfare of communication leading up into all our homes, schools and colleges," enraged Comstock. But then he realized, what better way to entrap the scoundrels than to do just as they invited him to do? He drafted a letter to H. Cameron & Company. He enjoyed fancy goods, he wrote; could the company send him its catalog and some rare photographs? He enclosed payment. He signed the letter John Beardsley, with a return address in Ohio. He signed a second letter George Nicoll, P.O. Box 50, Norwalk, Connecticut, and wrote others to the American Publishing Agency, Professor Rogers, and Edward Grandin. Dropping them at the post office, he arranged for an official to intercept the replies before they headed to Ohio and Connecticut.

The dealers were responsive businessmen. With a week left in July, "Beardsley" had received obscene publications from each. In August, two sent obscene pictures to "George Nicoll." Comstock hauled his evidence into US circuit court. Commissioner John Osborn, an official who handled pretrial matters like warrants, arraignments, and bail, issued warrants authorizing federal marshals to arrest the perpetrators. Two marshals headed out with Comstock.

On Bleecker Street, they watched an elderly man pick up the day's mail. As the address appeared to be only a mail drop, they followed him to his place of business, then pounced. The man's name was Henry Camp, they discovered upon serving the warrant. H. Cameron & Company was his front. He had fifty first-class letters containing obscene books ready to post.

Professor Rogers used a similar setup. Comstock and a marshal watched him sneak into the building at his Broadway address, climb to a top floor vacant but for a tin letter box, and snatch his mail. Rogers proved an alias for David Massey. They collared Charles Mackey, proprietor of the American Publishing Agency, the same day. The raid on Grandin's "Sporting Man's Emporium" netted the owner and twenty-five hundred books.

The men went before Commissioner Osborn for arraignment. Comstock's new friend Noah Davis, US Attorney for the Southern District of New York, pressed the case with none of the hesitation of the New York district attorney. Osborn set bail at $10,000 each. He committed the men to Ludlow Street jail until they posted it. The *Times* praised Comstock for rounding up this whole "tribe" and the "inflexible resolution" of Osborn and Davis to destroy the infamous business, root and branch.

The season would turn to autumn before the men came to trial. The indictments read that the obscene literature mailed was "too indecent to be herein set forth." Judge Charles Benedict agreed. Though Grandin had mailed only a catalog and a business card, a book's title alone could be obscene, in the judge's opinion. Massey's photos reportedly displayed women on stage in *The Black Crook*, the show that had run for hundreds of performances at Niblo's Garden. Their legs outlined in tights beneath short skirts were too risqué for the judge as well. To the defense's claims that prosecutors presented no evidence indicating any defendant himself had deposited the material at the post office, or that Comstock's letters had entrapped the men into committing the crimes, or that Comstock himself had supplied the obscene items from the tons of material he had collected, Benedict turned a deaf ear. Juries convicted Grandin, Massey, and Mackey. Henry Camp confessed. Benedict sentenced each to one year's imprisonment at hard labor and a $500 fine. The penalty was the maximum allowed under the law but entirely insufficient for the offense, the judge noted.

Comstock could exult. He had found a path for circumventing the local corruption. Yes, the federal penalties were too soft. But he would rise to that challenge.

15 | "SOCIETY . . . WILL HAVE ITS GHASTLY MEAL OF CURIOSITY"

FOR A DECADE, a neoclassical palace of marble and granite had been rising behind city hall. The new New York County Courthouse fronted on Chambers Street. A massive stairway led to a portico supported by Corinthian columns. Scaffolding encased the entire building. Work had ground to a halt.

The *Times* reported the costs so far totaled $12 million, against an original budget of $250,000. One lucky carpenter had earned $28,000 for woodworking in a single courtroom. A prince of a plasterer charged over $1 million for two months' work putting up walls and ceilings. Expenses for carpeting suggested the material would cover City Hall Park three times over. Those items were just the tip of the graft that had stuffed the pockets of Boss Tweed and his Tammany Hall Ring.

Despite the work stoppage and financial scandal, the courthouse had opened for business. Among the first occupants was the family of Edward Haggerty, the voucher thief whose cell Ned Stokes had admired when he entered the Tombs. Those vouchers related to construction expenses Tammany Hall needed to hide. As a favor for making them disappear, Tammany moved Haggerty's family into an elegant suite set aside for the janitor. Released from the Tombs, Haggerty took that job.

Haggerty's janitorial efforts did not earn good marks. "Filthy as a Digger Indian's cave," *Pomeroy's Democrat* described the building. Cigar stumps, cuds of tobacco, and a half-inch coating of dirt and tobacco juice littered the marble floors. The stairway balustrades were greasy to the touch, the steps laden with quarts of decaying and disease-breeding slime, a birthplace of contagion. The water closets assailed anyone opening their doors with a gust of noxious fumes, turning the stoutest stomachs.

Nevertheless, hordes climbed the courthouse steps one morning the last week of June. Before opening hour, people packed the hallways leading to the Court of Oyer and Terminer, responsible for trying crimes punishable by life imprisonment or death. Soon they were pushing and shoving as though their very existence depended on gaining entrance to the courtroom. The commotion attracted passersby ignorant of the cause.

They, too, joined the fray upon learning testimony was to begin in the trial of Edward S. Stokes for the murder of James Fisk.

"Society . . . will have its ghastly meal of curiosity," observed the *Herald*. The crowd would grow tenfold the next day. The usual scum attending murder trials joined the scrum, those prone "to squat in grog shops from early morn" and the "better-to-do Tony Crackit who ogles you and your watch chain." For this case they scuffled with so-called respectable spectators who proved their match in fighting into a gallery so crushing that locomotion from one side to the other was impossible. Ladies, too, clawed through, those of the "lean and lanky class" with nothing "at home to busy their minds, no babies to care for or husbands to please." Women "of all grades of homeliness" stared upon the prisoner, exclaiming, "Isn't he good looking?"

On this first day of testimony, a crossbar blocked the corridor. Police dispersed those remaining once the benches filled. At the last moment, two ladies, faces veiled, squeezed by. They passed through the rail separating the unruly masses from the participants in the trial and the friends and family of the defendant and of his victim. Hoots and hisses followed them as people realized the infamous woman who inspired the shooting dared to arrive simultaneously with the widow, Josie Mansfield and Lucy Fisk side by side. A closer look dispelled that atrocious idea. Lucy Fisk hid behind one veil; the second covered the face of Jim Fisk's sister.

District Attorney Samuel B. Garvin led the prosecution. Private counsel hired by the Fisk family assisted him: William Beach, who had so viciously cross-examined Mansfield and Stokes on the day of the shooting, and William Fullerton. The defense team sat opposite: John McKeon, who had served as Mansfield's attorney on that fateful day and repeatedly objected to Beach's insinuations about his client, along with Lyman Tremain, A. J. Daily, and John D. Townsend. Judge Daniel Ingraham presided on the bench. The press occupied its own table. An overflow of reporters leaned against a wall.

The sheriff led the defendant in. Deputies followed, one ready to pounce like a grizzly bear should his prisoner break for freedom. Stokes had waited too long to want anything but a judgment by his peers. For the past week the attorneys had interviewed hundreds of potential jurors, the defense refusing one after another who had formed an opinion that might influence his decision, the prosecution rejecting any opposed to capital punishment. Day after day, Stokes stood and faced the one or two chosen, until at last twelve men were found "whose minds were as nearly as possible utter blanks" when it came to the killing of Jim Fisk.

"Oyez! Oyez!" called the court crier. From the moment his voice opened the session, the solemnity of the occasion struck everyone. Every word the witnesses uttered, every question the counsel raised, every ruling the judge delivered would drive the defendant toward his moment of deliverance or his hour of death.

Stokes wore an air of nonchalance, any nervousness controlled but for biting his fingernails and running a hand through his hair. He stared vacantly at the woman sitting hardly ten feet away until she turned to speak to the prosecution attorneys and he realized the murdered man's widow was behind the veil. His gaze never again wandered in that direction.

For the next five days, Stokes listened to how he'd killed Jim Fisk. Hotel managers, hallboys, and guests laid out his steps from the moment he burst through the ladies' entrance to his near escape out the Mercer Street door. They described him lying in wait, spotting Fisk, mumbling "I've got you now," raising his pistol, and firing the shots. Doctors described rushing to Fisk's aid, ripping off his clothes, probing the wound, and administering to their patient as he declined and rallied through the night, finally drawing his last breath. The district attorney led each witness through mind-numbing detail. In cross-examination, the defense team impeached each witness at the same level, or tried to.

At every turn, the opposing attorneys went for each other's throats. Defense counsel McKeon berated the private prosecutors Beach and Fullerton for taking "blood money" from the Fisk family, bringing shame on the legal profession. The district attorney shot back that McKeon and his team had stained their hands and filled their pockets on many prior occasions. As these howls arose again and again, Judge Ingraham gaveled them down and harangued the opposing sides for their vicious personal attacks.

Not only tempers flared. The trial started in a hot and sultry courtroom. The mercury climbed every day, reaching ninety-five degrees and turning the place into a sweatbox. No breeze came through the windows, only "the rumble of ambulance trains carting to the hospitals the dead and dying men and women whose life-blood has been paralyzed by the lightning-like bolts of the burning sun," as the *Herald* described the ghastly heat.

Through it all, Stokes appeared in good spirits. He arrived nattily dressed, one day in black-striped linen trousers, the next in white ducks, his white or dotted shirts fastened with a black bow or a spotted necktie, a diamond on his chest. During the ceaseless babble of the lawyers, he showed no sign of losing his nerve or his heart. Members of his family greeted him in an anteroom each morning. When called inside, friends warmly shook his hand. His eyes brightened and a smile came to his lips. He listened attentively, occasionally whispering advice to his counsel.

Judge Ingraham leaned toward the breezeless window. The district attorney languidly fanned his face. Jurors slumped as if in despair over the bodily flesh they would lose during a fortnight serving the court. Court officials napped on the rails, the gallery against one another. Stokes took little notice of the heat but for momentarily wiping his handkerchief across his forehead as the sessions began.

After five days of testimony, the prosecution wrapped up. On only one point did the two sides agree: Ned Stokes had pulled the trigger of the gun that sent a bullet flying into Jim Fisk's guts.

———————————

The defense waited two days to put Stokes on the stand. By then everyone knew the strategy was to throw a half-dozen escape hatches against the wall and see which stuck. That some were contradictory didn't matter so long as the jury bought one.

Stokes was not to be the only star attraction this day. As the opening hour approached, Josie Mansfield strode into the courtroom. The modern Cleopatra, the magnificent Medusa, the Aspasia of the trial—the *Herald* found no end of classical references to describe the woman around whom Fisk and Stokes fluttered like birds fixed by the eyes of that fabled serpent, the basilisk. Mansfield had not shown herself in public since the shooting. Today she displayed all the magnificence that gold, silk, diamonds, and lace could bestow. She turned her dark, liquid eyes on the lover she had not seen since that January day they had also been in court together. She mouthed, "What a change has taken place." Stokes bowed. His mother regarded her son's paramour "with a look that only a mother could fathom."

When the crier called "Edward S. Stokes," the defendant walked to the bench, placed his hand upon the Bible, and took the oath. For three and a half hours he told his story, interrupted by tirades over legal matters between the opposing counsel and recess for lunch. When the year opened, he was on bad terms with Jim Fisk, he admitted, due to the latter's theft of the Brooklyn Refinery and the threats Fisk and his armed ruffians had made against him. On January 6, he had testified in Mansfield's libel suit against Fisk, then taken oysters at Delmonico's with the attorneys prosecuting that case. Upon leaving the restaurant, he stopped at a legal office to hear news regarding an indictment Fisk was seeking against him. The attorney told him the indictment had been dismissed so Stokes could go to Providence for a hearing on whether he had welched on a horse-racing bet. He flagged a coupé, stopped at the Hoffman House for papers related to the hearing, and drove to Mansfield's house. As the house was shut up, he decided she was too sick for callers. He ordered the hack onward to Broadway. There he darted in and out of a saloon before running into a friend. He asked that gentleman to walk with him down Broadway to the Metropolitan Hotel, where he intended to buy tickets to *The Black Crook*, again playing at Niblo's. As they passed the Grand Central Hotel, Stokes looked in a window and spotted a woman he had met at Saratoga. He dashed in and up the stairs, only to find he had mistook the lady.

Heading back down, Stokes saw Fisk alone on the landing. Fisk spotted him and drew a silver-plated pistol. Stokes cried, "Don't fire!" But Fisk raised and cocked the gun. "He wanted to kill me," Stokes testified. So he jumped aside, drew the pistol he carried in his coat, and fired. Fisk was still holding his pistol, so Stokes fired again.

To that point, Stokes had no idea that the man he shot was Jim Fisk. He dropped his pistol. He climbed back to the hallway, and when he found a hotel employee, said, "A man is shot below stairs. Get a doctor." He knew not what happened after that other than he found himself among several people and an officer. He recollected no one asking him about the shooting, nor did he recollect denying he did it. He remembered only that the officer took him to where Fisk sat on a sofa. Fisk looked up and said, "That is Stokes." Only that—Fisk said nothing about Stokes shooting him. And had Fisk done so, Stokes testified, he would have asked Fisk to admit to drawing his own gun first. Even when Stokes was booked at the police station, he had no inkling Fisk might accuse him of a crime.

At its simplest, Stokes's story amounted to this: he had shot some unknown man in self-defense. But the defense was planting seeds far deeper than a self-defense claim. His actions on the day of the shooting proved his arrival at the Grand Central Hotel was coincidental. He could not have anticipated finding Fisk, so any murder could not have been premeditated. Even had he premeditated the shooting, his harassment by Fisk and his ruffians, plus his worries over the horse-betting hearing, had driven him insane, at least temporarily. Medical testimony the next day added that even if Stokes had intentionally shot Fisk, the bullet had not killed him. The doctors were responsible, with their excessive probing of the wound. And if the probing hadn't killed him, the lethal quantities of drugs they administered, morphine and chloroform, had.

For several days, the defense introduced witnesses to build on these themes. Mansfield took the stand after Stokes. Fisk "said unless I returned to him, he would kill Mr. Stokes," she testified. When she refused, Fisk repeated the threat: "I shall shoot Stokes. There'll be bloodshed in this thing." Then he pulled out a silver pistol. The next time she saw Stokes, she told him to be careful. With Stokes in such fear of Fisk, the defense contended, was it any wonder the man shot in self-defense when Fisk aimed a pistol? Or that Stokes was driven out of his mind by fear? The arguments were rather curious after Stokes's claim he hadn't recognized the man he shot. But if the jury didn't buy that Stokes hadn't recognized the man, it might buy that he was defending himself against a known enemy, and if it rejected self-defense, it might buy that insanity drove the shooting.

In subsequent days, witnesses argued over whether Fisk carried a gun. None had been found on his person or in the hotel. Perhaps it was secreted away, the defense suggested. As for insanity, it ran in Stokes's family, his father testified. The old man's brother died mad, and his wife's nephew spent six months in the Bloomingdale Asylum. His son Ned, too, exhibited abnormal mental excitement during his quarrels with Fisk. He got pains in his head, so great he would hold it with his hands. He flew off the handle at little things, hurled insults like he was maddened. His eye, his countenance, grew so threatening the old man could hardly describe it. And Stokes understood his troubles—he feared going crazy. Opposing doctors argued over whether Fisk had died from the bullet or from incompetent treatment and drug poisoning, slashing so viciously one would have thought the medical profession were on trial.

On the trial's eighteenth day, defense attorney Tremain summed. The charge was murder in the first degree. If Stokes had not gone to the hotel with a premeditated design to kill Fisk, the jury could not convict. If Stokes had any justifiable cause for firing his pistol, such as fear of imminent harm from a pistol in Fisk's hand, they could not convict. If when he fired the pistol Stokes was insane, they could not convict. If Fisk died from anything but the gunshot wound, such as probing of the wound or drugs administered, they could not convict. If the jury held reasonable doubt on a single of these points, they must acquit Stokes of murder.

Well into the next day, Tremain sowed doubt on each point. He issued a final plea independent of them entirely. A man had a right to testify or remain silent in his own defense. A guilty man would remain silent. The ordeal of examination for his crime would be too terrible; the jury would detect the truth in his manner. The innocent, however, enjoyed telling his story, as Stokes had told his. His testimony itself demonstrated Stokes was an innocent man.

With the final word, the district attorney did not dispute Tremain's interpretation of the law. But he dispelled any doubt on each of those reasons for not convicting. The whole of the evidence showed that Stokes's sole purpose on that fateful afternoon was to go to the Grand Central Hotel and assassinate Jim Fisk. Stokes had washed his hands in the blood of his fellow man, he told the jury. They must do their duty manfully and let the consequences take their course.

As the judge delivered final instructions and the jury exited, a pallor came over Stokes's face. Anxiety asserted itself, reported the *Herald*. The transformation represented "nature speaking in defiance of will at the sight of the fingers of fate raising the curtain of doom." Then came the waiting, when the imagination played with the anguish of doubt, when "the imprisoned mind bursts its bars and riots in a fancied freedom, to find the iron of the dungeon on the limbs and a perspective bounded by a gallows and a patch of sky," thoughts no man could vanquish.

During hours of waiting, family and friends stood by Stokes. The morbid masses enjoying the spectacle didn't move. When the sun set, the jury had not agreed. Judge Ingraham locked them up for the night. The courtroom emptied. The sheriff led his prisoner back to the Tombs, Stokes wondering if he would ever see freedom again.

———————

The next day was Sunday. On the Sabbath, Chambers Street emptied of its usual rush of vehicles—drays, beer wagons, lumbering stages, fancy coupés, so many that the way was usually impassable from Centre to Church Streets. On this particular Sunday, however, an immense crowd gathered, eager to know if the jury in the Stokes case had reached a verdict. By eight o'clock, thousands swarmed the block and the courthouse steps. Others perched on every vantage point of the scaffold shrouding the building. Like the jurors so far, the crowd could not agree on anything, or even a man with himself. One who yesterday swore the trial was a farce if Stokes did not hang today might harangue Fisk as the murderous villain. So intense were feelings on each side that the Civil War seemed to have returned, a time when men went mad over every rumored defeat or victory. Police settled angry disputes with a beating, then sowed peace by sending the antagonists for a cooling draft of Weiss beer. But alas, at this hour of the Sabbath, no drinking place was serving.

Judge Ingraham arrived before eleven o'clock. Five hundred of the clamoring masses had squeezed inside. In an anteroom, Stokes paced, chalking up fifteen miles over the past two days, in the *Herald* man's estimation. Any observer could see he was not afraid to die. Some perhaps disagreed with that reporter's assessment.

As the jurors filed in, the rustle of a lady's silk broke a deathlike silence. Judge Ingraham scanned the faces of the twelve men. "I understand, gentlemen, that you have not agreed upon a verdict."

"No judge—Your Honor," said the foreman. "There is no chance of us agreeing."

Ingraham was not pleased. Further consultation was required, he insisted, and when the foreman protested, Ingraham cut him off. "I do not care where you stand, and I don't want to know until you agree."

At 2:00 PM, the sheriff's deputies escorted Stokes back to the Tombs. Another long night was in store. Still, Stokes seemed relieved at the foreman's protestations. Perhaps he had heard the consensus that any agreement was improbable, that at the very least he would obtain bail awaiting a new trial. And how many hung juries led to second trials anyway? Could he get off scot-free with no verdict at all?

The next morning brought him half the answer. No agreement whatever, the foreman told Judge Ingraham. The count was seven for a murder conviction, two for a slap-on-the-wrist manslaughter in the third degree, and three for outright acquittal. Ingraham gave in and declared a mistrial. As his attorneys celebrated, Stokes showed little emotion—relief, maybe, but tinged with disappointment. He thanked the jurors who judged him innocent and the friends who stood steadfast beside him. As the sheriff accompanied him to the carriage to return to the Tombs, he heard no outrage or anger. Everyone seemed gladdened that he had received a respite from the noose. He was a man to be pitied, not condemned.

By the afternoon, a second trial sounded unlikely. How could another jury be procured in the city, twelve men willing to face the ordeal of a three-week trial, who could honestly judge the accused after the torrent of coverage in the press? The district attorney had acknowledged as much, or so the papers said.

That night Stokes enjoyed his first good night's sleep in a long while.

———————

During his childhood in England, murder had fascinated William Howe. Reading of the murderer James Greenacre thrilled him, of how the man cut up the body of his fiancée, wrapped her head in a handkerchief to carry aboard a streetcar, then nearly fainted when the conductor called, "Sixpence a head." And of the coachman Daniel Good, who buried his limbless and headless victim beneath the hay in the stable where he worked, and of other atrocities tried at London's Old Bailey. The stories bent him toward the criminal law, Howe wrote later. He possessed no conscious affinity for the business, simply a fresh and buoyant mind that tended in that direction.

In 1872 he was having a good year. By summer, he had represented over a dozen charged with killing or trying to. Through the full year, he would defend twenty-three of the twenty-five accused murderers who awaited trial in the Tombs. But not Ned Stokes.

Why he skipped that sensational trial was anybody's guess. The least likely reason seemed that Stokes refused him. Certainly, Howe wouldn't have shied away because Stokes had indisputably pulled the trigger. Eight of his clients this year had wielded the instrument of death, from a pistol to a blade to a stone. The jury acquitted the first without leaving its box, the twelve men agreeing the circumstances justified the killing. Similar defenses got a second client off, a third convicted only of a misdemeanor, and a sixteen-year-old found guilty of a still lesser crime when both the DA and Judge Bedford agreed the youth had been tortured in the House of Refuge.

Another two killers won acquittal on grounds of insanity. After they served brief periods in the state lunatic asylum, Howe delivered affidavits to the court in which each declared he was insane neither now nor when he had committed his crime. That amazing gall had so far won them writs of habeas corpus—court orders that they be brought before a judge to determine whether holding them was warranted. Whether they would walk entirely was still pending. In only one case had a jury convicted a Howe client of first-degree murder. While that man was scheduled to hang in August, the date would come and go. Before another year passed, Howe would convince two New York Supreme Court judges to recommend the governor grant him clemency.

When the Stokes jury hung, Howe couldn't argue much with the result. But he likely looked upon the defense as yeoman's work. He could approve of the many reasons the attorneys gave the jury to acquit, from self-defense to insanity to assertions that doctors—not the bullet—killed the victim. Howe used them all himself. He could applaud the rebuttal of prosecution witnesses, particularly of the closest the prosecution came to an eyewitness, the hallboy whom Stokes's attorneys impeached by convincing the jury that $1,000 bought his testimony. But the beginning, seven days of jury selection and 750 men considered? That was ridiculous. Howe accepted almost any man so long as the twelve varied. A Catholic and a Protestant, a poor soul and a wealthy one, an ethnic minority or two—that mix comprised fertile enough soil for dissension to grow. And the summation was little more than a review of the many technical reasons the jury might acquit. Where was the emotion? Howe could have had the jury crying over Mansfield's broken heart as she watched the love of her life standing upon the scaffold with a noose around his neck. Or had the jurors quaking in the same fear that had overwhelmed Stokes as Fisk pointed a gun at his heart.

All that was academic to Howe, though. He understood what truly had turned the tide of the trial even if the judge and the attorneys, the press and the public, were in the dark. A strong eyewitness, one better than the hallboy bribed in the House of Detention, would have led to conviction. But Howe and Hummel had gotten to the hotel guest first, the doctor who had watched the shooting unfold. They had filled his baggage with loot and put him aboard a ship bound for they knew not where. They asked only his promise he would never again set foot on American soil.

Howe would be long dead—and so would Stokes—when decades later Hummel spotted the man in a rickshaw in Yokohama. His red, bulbous nose was unmistakable, rivaling even J. P. Morgan's enormous proboscis. "My God, that was a ghost that I never expected to see," Hummel said, grabbing the arm of an American expatriate showing him around the city. "So this is where he landed!"

16 | "RELIEF FROM TROUBLE"

AS SUMMER CLOSED, Anthony Comstock's success in US circuit court led him in a new direction. While he was investigating David Massey, one of the smut dealers he would soon convict of a federal crime, he got wind of his associate Dr. Charles Selden. Thinking he could find further evidence against Massey and perhaps corral another dealer, Comstock introduced himself to the captain at the Wooster Street precinct.

He had been surveilling Dr. Selden for several months, the captain told his visitor. He suspected the doctor of malpractice. Selden's advertisements as a "Ladies' Physician" ran in the *Herald*'s medical classifieds.

Comstock hoped only to find more of Massey's obscene literature at Selden's house. The lust such wicked books inspired was the most insidious force in the community, a frightful monster defiling the home, wrecking the family, and degrading society. But what the captain had uncovered was an immeasurably greater evil. It did more than inspire lust, Comstock thought. It enabled its fulfillment.

God had built certain safeguards into humankind, but they couldn't prevent smut from inflaming passions, not even of the gentler sex. Comstock had seen how wives worked hand in hand with the likes of Haynes and Simpson, how schoolgirls borrowed filth from Mrs. Simpson's "library." Fortunately, the safeguards created fear, which could stop a woman on the brink, preserve her chastity. Bearing a child would destroy her reputation. Society would banish her. But "ante-natal murderers and murderesses," as Comstock labeled abortionists, promised "security," "relief from trouble." They allowed women to step over God's barriers without risk of shame.

Comstock did not let his outrage sway him from the task at hand. He and the Wooster Street captain marched into the Jefferson Market police court and presented their case that Selden held obscene literature for the smut dealer Massey now awaiting trial. A judge signed a search warrant.

Selden wasn't home when the captain and Comstock rang his bell. After the detective they left behind observed two men entering the house, they rang again. The housekeeper again denied the doctor was in. They pushed past. The detective rushed to bar the back door. Hearing the commotion, Selden bolted for the front and landed in the arms of the captain. His patient Barbara Voss, age seventeen, lay almost nude in the front parlor. Shivering in fright, she admitted this visit was her third to the doctor in two weeks. On the first, Dr. Selden had hooked a galvanic battery to her stomach and back and turned on the juice. Evidently, he was less than confident the electricity would induce Voss's desired miscarriage. He had also thrust a long stick into her insides, hoping the screw at the tip would effectuate the deed.

It didn't. A week later Voss had come for another treatment, this time with a curved piece of steel as Selden's instrument. Another failure, Voss concluded, so she had returned today. The electrical apparatus seized lent credence to her story.

The police arrested Selden and his housekeeper, along with a male family friend who was helping Voss. In no way was he responsible for Voss's condition, the friend insisted. That denial didn't prevent him from landing in a cell at the Wooster Street station house. Voss went to the House of Detention as a witness. Two weeks later and two months into her pregnancy, she miscarried the child she didn't want.

While a federal court was hearing the Massey case that had instigated Selden's arrest, abortion was a state crime, with the New York district attorney responsible for prosecution. After a grand jury indicted Selden, the DA's office fixed the case, Comstock recorded. The culprits went free.

Comstock vowed revenge. He would go after Selden again, and then again, and after dozens more of his ilk. And he would make sure a federal statute landed them in a US court and then in the penitentiary.

17 | "WORTH A HOT NIGHT IN THE THEATER"

BY THE CLOSE OF THE STOKES TRIAL, legal sensation had exhausted the public's interest. Yet one more act was opening upstate. The New York Assembly had impeached New York Supreme Court Judges Albert Cardozo and George Barnard in May. Cardozo immediately resigned. Barnard refused. The trial to remove him from office began two days after the Stokes jury hung. Attorney Beach and Judge Ingraham had immediately decamped for Saratoga, the first to join Barnard's defense team, the second to testify. Josie Mansfield followed as another witness. Many of Barnard's transgressions had occurred in her parlor. William Howe waited until the beginning of August as he needed to get his formerly insane clients out of the state asylum first. Even then, no one quite understood why he headed upstate. Though his name figured prominently in the testimony, he was dodging the court's subpoena to appear.

During the first week of August, the *Times* ran the Barnard drama front and center on page 1. By the tenth, the editors understood the public was fed up with trials. They buried the case on page 4 beneath Amusements. By the end, the conclusion was so foregone the editors pushed Barnard's removal to page 5.

For those seeking alternative entertainment, the midsummer theatrical season was getting underway. Lydia Thompson and her British Blondes were reviving *Blue Beard; or, the Mormon, the Maid, and the Little Militaire*. As a packed house hooted for Thompson, the orchestra struck its notes. The curtain drew on the Turkish village of Bishmillah, aglow in the setting sun. Thompson waltzed in, costumed as the sultan's dragoon Selim, or at least her upper half was so costumed, complete with riding crop and fez. Her jacket ended where her legs, encased in sheer tights, began. She pranced around searching for Selim's lost love Fatima. Blue Beard would soon have the maiden in his clutches. Could Selim overcome this archvillain and save his beloved from seduction and murder?

This plot was a backdrop for the point of Thompson's burlesque: song, dance, buffoonery, and sparsely covered flesh. Nimble of foot, sweet in voice, and statuesque in form, Thompson excelled in all these particulars. Camille Dubois played the much-coveted Fatima, Henry Beckett the polygamous murderer with the azure beard who had

138

already disposed of six wives. Through twenty-five songs and dances praised as "skillful and grotesque," the audience demanded encores. "Worth a hot night in the theatre," the *Commercial Advertiser* concluded, no matter that the performance seemed never to end.

For those seeking a more sordid story, *One Wife* opened at the Olympic Theatre. *One Wife Too Many* was the more appropriate title employed when an enterprising publisher advertised the script. The plot? The maid that newlywed Mrs. Van Dyke tasks with tracking her millionaire husband reports his assignation with her bosom friend Mrs. Hoffman. Upon his return home, the unfaithful gentleman learns of his wife's discovery from the valet. As the secret spreads, he pays half his fortune to his mistress's husband, reconciles two or three times with his forgiving wife, and engages in further amorous liaisons. Finally, Mr. Hoffman kills him. "Adultery served up in a style more naked and shameless than our most intrepid purveyor of dramatic uncleanness have [sic] hitherto attempted," reviewed the *Times*. People flocked to the theater.

Audiences hoped for a more uplifting experience when Booth's Theatre reopened after a refurbishing. Proprietor Edwin Booth's career had survived the assassination of President Lincoln by his brother John Wilkes Booth. Unfortunately, this most renowned of America's Shakespeareans was not taking the stage himself this summer. Nor was he producing one of the Bard's masterpieces. *The Bells* aspired to be a psychological thriller of a tormented soul to rival Hamlet. Despite excellent reviews for the lead actor, the *Times* doubted "so gloomy and monochromatic a composition" would prove attractive after a short-lived curiosity.

For those disappointed in these early openings, the city's leading impresario promised a spectacular on August 20. Lucy Fisk had leased the Grand Opera House to Augustin Daly, whose Fifth Avenue Theatre had long been the premier venue for the dramatic arts. He was spending $90,000 to renovate the opera house and stage his production of *Le Roi Carotte*, or, in his version translated from the French, *King Carrot*. Carpets of Wilton velvet now paved the hallways and auditorium. Fresh upholstery burnished the boxes. The lobby exhibited the best works of the best-known European and American artists. A ladies' toilet with the latest conveniences and a full-time maid stood ready to attend the finest society.

For the opening, Daly had installed ingenious machinery beneath the stage that promised almost instantaneous transformations between scenes. Renowned painters had worked months on the tableaus. Paris designers shipped two thousand costumes. The choicest actors of the English and American stages and a chorus drawing from companies throughout European opera had rehearsed.

Hitherto the Grand Opera House stood for failure, the *Times* noted. The paper recognized the great pains Daly had taken to reverse that reputation, and the risk. Wherever performed to date, *Le Roi Carotte* had been a failure, or at most a succès d'estime. The *Evening Post* was blunter. "We have our doubts," the editors wrote.

The start was not auspicious. On opening day, Daly canceled the performance. An intricate piece of machinery had arrived a week earlier. The mechanism would operate with only a winding up like a watch, or such was the promise. In fact, it required reconstruction of the stage.

With the postponement whetting the public's expectations and the producers' anxiety, a well-heeled crowd jammed the entrances six days later. Elegant ladies and their gallants loved the picture gallery, lingering until church bells struck one in the morning. The critics praised the scenery, the magnificent costumes, the dramatic interpretation of the actors. Especially noteworthy was Daly's refusal "to brighten the stage with nude female limbs." Not a single ballet dancer exposed her charms. About time, concluded the *Herald*; even the most foolish of fast young men should realize a woman looks quite as well in a dress as without one. Perhaps leggy burlesques were giving way to some salutary improvement in theatrical taste, the paper hoped.

But as for the play—the plot was at least consistent to its own vein of extravagant improbability, remarked one reviewer. Others complained of a total lack of ingenuity, the commonest sort of language in the libretto, and music largely stolen but at least not spoiled in the stealing. And really, critics griped, Daly should have known to prune hackneyed political commentary from his script. A score of apes in the "Island of Monkeys" scene afforded the most merriment of the night, and the acrobats hired to entertain the audience during set changes received the most enthusiastic ovations.

Still, no one wanted to incur Daly's wrath. Taken as a whole the piece "brilliantly inaugurated what will probably prove the most successful management the Grand Opera House had yet enjoyed," one critic said, summing up the consensus. Jim Fisk had set a low bar with the Demon Can-Can he staged there.

V

AUTUMN

Inside Plymouth Church.
Lyman Abbott, Henry Ward Beecher, A Sketch of His Career, *1883*

18 | "I BELIEVE IN PUBLIC JUSTICE"

DURING SLEEPLESS NIGHTS ON the floor of her Broad Street office, Victoria Woodhull had countless hours to ponder how her life had grown so entangled with the Beecher family. The patriarch, Lyman Beecher, had risen to prominence as a radical evangelist and temperance advocate during America's Second Great Awakening, a religious revival sweeping the nation early in the nineteenth century. The next generation carried on the family's theological and social leadership, the seven sons as Congregational ministers, the four daughters as authors and educators. Turning abolitionists, two of the siblings made the Beecher name one recognized throughout the country. Harriet Beecher Stowe painted the evils of slavery in her bestselling novel *Uncle Tom's Cabin*. Reverend Henry rallied the North with a cry: "Give me war redder than blood and fiercer than fire!"

Youngest sister Isabella Beecher Hooker became Woodhull's most loyal confidante. When Woodhull was feeling the world against her, she unburdened herself in letters to her friend. With all the curses and imprecations heaped upon her, she wrote, "I need some little sustaining presence from those who I believe comprehend me." Hooker responded with comfort, despite relentless browbeating from her family to disown the vile woman. Hooker understood when Woodhull said a power compelled her to do things from which her sensitive soul shrank. Woodhull could happily live a sanctified life focused around the home, children, and husband she loved, yet that was not the mission chosen for her. Hooker urged Woodhull on with the promise of her allegiance to "My Darling Queen."

Harriet Beecher Stowe and eldest sister Catharine Beecher treated Woodhull as anathema. Hardly had Woodhull finished presenting her suffrage memorial before the House Judiciary Committee in 1871 than Catharine delivered to Congress a remonstrance protesting against the vote for women. In the following months, the two sisters penned diatribes against Woodhull, and though some were signed simply "A Citizen in Hartford," Woodhull harbored no doubt about the source. Lest she try to lecture in New England, Catharine lobbied governors to deny her and newspaper editors to revile her. Harriet mocked her in a serialized novel running in her brother's *Christian Union*.

My Wife and I featured a brazen hussy named Audacia whose family row spilled into the street amid charges of blackmailing and swindling and a "terrible wash of dirty linen." With the novel appearing only weeks after Annie Claflin, her daughters, and Colonel Blood were feuding in court, no one doubted Woodhull was the model. To reporters questioning her, Harriet protested no, she only meant to depict the type. Their mistake if the papers believed Woodhull was represented. *Pshaw!*, as Audacia would say. Woodhull was fed up with the Beecher sisters smearing her every chance they got.

Isabella played the peacemaker, persuading Catharine to call on Woodhull that spring. Woodhull had welcomed Catharine to her Murray Hill mansion; then the pair settled into Woodhull's carriage for the afternoon parade in Central Park. Catharine lectured Woodhull on the dangers of women challenging men. When she got a word in, Woodhull called her guest misguided and advised her of rumors about her family that Catharine did not wish to hear. Catharine yelled, "Remember, Victoria Woodhull, I will strike you dead. . . . I can and will kill you." She clambered out of the carriage and fled across the park.

Their reverend brother Henry Ward Beecher was the enigma who most intrigued Woodhull. He had arrived in Brooklyn twenty-five years earlier. He entered the pulpit of Plymouth Church so penniless that the elder who recruited him paid off his debts, which totaled $800. Today he was the most popular preacher of the most popular church and by general agreement the most famous man in America. He was also the cornerstone of a financial empire. Books, lectures, and journals fed its coffers, not to mention astounding fees for one's own pew. That church elder, Henry Bowen, had recouped his investment many times over.

On Sundays, thousands of Manhattanites piled into "Beecher Boats." In the morning light, Brooklyn Heights loomed across the East River like the Shining City upon the Hill. From the ferry landing, the faithful surged up to Plymouth Church. The redbrick building rose like a barn from the Connecticut countryside where its pastor grew up. It was unabashedly square and unornamented but for the cornice of its peaked roof. Sunlight filtered through high windows as if casting the aura of heaven inside. At precisely ten minutes before the service, pew holders were presumed to be seated. The masses were unleashed through doors wide enough for a team of horses. Within minutes they filled every seat on the floor, the gallery above, the aisles, stairways, and vestibules, waiting anxiously for the metropolis's greatest thespian. Though his congregation would never stand for its pastor sanctioning a theatrical at the Brooklyn Academy of Music several blocks away, Henry Ward Beecher surpassed any actor appearing on its world-renowned stage.

To open, the organist filled the pipes of the largest church instrument in the land. The choir and congregation sent out a melody seldom equaled this side of heaven. Beecher bounded through a small door at the rear of the platform, tossed his floppy hat to the floor, joyfully sniffed a vase of flowers, and plopped into the armchair placed where the platform extended into the congregation. He had designed his stage on the principle of "personal and social magnetism" emanating reciprocally from the speaker and a close throng of hearers. "I want them to surround me," he said, "so that they will come up on every side, and behind . . . [and] surge about me."

He began the sermon he wrote that morning. "Some men like their bread cold," he said in explanation of the extemporaneous and emotional effect the last-minute composition imparted. "I like mine hot." He had abandoned the strict Calvinism of his youth focused on fear of God. He preached a "Gospel of Love" celebrating the boundless opportunity of America, the beauty in flowers and sunsets and all of nature, the faculty for enjoyment God gave humanity. His audience glowed as his passion reached a level beyond reason. He described this state as "I do not seem to think, I *see*."

Was it any wonder such a man would fascinate a woman who lost herself to the spirits when she mounted the platform, who in this trance of the spirits mesmerized her audience?

Woodhull had not met Beecher when she learned his secret. Visiting Woodhull's home early in 1871, Paulina Davis had told her of a recent visit to Theodore and Lib Tilton. As a promising journalist of twenty in 1855, Theodore had moved to Brooklyn Heights to marry Lib, who grew up attending Plymouth Church. Her pastor Henry Ward Beecher performed the ceremony. Theodore and Henry began working together on the Christian journal the *Independent*, founded by Henry Bowen, the church elder who brought Beecher to Brooklyn. Over the years, Theodore developed a reputation as a brilliant writer, journalist, and lecturer. With Beecher's theological contributions, the creative editorship of Tilton, and the business acumen of Bowen, the *Independent* thrived as a leading Christian journal of the time. Beecher, Tilton, and Bowen became known as the "Trinity" of Plymouth Church.

Beecher treated the Tiltons' as his second home, the sanctuary to which he escaped when his own oppressive home life was too much to bear. Of Henry, Theodore said, "I came to love him as I had no other man."

On the evening Davis visited, Lib Tilton answered the door and she burst into tears. "Have you come to see me?" she cried. "For six months I have been shut up from the world, and I thought no one ever would come again." The spigot opened, her words poured out about the years-long intimacy she had with her preacher, Beecher, her love for him predating her marriage, her husband's rage upon discovering the affair, the abuse she suffered in retaliation, the miscarriage not three weeks past of the child her husband was sure Beecher had fathered. "I came away from that house, my soul bowed down with grief at the heart-broken condition of that poor woman," Davis told Woodhull. "I felt that I ought not to leave Brooklyn until I had stripped the mask from that infamous, hypocritical scoundrel, Beecher."

Visiting Woodhull a few months later, Elizabeth Cady Stanton added to the story. She and Susan B. Anthony had recently stayed in Brooklyn Heights. Stanton and

Theodore Tilton dined at the home of another leading suffragist. Due to a mix-up in the arrangements, Anthony remained with Lib at the Tiltons' home. Over the meal, Theodore unburdened his soul, relating details of the family secret with such agony that he raved and tore his hair, seemingly on the verge of insanity. "That that damned lecherous scoundrel should have defiled my bed for ten years, and at the same time have professed to be my friend," he raged against Beecher. "Had he come like a man to me and confessed his guilt but to have him creep like a snake into my house leaving his pollution behind. . . . And when I think how for years she, upon whom I had bestowed my heart's love, could have lied and deceived me so, I lose all faith in humanity."

The next day Anthony reported that Theodore had stormed back to his house. In an angry argument, Theodore and Lib spilled how each had broken their wedding vows. Anthony withdrew to her room, only to find Lib dashing up the stairs with Theodore chasing behind. Lib rushed in. Anthony slammed and bolted the door as Theodore pounded outside. "No woman shall stand between me and my wife," he screamed. Protected by Anthony, Lib again poured out the tale.

By the time she related it to Woodhull, Stanton understood the scandal was an open secret. Money was keeping it contained. Men like Henry Bowen and Stanton's brother-in-law Sam Wilkeson had huge sums tied up in Beecher as stockholders in Plymouth Church, in the journals he contributed to, and in the multivolume *Life of Christ* he was failing to write despite pocketing a $10,000 advance.

An infamous scoundrel, a damned lecher, a creeping snake. How others saw Beecher in this story of adultery, Woodhull did not. She saw a kindred spirit. She saw a free lover.

Yes, Woodhull proclaimed, she believed in free love. When a man and a woman were mutually attracted and a feeling within them deepened to love, or whatever they wished to call it, they had every right to pursue that love, to consummate it through any physical act they chose.

Lib Tilton loved Henry Ward Beecher. Woodhull did not question her sincerity, nor did she doubt that he reciprocated. In consummating their love, Lib and Henry exercised an inalienable and natural right. They practiced what she preached. If Woodhull had any issue, it was that Henry did not announce his belief in free love to the world.

But shortly after Woodhull heard Stanton's story, the war in Woodhull's Murray Hill mansion spilled into the street and the court. The headlines blared of Woodhull's mother and husband duking it out, of blackmail plots, of her two husbands living under one roof. Of free love. The attacks against her crescendoed, from the Boston women who hated her; from the Beecher sisters Catharine and Harriett; from their brother Henry's journals, the *Christian Union* serializing Harriett's novel and the *Independent* damning her for forcing her free love views on women seeking the vote.

How could Woodhull help but feel the weight of the Beecher cabal upon her neck when she defended herself in the *Times* and the *World*, when she wrote that helping her ailing first husband was one of the most virtuous acts of her life? The weight was too great, so she put the cabal on notice. "I do not intend to be made the scape-goat to sacrifice," she added to her letter, "to be offered up as a victim to society by those who cover over the foulness of their lives and the feculence of their thoughts." Yes, she advocated free love in the highest, purest sense. But "my judges preach against 'free love' openly, [and] practice it secretly. . . . They are full of dead men's bones and all manner of uncleanness. For example, I know of one man, a public teacher of eminence, who lives in concubinage with the wife of another public teacher of almost equal eminence."

Woodhull named no names. But she declined to play "the frightful example" without examining other lives. "I believe in public justice," she closed.

Looking back on those days, perhaps they didn't seem so dark compared to sleeping in the Broad Street office with her children. Her warnings had been just that. She hadn't ever carried out a threat, hadn't exposed any hypocrites practicing free love out of sight. She had done no more than pressure the women who vilified her to shut their mouths. In Beecher's case, she was more eager to meet the man than to unmask him. Could she sway him to her cause? She wondered.

Her opportunity came the day after the *Times* and the *World* published her letter in May 1871. Theodore Tilton stormed into the Broad Street brokerage. "Whom do you mean by that?" Tilton asked, pointing to the *World*, to her letter referring to public teachers of eminence.

"I mean you and Mr. Beecher," Woodhull said.

And so began her immersion in the tight community of Brooklyn Heights protecting its precious gem, the Reverend Henry Ward Beecher.

Late one evening, roughly a year before she found herself homeless, Victoria Woodhull had ferried across the East River. As she hurried along the streets of Brooklyn Heights, she could see few reminders of the place Henry Ward Beecher had arrived a quarter-century before. Brooklyn had been a village ruled by women then, or so it was said. Each morning Satan tempted the men across the river with the riches of Wall Street, the dazzle of Broadway, the depravity of the Bowery. Each evening they returned to welcoming wives who kept the hearths warm, the life simple, and the community pure. At week's end, happy couples sought no more diversion than joining neighbors for prayer.

In those days an influx of New Englanders and their Puritan values labeled this side of the river Little Boston. Canopies of oaks shaded simple frame houses, the sort with wide porches where a family might gather after dinner for Bible reading and neighborly conversation. The sort that were rapidly disappearing as the marriage of Yankee shrewdness and New York ambition brought newfound wealth and the displays of elegance and ostentation it could buy. While the Heights still held itself up as God's model of Christian virtue, Brooklyn's men today leaned more to velvet-lined coats and silk hats than homespun and coarse woolens. Their waiting wives were more likely fussing over the mahogany and satin furnishings of an elegant brick or brownstone than stoking the fire of a clapboard homestead. Art and music would occupy the evening, or among the more daring, dancing and cards under glittering chandeliers.

Woodhull climbed the porch of a house that harked back to the old days. Theodore Tilton had first invited her to his home when he learned she knew everything. He wanted her to meet his wife, Lib. Theodore hoped compassion for Lib would silence her. Woodhull came, and she gave Lib a sympathetic ear. Over several visits, the ladies shared confidences, called each other friend. Woodhull sat by Lib's side as she sewed a dress for her daughter. At times Lib dropped her work, encircled her arms around her friend's neck, and kissed her.

Woodhull's friendship with Theodore developed into an infatuation between the two. In that summer of 1871, they swam off Coney Island, rowed in Central Park, watched stars from her rooftop. Woodhull poured out her life story for a biography he published in September. He relived the horror of his wife's adultery with Beecher, telling her more than she already knew. How his suspicions grew so aroused he questioned his daughter about the comings and goings in his house. How terrible orgies were carried on within, in the presence of his children. How he ripped Beecher's picture from the wall and pounded it to pieces. How he stripped the wedding ring from his wife's finger and stamped it in the dirt. How Beecher infiltrated his house once more and demanded from Lib a letter denying everything. How his friend Frank Moulton went with pistol in hand to Beecher's home to retrieve that denial.

Detail after sordid detail, Tilton told Woodhull. She learned more from Frank Moulton and his wife, Emma, who invited her into their home. So many evenings she had ferried to Brooklyn before this one on which she was again ringing the Tiltons' bell. But tonight Woodhull was not seeing Theodore or Lib.

At 10:00 PM, Woodhull sat beside a man who looked his sixty years. A great bulk had settled around his middle. Stringy gray hair hung to his shoulders. His jowls drooped into fleshy wrinkles. His eyes, at least during moments of stillness late in the evening, appeared tired. He did not want to be here. He had come not because the woman beside him wanted so eagerly to meet him. Henry Ward Beecher came because he feared her.

She seduced him. Perhaps not to some physical act, though she would never squarely say, despite the speculation that swirled. Perhaps she only reached into his pocket and withdrew one of the loose gems he kept there, his "opiates" as he called them, his well-known addiction that New York jewelers vied to feed. She could have rolled it in her palm, taken his hand and placed the stone in his, letting him gaze upon it in their hands together, feeling its warmth and hers. Or perhaps he pulled the stone out himself, for that was how he calmed himself in moments of stress. Perhaps he placed it in her hand.

Or perhaps she was right about him, that in their hearts they were kindred spirits. She recognized the sensuous nature of which his passion for gems was a symptom. She understood the hunger for intimacy that drove his passion in the pulpit and the lust in his heart. Whether standing over his flock in Plymouth Church or welcoming a visitor under the cloak of darkness, he peeled away the curtain that hid the essence of the creature before him, penetrating it with the indomitable urgency of his love. That evening, and on subsequent nights in Brooklyn Heights, the curtain fell from both of them.

He was a free lover in every fiber of his being. *No person on earth could more quickly end the injustice of our social system than you,* Woodhull told him.

The social system, yes, he agreed. *Marriage is the grave of love.* Never once had he married a couple that he did not feel was condemned.

A single sermon could free women from the slavery of marriage, could release husbands from the loveless unions that drove them to debauchery, could rescue once-innocent young women they paid to service them. *A simple acknowledgment of the life you lead could ignite a social revolution,* she told him.

He was twenty years ahead of his church, he replied. He preached the truth as fast as his people could bear it.

Then you are a fraud, she said. *You confess that you do not preach the truth as you know it, while your people persuade themselves you are giving your best.*

He would preach to empty seats, he said. He would ruin his church.

She was a revolutionary, she told him. She aimed to overthrow the social slavery in which the country was trapped. She would mount the ramparts. Would he join her?

They were intimate moments, these arguments. He agreed with her in so many ways, he admitted, even if he was not brave enough to bear open testimony to his beliefs. She would wheedle until he could resist no longer, until he joined her on the platform. He would do so, she was sure, Woodhull wrote his sister Isabella. Henry was her true friend, as much as Isabella herself.

That November 1871, Woodhull planned a speech at Steinway Hall. Her topic was Social Freedom. It covered issues she and Beecher argued over and agreed on—the slavery of marriage, the injustices it produced, the right of individuals to govern their own actions. She toned the words down as much as she conscientiously could. She did not want to frighten Beecher away when she asked him to introduce her. She carried the speech to his office seeking his opinion. She followed up with a note asking him to preside. She solicited Tilton and Moulton to convince him this was his opportunity to come out as an advocate of social freedom. Alarmed by her request, Beecher sought out Tilton and Moulton. *Accept,* they advised. *The course Woodhull offers is the safest option. Accept before the facts emerge of their own accord.*

When she received no answer by the day of the speech, Woodhull went to Brooklyn Heights. She pressed Beecher. He agreed perfectly with what she planned to say, he told her. But he could not stand with her at Steinway Hall. He should sink through the floor. Yes, he was a moral coward. He was not fit to be beside her. She would speak the truth, he would stand there living a lie. She insisted. On the sofa beside her, he got on his knees. He took her face in his hands, and with tears streaming down his cheeks, he begged her to let him off.

Disgusted, she walked out. Tilton and Moulton brought her back in. "Some day you have to fall," Tilton told Beecher. "Go and introduce this woman. . . . It will break your fall."

"Do you think that this thing will come out to the world?" Beecher asked.

"Nothing is more certain in earth or heaven," Tilton said.

"I can never endure such a terror," Beecher said. "Oh, if it must come, let me know of it twenty-four hours in advance, that I can take my own life."

Enraged, Woodhull said, "Mr. Beecher, if I am compelled to go upon the platform alone, I shall begin by telling the audience why I am alone, and why you are not with me." She turned on her heel.

A frightened Beecher promised Tilton and Moulton he would come if he could rouse his courage. Despite a wet, miserable evening, Steinway Hall filled to bursting an hour before the program. Four minutes before she was to take the stage, Tilton and Moulton found Woodhull weeping in an anteroom. She would faithfully keep her word regarding Beecher, she told them. Let the chips fall.

Tilton intervened. He insisted on introducing Woodhull if only she did not mention Beecher. She reluctantly agreed, and she channeled her anger into two hours of a ringing speech. She moved from religious freedom to marriage slavery, from human bondage to prostitution, from inalienable rights to individual sovereignty, from the Ten Commandments to sexual freedom. The *Times* ranked the crowd as one of the largest ever assembled at a public hall in New York. Twice the audience condemned the speaker's theories with loud hissing. At one point, they hounded her from the stage.

She returned undaunted. She cried, "Yes, I am a free lover. I have an inalienable, constitutional and natural right to love whom I may, to love as long or as short a period as I can; to change that love every day if I please, and with that right neither you nor any law you can frame have any right to interfere!"

The papers were not kind. Summed up one, "The lecture in itself was a disgrace to the hall in which it was held, the city in which the hall is situated, the State in which the city is located, and the Union of which New York is a member." Her enemies would use her words to vilify her as she ran for president the next year.

Yet the night was a huge success. Within forty-eight hours, thirteen cities plus two more venues in New York invited Woodhull to repeat her lecture. Two hundred more times she would deliver the speech over the next year, she promised, reaching half a million people, "though its thunders fall upon some terrified ears," a goodly number of which would undoubtedly belong to a "braying Ass."

One such ass brayed in that organ of Plymouth Church, the *Independent*. Henry Bowen called the lecture "one of the dirtiest meetings that has ever been held in New York."

From Henry Ward Beecher, Woodhull heard not a word. That day was the last the two met. She did not forgive him.

———————————

Days before she ended up homeless, Victoria Woodhull contacted Beecher one last time. Made desperate by her threatened eviction from the Gilsey House, she set her pride aside and begged. The fight against her had become hotter than she could endure, she wrote Beecher. Her business, her projects, everything she lived for suffered from the persecution she was under. Her enemies were hunting her down, determined not to let her live. She wanted his assistance to keep her place in the Gilsey. "Will you lend your aid in this?" she asked. Beecher rebuffed her without reply. He would not take a single step in that direction, he told Moulton. Would Moulton be so kind as to pass that along? "And please drop me a line to say all is right," Beecher added.

So for weeks Woodhull, her children, Claflin, and Colonel Blood lived on Broad Street. At last her sister Maggie Miles found another house. When autumn arrived, Woodhull and the others at the office had moved in. So had much of the quarrelsome clan from Murray Hill—Woodhull's mother and father, a fourth sister, brothers-in-law, and nieces. Thirteen inmates, as a visiting reporter called the family, plus lodgers on the upper floors to help pay the rent. They packed the place like a tenement. Woodhull and Blood secured a bedroom. Tennie's boudoir was a curtained-off portion of the parlor.

Woodhull was exhausted and discouraged. Slander and innuendo had destroyed her character. The trust she had spent years building had evaporated. As to her mission, she knew she had done right championing social freedom, but she could see no path to carrying it out. Even the spirits seemed to abandon her, though she did not abandon them. Her abiding faith in their wisdom kept her from losing all hope.

In September Woodhull dragged herself to Boston for the annual convention of the American Association of Spiritualists. As the association's president for the past year, she felt a duty to render an account of her stewardship. Afterward she would surrender her office. At this point the association was a rump group of Spiritualists that others in the movement considered heretics for not deserting the vile woman serving as their president.

As Woodhull stood offstage readying to deliver a speech urging political action, she listened for hostility. She detected nothing unfriendly, rather a sense of uncertainty and doubt. She stepped into the light.

The spirits seized her.

———————————

E. A. Meriwether was a southern woman. She happened to be in Boston with her family in September. She didn't think much of the North. These New England Puritans looked upon themselves as the "trooly loil" and upon the South as "degraded secesh." She didn't appreciate the attitude.

She thought even less of Union newspapers. Through four years of war, nearly every northern editor lavished on southern women every abusive adjective the English language contains. *They called us secesh shriekers, she-adders, she-devils*, Meriwether complained. One widely circulated pamphlet asserted almost every southern white woman, especially "the proud daughters of the slave aristocracy," carried on liaisons with their fathers' enslaved men. Indeed, southern women "preferred the illicit loves of Negro men to the honorable loves of the white men," the pamphlet charged. It took the *London Times* to call out the outrage of decency that pamphlet perpetrated. Not a single northern editor condemned the lies, so far as Meriwether could tell. Yet after the war those chaste Puritan newspapermen held their hands up in holy horror at any mention of the secret licentiousness of the North's rich and powerful men.

So, when Meriwether heard those same editors smear Victoria Woodhull, she wasn't about to condemn the woman. On the contrary, when the northern press so grossly abused a woman, she was inclined to believe the woman had some noble qualities. That's why she dragged her husband into the Boston hall where Woodhull was speaking.

The program plodded along while a half-dozen men droned about motions and resolutions. The crowd grew restless. They hadn't come for pontificating; they had come to hear Victoria Woodhull. Without warning the woman flashed onto the platform. An electric shock swept over the assembly, striking it to dead stillness.

The speaker was a delicate creature, plainly dressed, her skin smooth and pale but for two crimson spots burning on her cheeks. Her face was sad, telling of wrecked hopes and a cruel battle for life. Her expression evoked a tragic queen. Suddenly Woodhull tossed back her hair and poured out a torrent of flame. Meriwether felt her flesh creep, her blood run cold. A profound pity rose inside her as Woodhull poured out her struggle against great powers that had driven her to this night. The experience was like watching a hunted creature at bay, a creature trying to escape its enemies but overtaken, turning for a last desperate fight.

Woodhull's words blasted over the audience. *Society is a whited sepulcher, fair on the outside but festering rot within*, she charged. *My mission is to show up the shams.*

Editors, teachers, preachers, she spared not. She tore aside the religion and morality and respectability they wrapped themselves in and exposed their sins to the glare of day. Everyone watching shuddered, especially the high and mighty Boston men dreading she might raise their sins before the world.

Woodhull called out the names of her targets and stated their crimes. *The world worships Henry Ward Beecher*, she cried, *but he lives a lie. He preaches a Christlike purity of life, yes, yet every Sunday his words ring out to his mistresses sitting in their pews, robed in silks and satins and high respectability. For years he carried on a criminal intimacy with a member of his church, Mrs. Tilton.* She had heard it firsthand from many different people.

When Woodhull finished off Beecher, she moved on to S. S. Jones, leader of a dissident faction of Spiritualists who attacked her as a disgrace to the movement. He kept the medium Mrs. Robinson as his mistress. Woodhull named an editor who had sought her clairvoyant powers to foretell whether his sick wife would die soon. He might then enjoy the charms of his mistress unhindered. Woodhull didn't spare the women either, the Livermores and Hanafords of the world, those free-loving hypocrites pretending to be holier than thou.

Woodhull vanished from the stage as quickly as she had entered. The audience didn't move. The speech had been a bitter, burning denunciation. Meriwether knew not what truth it held. Let the ones called out deny the accusations, she concluded; let them charge that Woodhull's story was but the crazy chimera of her brain. The world would believe them. It would not believe their silence.

Whether Woodhull's words were true or not, her opinions misguided or utterly vile, Meriwether could feel only sympathy for her. With all that Woodhull had suffered—not so much the persecution of recent years as her unbearable marriage at age fourteen, to a debauchee and drunkard who beat her, starved her, steeped her in the dregs of poverty for the next sixteen years—the wonder was not that she shuddered at the words *marriage* and *husband* but that she did not go mad and hate all humanity.

One thing Meriwether knew for certain. Woodhull had not uttered a single word that was obscene.

The papers didn't agree. Most ignored Woodhull's speech. Others simply reported that she spewed "a disgraceful tirade," "vile vituperation," or language "never equaled in vulgarity." They didn't bother with what she actually said. The few that observed she had targeted Beecher exonerated the preacher, one saying Woodhull was fit for the lunatic asylum, another that Beecher would be foolish to even deny her "obscene calumnies."

As far as the press was concerned, that ended the matter.

19 | "THERE IS NOTHING SECRET THAT SHALL NOT BE MADE KNOWN"

VICTORIA WOODHULL got another surprise before she returned to New York from the Spiritualists convention. With a power stronger than herself taking over her body, she could hardly remember giving the speech. Afterward, tears streamed from the eyes of many who heard her. *You spoke in a rhapsody of indignant eloquence,* they told her, *and poured out the whole history of the Beecher and Tilton scandal in Plymouth Church. And yes, you used some naughty words. But you swore divinely.* No matter what the newspapers printed, the Spiritualists attending were not horrified. They elected her to another term as their president. They refused all her efforts to decline.

Woodhull arrived home heartened. As autumn progressed, the house turned into a home. Tennie hosted dinners of oysters and brandy and the ginger ale she particularly liked. Woodhull lovingly tended her son, Byron, who scrambled about overwrought and underfoot. With the leaves turning, they joined Woodhull's husband on carriage rides in the park. Her twelve-year-old daughter, Zulu Maude, and her nieces enlivened evenings playing the piano and singing. The elder niece had attracted the interest of the impresario Augustin Daly and was undertaking minor parts at his Fifth Avenue Theatre. Tennie, too, had theatrical aspirations and was rehearsing for her debut as Portia in *The Merchant of Venice*. As the family welcomed visitors, one recalled his reception "as refreshing as a midsummer shower." A "jubilant joy" pervaded the place.

The clearest sign of Woodhull emerging from the doldrums was her going back to work. With blackmail accusations still stinging, she and Claflin hired Boston attorneys to sue "Warrington," the pseudonym of a newspaper correspondent who spread the rumors. The suit also named the *Woman's Journal* and the *Springfield Republican*, which published Warrington's reports. The sisters were considering a second suit against the Gilsey Hotel for their eviction. After the New England papers damned not just her Boston speech but herself personally, and did it with innuendo rather than any words

154

she actually had spoken, Woodhull called in the New York papers to offer her version of the event. They gave her no better coverage.

And Woodhull began plotting with her closest circle, Claflin and Colonel Blood and Stephen Pearl Andrews, who had played a crucial role at *Woodhull & Claflin's Weekly* from the first issue onward. Her cabinet of confidential advisors, she called them.

She gave many versions of her thinking during these days debating how to proceed. When she was on the verge of abandoning her mission, had not the spirits demanded she resume it? Did she not face a choice after her Boston speech: either endure being labeled a slanderer or place the facts before the public and let the people judge? After so long battling for social freedom, had she any right not to use the weapons Providence handed her? If she withheld what she knew, was she not partaking in the crimes she decried? Did not the sacred cause of human rights hold a paramount claim over her conduct?

Asking these questions, she contemplated her mission on earth. She thought about narrow objectives—to make women independent and free—and broader goals—to better mental and moral and physical conditions throughout society. She pondered the paths to winning the revolution these goals represented; how to leverage the system of warfare that had abolished slavery; how the sins of society, like the sins of slavery, had to be exposed. It wasn't the abstract sins that had defeated slavery; it was sins in the concrete, the exposure of specific acts of horror, the naming of the men who had perpetrated them. It would be the same in the social realm. The airing of specific hypocrisies was needed, along with the naming of the hypocrites themselves. It couldn't begin with little people and their peccadilloes. That would be cowardice. It had to vent the offenses of the powerful.

She considered how painful the battle would be. So what if it brought sorrow, trial, affliction, poverty, disgrace? She had long demonstrated she could survive any torture. She was a prophetess, an evangel, a revolutionary. If her fate be a martyr as well, let it come.

She deliberated slowly, methodically, reluctantly, within her mind and with her cabinet. She reminded herself what Christ had said: "There is nothing secret that shall not be made known; nothing hidden that shall not be revealed." Did Christians believe that, she wondered? Did Plymouth Church?

Yes, all the times she went around and around, she circled back to the Reverend Henry Ward Beecher and his church. So she decided. She would burst the bombshell.

The story was already written. A reporter had interviewed Woodhull. He had recorded the full story of the Beecher-Tilton scandal that poured from her mouth. Woodhull and Claflin with Blood and Andrews would publish the interview, or at least that's the conceit they adopted for the revival of *Woodhull & Claflin's Weekly*. It would fill four pages. A full issue was sixteen, and there was so much more to say. They went to work.

Four months had passed since they shut their presses without a word of notice. Their readers deserved an explanation. So, under the headline To the Public, they laid out what the paper meant to them, how it was their lifeblood. They described the trials that had driven it under, from the loss of their home and their friends to the paralysis of strength, health, and purse that resulted. They foretold where they were taking it now, from their aims for a social revolution to their declaration of war—that whenever a person they knew lived a lie or denounced them for their doctrines while he secretly practiced those doctrines, they would unmask him. They fired a warning bullet—they held biographies of five hundred such persons.

Claflin insisted a precedent be set. She outlined a recurring column, The Philosophy of Modern Hypocrisy. It would hold up for inspection gentlemen who debauched women without consequence while driving those women to eternal shame. She had met its first feature when she and Woodhull attended the French Ball early in the year. They had purchased a box at the Academy of Music. Two gentlemen they hadn't met, Luther Challis and a friend, joined them there, bringing along two women from Baltimore. The men called for wine. They drank little themselves but plied the others, and when Claflin begged the women to drink no more, the men told her to shut her mouth.

Challis began calling on Claflin after the ball. During these visits, Challis boasted of his exploits and of his particular taste for deflowering young maidens, or as he called them, "spring chickens." Claflin led him on. Eventually she tracked down the Baltimore women and heard the story of their seduction. She learned of another woman Challis seduced. For several days afterward, Challis proudly displayed on his finger "the red trophy of her virginity," Claflin noted in her column.

Woodhull's speech written for the Spiritualists, the one superseded when the spirits overtook her, occupied several pages, and soon the sixteen pages were filled but for the first. That one required advertising be sold, or at least bartered. Or given away, for that was better than empty space. They rounded up fourteen spots, mostly from their fellow brokers and bankers.

They placed the centerpiece nine pages in. Woodhull headlined it simply The Beecher-Tilton Scandal. She took full responsibility in the subhead: The Detailed Statement of the Whole Matter by Mrs. Woodhull. An introduction reinforced her reasons for publication.

She was engaged in moral warfare, she said. She encapsulated it as "social revolution on the marriage question," but she explained her aims as upending the unjust roles and relationships between the sexes. The betterment of society impelled her to ventilate one of the most stupendous scandals ever to occur. She bore no hostility whatever to Beecher—quite the opposite. He was every bit as good, pure, and noble as the world held him to be. She lauded his immense physical potency, his indomitable urge for intimacy, his amative nature. From these pieces of his character flowed the zest and magnetism that powered his preaching and impassioned his audience. These same traits engendered his private practices for which the world might condemn him. But she never would. The world had no more right to inquire into such matters than to ask what she ate for breakfast.

She knew firsthand those practices. Beecher lived the doctrines she preached, that every individual had an inalienable right to love whom he or she wished, for as long or as short as he or she wished it, and to change that love when he or she so chose. In his heart, Beecher was an ultra social reformer. Yet public opinion overawed him. He professed a false morality under which he privately chafed. For the infidelity in his heart and the hypocrisy in the image he presented to the world, and for that only, she condemned him. Beecher was a powerful man exerting tremendous influence. The world needed him to champion the rights he exercised, not hide them.

This was war. Woodhull invoked an adage she attributed to Bismarck: "If an omelet has to be made, some eggs have to be broken." So, with humble apologies to Beecher the individual, Woodhull compelled Beecher the Divine into the public realm, where he lacked the courage to go of his own accord. By acknowledging his true self, he could accomplish a hundred times greater than all he had up to now, she claimed. The ordeal would emancipate him. He would not stand alone for even an hour, Woodhull prophesied. An army of glorious and emancipated others would surround him. Together they would establish a new social order for all time.

Composing the issue was the easy part. Few people beyond Woodhull and her cabinet needed to know the contents as it developed.

Printing required releasing the manuscript to the printer, who would contract with the typesetter. Proofs would come back for checking. Once approved, the set type would go to the stereotyper to create plates and hand them off to the pressman for printing the pages. Add in messengers, bookkeepers, assistants, and managers—who knew how many people had a finger in the process or an inkling of the contents? And once printed copies went into the distribution system, all control was lost before a single reader opened the paper.

Secrecy was imperative. Beecher was not just a preacher. He was a business, and a very lucrative one. The investors in that business were powerful men who had contributed substantial capital to the enterprise. They would not sit idly watching their investments sucked down the drain. One leak and they would show no scruples in getting their hands on every copy and burning the lot.

And how would Woodhull and her colleagues pay for it all?

Early on, Woodhull began negotiating for lectures to bring in the money. She hoped for a swing through the South and West. It did not pan out but for a lecture in Chicago scheduled the last week of October. She accepted that invitation, but the fee could nowhere near cover the print run they planned. By hook or by crook they cobbled together the cash or the credit to get going.

Blood called on his colleagues along Nassau Street. At the printer he knew, a Mr. Smith, Blood arranged the run. *Not the usual number*, he told Smith, *several times more*. They were gambling that the sensation in the upcoming *Weekly* would boost demand far beyond the twenty-seven thousand circulation the *Weekly* claimed earlier in the year. Blood moved on to his typesetter, near the corner of Ann Street, and then to the stereotyper.

As the middle of October approached, a messenger delivered the manuscript of *Woodhull & Claflin's Weekly* to Nassau Street. The type was then set and proofs returned. The Woodhull household began reading them aloud in the parlor.

With a week left in October, Woodhull boarded a train for Chicago. A few days before, the *Chicago Post* ran an advertisement for her lecture at the Academy of Music on Sunday. It promised an "Eloquent and Thrilling" lecture on social freedom, involving questions of marriage, love, and divorce, along with commentary on the upcoming presidential election. Tickets sold well at fifty and seventy-five cents.

Beforehand, a reporter for the *Chicago Times* interviewed her. She was "animated and dashing," noted the paper, and showing off "a new, simple style of dress" she and Claflin had recently inaugurated, a plain blue broadcloth trimmed with black. The reporter admired how the tight jacket set off her graceful figure and fit her intellectual face. Since the sisters had adopted the fashion, the department store A. T. Stewart & Company had sold thousands of yards of the cloth for such dresses. Woodhull attributed its popularity to women dispensing with one of the chief causes of their ruin—extravagance in attire, whose days were as numbered as those of Saratoga trunks.

Woodhull's conversation was feisty. Their brokerage business was excellent, she said, invoking Vanderbilt's ongoing backing as a key factor. Claflin's clairvoyance had been a huge help to the Commodore's family, though the sisters no longer practiced it. The sisters were still settling past injustices, however, such as their eviction from the Gilsey, one of many hotels run as houses of assignation. Its proprietor would lose his license before Woodhull and Claflin finished with him, Woodhull threatened.

Pushing a hand through her hair, she slipped out a hint. The next number of their paper would be a rouser for a prominent Brooklyn divine. She moved quickly to other matters before the reporter could question her further.

That evening, a full house attended her lecture. Not at all a select audience, reported another paper. Hisses mingled with applause.

Woodhull headed home.

Three days before the Chicago speech, Claflin and Blood returned to Nassau Street. The printer and typesetter waited as they reviewed the final layout. One of them gave the order. *Go to press.*

This first run took two days to print and package. No copies would be sold in New York. Instead, between Saturday evening, October 26, and Monday morning, they quietly dispatched copies to their subscribers and to the entire list of newspapers in the United States, Canada, and Great Britain.

On Monday afternoon, a person appeared at the Broad Street office asking for the "*Weekly* with the Beecher Scandal." He couldn't find it on the newsstands. They gave him a copy, the first distributed in New York. Others dribbled in, word spread, and by the close of the day people clamored for the issue.

They shipped the usual number to their distributor, the American News Company. The company refused to deliver and shipped them back. But the dealers operating the stands and the boys hawking papers on the street weren't missing the opportunity to make money. They descended on the office, carrying off a hundred and a thousand copies at a time.

Two presses rolled off copies through the week. It wasn't enough. The paper, cover price ten cents, reached fifty cents, then a dollar, then two-fifty. Eager readers who could find no copies bid five, ten, and twenty dollars for a copy, and one went for forty. Some lucky enough to secure the issue rented it out for a dollar. It was not just New York. Across the country, people paid exorbitant amounts.

On Wednesday, papers in Maine and Massachusetts ran the first stories of a new *Woodhull & Claflin's Weekly*. The *Springfield Republican* called the issue a "last and most desperate bid for notoriety." A Portland paper would prove prophetic: "If there is any literature published in New York that calls for a more speedy application of the laws against obscene literature, we have not seen it." A news dispatch went across the country, generating a handful of stories over the next two days, from Virginia through the Midwest to Kansas. One predicted Beecher was so well anchored on moral ground that he would rise above the mountain of nastiness. But in the New York papers that had long castigated the sisters for their free love views—the *Times, Herald, Tribune, Evening Post, Commercial Advertiser*—not a word.

The office was jubilant. The exposé had gone off like buttered hot cakes. Hundreds of dollars per hour poured in. The extraordinary interest vindicated their belief that the social question touched the human heart more than any other. What else could have moved an entire people as with one accord? When a rumor floated in Wednesday that the forces behind Beecher were preparing a counterattack, it did not dispel the joy. Woodhull and her cabinet believed what they had written, and they would live up to the words. Only the sisters' father, Buck Claflin, worried. He didn't object to the Beecher story, he told them, but trouble was coming, and they should keep out of the way. They refused the advice.

20 | "A MALICIOUS AND GROSS LIBEL"

FRESH OFF HIS OBSCENE LITERATURE convictions in US circuit court, Anthony Comstock should have been pleased. Judge Charles Benedict sent Henry Camp and David Massey up the river the first week of October. Edward Grandin skipped his court date. The attorney he sent pleaded illness. The judge didn't buy it and ruled his bail forfeit. Within a week, marshals collared Grandin, and he, too, was doing hard labor.

True, all three were penned up for a ridiculously short sentence of one year. That stuck in Comstock's craw. And that maximum penalty was only one of the weaknesses of the federal law. The law wasn't the source of his displeasure, though. He had a plan for fixing it.

Comstock understood that the essence of the federal obscenity statute was on target—namely, to outlaw the stuff in the US mail. But three limitations kept all kinds of smut streaming through. First, the law classified nowhere near enough stuff as obscene. The great legal minds didn't think "obscene book, pamphlet, picture, print, or other publication of a vulgar and indecent character" included Frank Leslie's *Day's Doings* or the *New York Herald*'s advertisements for quack doctors killing babies, just for starters. And publications only? What about those rubber devices that were as bad, whether they protected men and women from the consequences of their sin or enticed them to pleasure themselves? And throw in medical advice dispensed by con men calling themselves doctors. The law must ban every bit of it.

Number two, how was one supposed to catch culprits when one wasn't allowed to look in the mail? Even if a postmaster knew a piece was obscene, he couldn't unseal the envelope. If he identified the sender as one of the offenders notoriously advertising obscene products, he couldn't confiscate it. Nor if he magically discovered obscene material in another fashion could he destroy it. No wonder the prosecutions under the law were minuscule.

And then there were the light sentences, which more encouraged than threatened the smut dealers.

The bill Comstock was drafting addressed these points. He had outlined his plan to Morris Jesup. His mentor at the YMCA promised that his legal contacts would get the bill in proper shape. Then Jesup would introduce Comstock to members of Congress who could get it passed into law. The $100 a month the YMCA paid Comstock enabled him to focus on the effort despite the bottom dropping out of his sales at Cochrane, McLean.

Criminals convicted, stronger legislation moving forward, powerful friends, and financial support all pleased Comstock. But now he faced a wall of obstruction.

Fainthearts filled the Committee on Obscene Literature overseeing Comstock's efforts on the YMCA's behalf. Despite abhorring obscenity, they were too cowardly to touch the stuff. *It's so unpleasant*, they argued. *Please don't bring it into public view. Stirring the pool will only harm sensitive souls and show people where to find it.*

Hogwash! You don't fight disease by pretending it doesn't exist, Comstock thought. You carry the battle forward, not sneak around like a thief in the night. Comstock had presented a strategy to win the war, and the fainthearts muzzled him. Some accused him of going too far in the arrests he had already made. Jesup seemed like the only man in his corner.

Comstock needed a way to overcome their objections. He must win a triumph so widely hailed they could no longer deny him; he must establish a reputation that demanded their loyalty.

But how? He had one ally more powerful than Jesup. As always, to Him Comstock prayed.

Suddenly a door opened.

Shortly after the latest *Woodhull & Claflin's Weekly* leaked onto New York streets, news of "The Beecher-Tilton Scandal" reached the office of the *Independent* across from city hall. The staff sprang into the street, buying every copy they could find. Rumor had Beecher himself carting off a hundred copies at a time. The news hawkers restocked as fast as the staff could dump loads at the office.

Copies migrated up Broadway to Cochrane, McLean, where Anthony Comstock still worked. He perused the Beecher story and Claflin's tale of Luther Challis and the French Ball. He made his way to the *Independent* and offered his services to its owner Henry Bowen.

The *Weekly* had grossly libeled Henry Ward Beecher, they agreed. Beecher had every right to file criminal libel charges against the women whose names were on the masthead and any others who had participated in printing the lies. But should he? A contrary view, advanced in the early newspaper reports, argued Beecher should not so much as respond to the scurrilous accusations. With the country's most popular and heroic preacher pitted against those loathsome free-loving women, the public would rally behind him. Let him rise above the fray.

Bowen embraced the silent approach, albeit for entirely different reasons. He knew the scandal was true. Irrespective of the verdict, a libel trial would expose every detail to the world. He had been intimately involved in negotiations between Beecher and Tilton. On more than one occasion he had threatened Beecher. On others he had conspired against Tilton. A trail of letters led directly to him and his duplicity.

Comstock offered salvation. Let Luther Challis sue for libel over the story about him seducing virgins, he proposed. They would charge Woodhull and her gang with distributing obscene literature through the US mail.

The first step was to receive the obscene issue through the mail. An employee of the *Independent* picked up two copies at the New York post office. Upon the employee reaching the *Independent*, his boss opened the issue and pointed to the Beecher-Tilton article. The employee then returned to the Broad Street office to buy the issue in person, one from the hand of Victoria Woodhull and one from Tennie Claflin. He paid ten cents for each.

Cognizant of the difficulties of prosecution, Comstock wanted belt and suspenders. He sent another man to Broad Street after hours. The man found one of Woodhull and Claflin's employees still there. He bought a copy and asked that it be wrapped and addressed to "M. Hamilton, 143 St. James Place, Brooklyn." Why not have a bit of fun, Comstock evidently decided. Hamilton was the maiden name of his wife, Maggie.

Upon leaving Broad Street, the man carried the package to the Nassau Street post office. He handed it to a clerk, who deposited it in the Brooklyn mail bag. The "obscene" copies were now in the US mail—for a few seconds. The clerk took the package back, marked it, and delivered it to the office of the US Attorney by direction of the special agent of the Post Office Department. The US Attorney was Noah Davis, Comstock's partner in prosecuting the smut dealers earlier in October.

Still not satisfied, Comstock visited Broad Street, finding Woodhull, Claflin, and Blood in the office. He watched several people buy papers. Claflin or Blood sold him a copy—his memory eluded him later on.

By now Comstock had adopted Saturday as his favored day for arrests. If an offender could not make bail by close of business, he would spend two nights in jail before another opportunity Monday. So Comstock waited until Saturday to appear before Commissioner John Osborn in US circuit court. Upon receiving the issue of *Woodhull & Claflin's Weekly* and affidavits sworn by the *Independent* employee, the man Comstock sent to Broad Street, and the postal clerk, Osborn granted warrants for the arrest of Woodhull and Claflin.

Woodhull spent Friday evening with her family. Around midnight word reached the house that an order was out for the sisters' arrest, along with seizure of the issue and the plates for printing it. Expecting this reaction, they didn't bother about it until morning. Woodhull awoke with a severe cold. The sisters sent word they were remaining at home but for the office to notify them if police officers called. When they heard two marshals were waiting on Broad Street, they ordered a carriage. In Woodhull's telling of the story, the marshals greeted the sisters rather rudely when the carriage rolled up around noon. After manhandling them back onto the seat, one marshal climbed up with the driver while the second plopped into their laps for fear they would leap out. Bankers and brokers rushed to find what the stir was about.

At the courthouse on Chambers Street, the marshals escorted them into a secret room. US Attorney Noah Davis introduced himself. Several others were present, including Commissioner Osborn, assistant prosecutor Henry Davies, and two men the sisters suspected were members of Plymouth Church.

To the prospect of being examined privately and without counsel, Woodhull said no, they had nothing to conceal; indeed, they wished the public to be thoroughly acquainted with this case. She and Claflin refused any examination until taken to a public courtroom. At one o'clock, attorney J. D. Reymert appeared on the sisters' behalf. Led into Commissioner Osborn's courtroom, they began their examination. The prosecutor's opening caught them off-guard.

"They are arrested on a charge of having circulated through the mails of the United States an obscene and indecent publication," Davies informed the court.

THE ARREST OF MRS. VICTORIA CLAFLIN WOODHULL AND TENNESSEE CLAFLIN, NOV. 2ND, 1872.

Victoria Woodhull and Tennie Claflin being arrested.
M. F. Darwin, One Moral Standard for All: Extracts from the Lives of Victoria Claflin Woodhull and Tennessee Claflin, undated

Over and over Woodhull and her cabinet had discussed the risks they ran, the efforts Beecher's allies would undertake to slaughter them. But obscenity? Libel, yes; they would face that charge and in defense prove the truth of the stories they published. They never dreamed anyone would call the *Weekly* obscene.

Reymert requested an adjournment. He needed to consult with his clients and read the affidavits. Davies insisted on immediate examination of the prisoners. Osborn sided with the accused. Davies agreed to hear the case Monday afternoon. So long as the prisoners were held until posting $10,000 bail, he demanded, with two sureties required for the full amount.

This was a grave and serious offense, he said, one that had done the greatest harm and injury to the community. The defendants had not only circulated an obscene publication through the mails but also committed "a malicious and gross libel upon the character of this gentleman, whose character it is well worth the while [of] the government of the United States to vindicate."

Without naming him, the prosecution had just placed Henry Ward Beecher at the center of its case. The ladies were charged with violating a statute against sending an obscene publication through the mail. Henry Ward Beecher and his character had nothing whatsoever to do with what was and was not considered obscene.

"The idea of the government vindicating or defending the character of a gentleman is entirely outside of this case," Reymert told the court. "The government are not called on to defend this gentleman from slander."

Davies won a lesser but still exorbitant bail of $8,000 when he invoked a similar obscenity case, that of an unnamed Edward Grandin, who two weeks past had skipped on $5,000. But his victory raised a question that would echo through the press for weeks: Was the US Attorney prosecuting these women for sending obscene materials through the mail or persecuting them for their accusations about Henry Ward Beecher, and for their free love views more generally? Weeks would turn into months and months into years while people puzzled over a related question: If Beecher was so viciously libeled, why was he not defending himself?

Before the day was out, a wealthy eccentric named George Francis Train offered to post bail for the sisters. By that time, the counsel they retained in anticipation of trouble had arrived. William Howe advised them to refuse Train's offer. For the federal obscenity crime, they would go to Ludlow Street jail, commonly known as Warden Tracy's Hotel for its relative hospitality. Were they to post bail, the New York district attorney stood by to arrest them on a libel charge filed by Luther Challis, he who had worn the red trophy of a girl's virginity on his finger. On that charge, they would spend the night at the notoriously worse Jefferson Market holding tank.

Besides, martyrdom had its uses. Why not enjoy it at Warden Tracy's Hotel?

———————

After meeting with Howe in Warden Tracy's office, Woodhull and Claflin adjourned to the jail's dining room for broiled chicken and potatoes. Their father arrived shortly, two other sisters joined, and soon visitors crowded the warden's office. Around eight o'clock, they climbed a stairway to Ludlow's "Fifth Avenue" and their new address, cell 11. Aside from the warden's family quarters and a "citizen's bedroom" currently occupied, the cell was as luxurious as the prison offered. One window looked out to the alley, another through the wooden door. Gaslights illuminated the interior. Iron bedsteads offered places to receive visitors. While the neighbors were not the most socially refined, the sisters befriended several. The men agreed to forego cigars in honor of the ladies.

Cell doors clanged shut at 10:00 PM. Wakeup calls came at 6:00 AM, followed by housekeeping and breakfast, lunch at noon and tea at 5:30 PM. Notable guests like the sisters enjoyed leeway. At midnight, a half-dressed Claflin beckoned a reporter to sit beside her while Woodhull suffered chills beneath her covers. The accommodations were not up to their standard, Claflin apologized, but the meanness of a Saturday arrest ensured a two-nights penance. In fact, the sisters settled in for a longer stay. Zulu Maude joined her mother for the duration. Visitors flocked in daily to break the monotony. Special friends stayed overnight. The sisters regained their celebrity. The day after their arrest, twenty reporters sought interviews. *We are not sorry for a single word we printed*, they repeated over and over. A million of their papers were circulating throughout the country. Whatever they suffered would be "the seed from which is to spring the perfect flower of a new religion of humanity," they predicted. As for their crime, nothing they had written was any more obscene than the letters of Jim Fisk and Josie Mansfield long since published in the papers.

Ludlow provided the accoutrements of a regular hotel, they would conclude upon their release—a generous table, bathing facilities, exercise in the open air, scrupulous cleanliness, an attentive staff of culture and refinement. Colonel Blood was not so lucky. While the federal obscenity warrant didn't name him, the libel suit filed by Luther Challis did. Blood was locked in Jefferson Market. The printer and the stereotyper were also incarcerated there. Stephen Pearl Andrews joined them Monday. Armed with a warrant issued by the mayor, police raided the Broad Street office, seizing furniture, books, and as many copies of the libelous issue as had not been sold.

As Woodhull and Claflin enjoyed their first meal at Ludlow, the choir of Plymouth Church assembled for its Saturday evening rehearsal. "I tell you, Nettie, I don't believe it," a contralto said to the soprano.

"Well, it's very strange," Nettie said.

A dozen singers weighed in on the scandal engulfing their preacher. Spotting a reporter from the *Sunday Mercury*, Deacon Hudson hurried over. "I know what you're after," he said.

"Yes, Deacon, I want to know how Brother Beecher takes this Woodhull affair," the reporter said.

"He ain't going to say anything about it. He's going to cut the whole thing and let it go."

Whatever details Woodhull provided to support her charges didn't matter. The Deacon had spoken to Beecher earlier and heard it straight from the horse's mouth.

"But, Deacon Hudson, will Mr. Beecher not take the trouble to refute these charges when they are made circumstantially?" the reporter asked.

"No, I don't think Brother Beecher will take the trouble. You see, we know him, and we don't propose to take anything that women like Woodhull says against him. I know Victoria Woodhull as well as Brother Beecher does, and she never told me anything about it. I think it is blackmail. She wanted him to preside at that free-love meeting, and he wouldn't so she came down on this Tilton thing."

"Well, Brother Hudson, do the Plymouth Church flock intend to stand by Mr. Beecher?"

"Of course we do. We know him, and we will support him."

On Sunday morning the packed church suggested Deacon Hudson read the situation clearly. Not even a breakdown in the streetcars kept people away. After the organist opened the service, Beecher bounded out in excellent spirits. "For it is God which worketh in you both to will and to do His good pleasure," he declared, and launched into a sermon about how those with faith in Divine Providence were happy Christians. If troubles came, they need have no fear. What was the worst that could happen—bankruptcy, death? Why worry when it was just as easy to be happy and trust to God?

Beecher seemed to be practicing what he preached.

When William Howe arrived at US circuit court Monday afternoon, a crowd clamored to hear the obscenity charge against Woodhull and Claflin. *You will be disappointed*, he could have told them. *The outcome is predetermined.* He had heard it earlier while working another case. Instead he decided to put on a show for the lucky few pummeling hard enough to squeeze through the door.

Howe greeted his clients. Woodhull looked somewhat cowed. Claflin bit her lips in contempt of the whole affair. *We are ready to proceed with the examination*, he told Commissioner Osborn.

Assistant US Attorney Davies intervened. He wished to inform the court that this morning the grand jury had indicted the prisoners on the obscenity charge. Accordingly, this hearing was moot. Commissioner Osborn no longer had jurisdiction over the case.

Osborn agreed.

He would be much surprised, Howe said, had he not heard that news this morning. In a state court, any magistrate with an examination pending would quash the grand jury's indictment and proceed himself. This was a well-established practice even if not mandated in law. It was also just. These ladies had a perfect defense, and they desired to express it to the court and the public. A party too cowardly to appear instigated their persecution, and now that party was making the grand jury and this court complicit in depriving the ladies of the opportunity to be heard.

As for their crime, the ladies were prepared to show their paper was no more obscene than the Holy Bible, the works of Lord Byron or Shakespeare. Those works would need to be prohibited from the mail under the same charge and subject to the same penalty. The Society for the Diffusion of the Bible had better close its doors for fear it be liable. Indeed, this prosecution was a blow at the freedom of the press, which, if allowed, would strike with a force the effect of which no one could contemplate.

He personally had read the ladies' paper word for word, Howe said. It contained not a word of obscenity and nothing whatsoever contrary to the act of Congress. He had not yet reviewed the grand jury's indictment, but he understood it carefully omitted any mention of the article related to Beecher, a reversal of the previous charge. Rather, the indictment referred solely to the article on Challis. The finding of such an indictment was nothing but a cruel persecution.

An eloquent speech, Davies observed, but totally irrelevant to the matter at hand. Again, Osborn agreed. The grand jury was a tribunal higher than the commissioner. He could not proceed with an examination. Nor would he pass comment on whether the paper was obscene, vulgar, or indecent. He dismissed the case from his court.

And could the government give some idea when it proposes to try the accused? Howe asked Davies.

I can't say, Davies replied. He would see the prisoners had timely notice.

And the bail?

He would leave the bail at $8,000 per prisoner, Davies said. Marshals moved in to serve warrants and return Woodhull and Claflin to Ludlow Street jail until such time as they made bail or a trial ended with acquittal.

21 | "THE GREAT PRESIDENTIAL BATTLE"

THE NEXT TUESDAY was the first in November, Election Day. Lest anyone overlook the hours allotted for casting ballots, the *Times* reminded voters five times—and that was just counting the first two columns on page 1. Reminded Republican voters, that is: "Let no Republican fail to be at the polls before 4 o'clock, as they close at that hour; remember this is a legal holiday; go to the polls early, and then spend the day in seeing that every other Republican votes the right ticket."

According to the *Times*, today was THE LAST CHARGE in the partisan political warfare. Louisiana, voting a day earlier, had vanquished the enemy, handing Grant a thirty-thousand-vote victory. Greeley was on the run, the fate he deserved for supporting secession in 1860 and throwing his lot in with the Ku Klux Klan. Yesterday his Klan friends in Kentucky had hanged a man, his wife, and his daughter simply for being Republican. *Watch out here too*, the *Times* warned. Greeleyism was tottering, but violence and fraud were awaiting their chance. The previous night Greeley men had attacked a Republican parade in Poughkeepsie. In Queen's County, fraudulent voter registrations were running rampant. Fake ballots were floating around to hoodwink Republican voters. *Don't be fooled!*

The *Tribune*, perhaps having more faith in the average voter's intelligence, reminded readers only once of the polling hours. Endorsing its owner, Greeley, the paper sized up the election prospects differently. Its candidate led Louisiana by twenty thousand votes. His breakaway Liberal Republicans had won four of six congressional seats and were running away with state races. All this despite federal troops intimidating voters from supporting the Liberals. The soldiers especially targeted black voters with tactics no different than the KKK. Ohio and Indiana, too, were swinging toward Greeley despite Grant's people dishing out vast amounts of money to pull venal politicians, election officials, and voters to the Republican side. Forget the predictions that Grant's victory was assured, the *Tribune* said. The Liberals' strength was underestimated, and turnout from Democrats supporting Greeley would secure his victory. The *World*, the Democratic Party's organ in the New York press, pitched in to encourage Democrats to vote the Liberal ticket, albeit with more berating of Grant than enthusiasm for Greeley.

As befit its role as camp follower, the *Herald* watched "the great Presidential battle" from the sidelines. Hear the opposing armies pounding on their weapons, giving "dreadful note of preparation," the editors urged readers as they proclaimed their paper independent of the partisans. *We have laid the great and weighty issues before the public,* they added, *and have exposed the intrigues to defraud people of their votes.* Now the citizen would take his turn to cast a ballot for the candidates he judged best. So long as the votes were honestly recorded, the *Herald* was indifferent to the results. "Let the Best Men Win!"

At 6:00 AM, the police force deployed around the city. Four citizens served as Inspectors of Elections at each polling place. Precinct commanders assigned two officers to each site. The officers delivered ballot boxes, protected the inspectors and observers each candidate was allowed, and prevented electioneering within 150 feet of the polling place. When inspectors completed counting, the officers returned locked ballot boxes to the station house.

Other officers kept order in the streets, arrested violators of the election law, and enforced the prohibition against selling or giving away intoxicating liquors. Commissioners stood by in US circuit court to deal with violations.

The Republicans turning out early were sticking with Grant, reports said. Black voters appeared especially enthusiastic. One quoted in the *Evening Post* swore if he had a thousand votes, he would give them all to Grant. Hungarians, Poles, Scandinavians, and Bohemians were voting Republican too. Germans were a mixed bag. Democrats were less than thrilled with their party's choice. Many refused to mark their ballots for any presidential candidate.

By midday, the police were performing commendably. Illegal voters had not swarmed the polls. Police dragged about twenty suspected violators into circuit court only to have the commissioner discharge them. Levi Dodd was a typical case. When the police failed to verify his registration, they asked around the neighborhood. Nobody knew a Mr. Dodd. He turned out to be a fixture of the area, but everybody called him "Old Kaintuck." Who cared about his real name? A more serious violator was a woman demanding to vote for Jimmy O'Brien, the Democrats' candidate for mayor. Officers hauled her away.

The police failed in one area, though. Drunks reeled through the streets. The fronts of saloons might be shuttered, but steady traffic traveled through the side doors. The flow of liquor hadn't led to much disturbance, and as far as the press could tell, the liquor wasn't buying votes. Rumor of one murder circulated. Whether the man was shot dead with a gun or a sling shot was in dispute. Investigating police learned the victim was an intoxicated Irishman who stumbled into an iron railing and fractured his skull. Hopes rose that the day might end without criminal bloodshed.

When the polls closed, crowds gathered around Printing House Square. The streets were a cauldron of rich and poor, friend and foe, sober and drunk, celebrating and disgusted. Police collared agitators threatening to turn the brew toxic. Thousands peered at the bulletin boards where papers posted returns.

Uptown a more refined crowd gathered around the Fifth Avenue Hotel, where the *Times* offered a special treat. The paper had laid a wire from its editorial room downtown to the Stereopticon Advertising Company opposite the hotel. As soon as editors received dispatches from around the country, they telegraphed them to the company. Writers transcribed the returns onto glass and slid them into the stereopticon. This contraption projected the election results in immense characters visible from the hotel vestibule. Men shouted, waved hats, and bawled in a Babel of voices, thrilled with both the medium and the message.

The next morning the *Times* patted itself on the back for how this marvelous innovation had enthralled its beholders. Mostly though, the paper gloated over the enormous victory of the Republican standard-bearer and his party. Its artists had started ridiculing Liberals the night before, flashing impromptu cartoons through the stereopticon with titles like HORACE GONE WEST, HIS HANGERS-ON, and a dozen other depictions of Greeley's checkered political career. The morning edition laughed at the disgusted crowd in front of the *Tribune* office slinking away. The *World* was so embarrassed over Greeley's defeat it couldn't bring itself to post the bad tidings until far into the night.

The *Times* carried on this way for days. In the wake of his complete rout, the graceless Greeley blamed everyone but himself. He described his whole army of followers as a pack of dirty, venal, cowardly, unprincipled scamps. They had scented the moneybags his enemies brought in. "There was nothing purchasable in the Keystone State that was not bought, whether of voters, electioneerers, or inspectors," the *Times* charged Greeley with saying. As for the Democrats who were supposed to support him, they were bought up like so many cattle. The *Times* wondered how anyone could argue with the words it gave the defeated candidate. If his supporters hadn't been of such a character, they never would have backed Greeley in the first place. Besides, Greeley had sold out his principles and the record of his whole life for the glittering prize of the presidency. Why shouldn't his supporters sell out for a little ready cash to save them from starving?

The *Times* dismissed its other rivals with equally scathing editorials. For backing Greeley, the *World* was "destitute of principle, honor, and ability" and "as much open to purchase as a horse at a fair." The *Herald* had backed so many defeated candidates for so many years, it might as well "confine its attentions henceforth to the Imam of Muscat. It is no good nearer home."

Better to be graceless in overwhelming victory than in defeat, and no one could dispute this victory was overwhelming. Grant won 56 percent of the vote and 81 percent of the Electoral College. The Republicans won supermajorities in both houses of

Congress. In New York State they regained the governorship and large majorities in the legislature. Every citywide office went Republican. In one, Anthony Comstock got a new friend on the New York Supreme Court with the election of Noah Davis, formerly the US Attorney. Tammany Democrats elected a measly six aldermen. Greeley's Liberals were shut out but for five seats in the New York Assembly and a single US congressman.

Greeley had a small consolation. New York City and Brooklyn handed him local victories of twenty-three thousand and four thousand votes. They were of course meaningless, as were the six states he won. A Chicago paper offered the loser another consolation: "He is not the worst beaten individual. . . . Victoria Woodhull did not get any states at all."

Even Woodhull's running mate fared better than she. Frederick Douglass won as an at-large elector for New York State. He would vote for Grant in the Electoral College.

––––––––––

Under the Election Day headline TODAY'S BREAKFAST TABLE, the *Times* urged women to throw their weight around to elect Grant. *So what if you don't get to vote; you control those who do,* insisted the paper. Surely no woman who had lost a husband or father or brother or son in the war could wish he spilled his blood in vain. *Make every man you can sway—and there are few you can't—promise to vote for Grant.*

Susan B. Anthony was putting up with none of that patronizing. She was going to the polls. She had been thinking about it for years. Her rigorous travel had previously prevented her from being home for thirty days leading up to an election, the residency requirement within an election district. This year she stayed in Rochester and qualified.

On November 1, Anthony gathered documents proving her right to vote. She intended to assert that right under the US Constitution's Fourteenth Amendment. She had effectively expelled Victoria Woodhull from the suffrage movement, but she hadn't rejected the argument Woodhull presented to the House Judiciary Committee almost two years earlier.

Anthony led her sisters to a barber shop, which was doubling as the registry office of the first election district of Rochester's Eighth Ward. She asked the gentlemen present whether this was the place to register. Mr. Beverly Jones, the chair of the three-member board of inspectors for the district, said it was. Several men watched, inspectors Edwin Marsh and William Hall, two federal supervisors of elections, a marshal, and a poll watcher employed by the Democratic Party.

She and her sisters would like their names registered, Anthony said. Jones informed her that as she was a woman, the New York State Constitution did not allow it.

She didn't claim any rights under the New York Constitution, Anthony said, nor was she appearing as a female. She was presenting herself as a citizen of the United

States and asserting her rights under the US Constitution. Was Jones conversant with the Fourteenth Amendment? she asked.

Jones was. A debate ensued between Anthony, the inspectors, and the federal supervisors. Anthony read the amendment and argued its points. Jones and Marsh came around. The third inspector, Hall, argued back. One federal supervisor could see no grounds for not registering the ladies. Hall relented since the supervisor was a respected friend. Anthony became the twenty-second registered voter in the district.

Anthony walked away amazed. She had hardly imagined prevailing. A denial would have served her goal, enabling an appeal to the federal courts as a test case. The act of voting, successful or not, promised more. Could she really get away with it?

Anthony carried her documents to Henry Selden, a leading Rochester attorney. She asked for a legal opinion—was she entitled to vote? Selden promised an answer before the election. Irrespective of his answer, Anthony resolved to cast her ballots. She wouldn't be alone. When registrations closed, eligible voters in the Eighth Ward's first district included fifteen women. In all the wards in Rochester, fifty women registered.

On Monday, Selden assured Anthony she was as lawful a voter as himself. Tuesday morning, Anthony appeared at the polls with several others. Inspectors Jones and Marsh were willing to proceed. The third, Hall, again protested. As the argument heated up, Hall was ready to throttle his colleagues. Finally, reason prevailed. The inspectors voted, and Hall acknowledged that majority ruled. The three men were caught between a rock and a hard place no matter what. Whether they denied an eligible person or allowed an ineligible one, they were liable.

Immediately another barrier arose. Anthony had been challenged, Jones told her. Although the law did not allow inspectors to identify the challenger, Sylvester Lewis was standing there. He was the poll watcher for the Democratic Party who had seen her register.

Anthony accepted the challenge. Jones presented a Bible. Anthony placed her hand upon it. "Do you swear that you will fully and truly answer all such questions as shall be put to you touching your place of residence and qualifications as an elector?" Jones asked. Anthony swore yes. Jones asked questions about residence and citizenship. Hearing the answers, Jones found no qualifications in which Anthony was deficient.

Jones turned to Sylvester Lewis and asked if he renewed his challenge. He did. If she persisted in her claim to vote, Jones told Anthony, she would have to take the general oath in the election law. Back came the Bible. "Do you swear that you are twenty-one years of age, that you have been a citizen of the United States for ten days, and an inhabitant of this state for one year next preceding this election, and for the last four months a resident of this county, and for thirty days a resident of this election district, and that you have not voted at this election?" Jones asked.

Anthony answered yes. Lewis threatened to round up twenty Irish women to offset these women if they voted. But the law was the law, and the general oath satisfied its requirements. Anthony handed her ballots to the inspectors for the seat in the Twenty-Ninth US Congressional District, New York State's at-large congressional seat, New York statewide offices, a seat in the New York Assembly, and electors to the Electoral College. With the ballots folded in half, no one could see which candidates she favored. The inspectors deposited the ballots in their respective boxes.

The women accompanying Anthony repeated the process. The news flashed across the country. Even the patronizing *New York Times* lauded Anthony's leadership, with one caveat. The editors assumed the "ladies at Rochester showed their capacity for an intelligent exercise of the franchise by voting for Grant."

That evening Anthony wrote Elizabeth Cady Stanton. She had gone and done it, she told her friend. She had been on the go constantly for five days. Now she was so tired. But it was worth all the effort. If the suffrage women worked to this end, what strides they would make.

Her ordeal was just beginning.

22 | "THE RED TROPHY OF HER VIRGINITY"

THE SATURDAY MORNING AFTER ELECTION DAY, William Howe eyed his wardrobe. Yesterday, for the first day of examination in the Luther Challis libel suit, he had wrapped a green waistcoat around his middle and donned a purple jacket. He had selected pantaloons striped with green. Today's morning papers entertained readers with how he'd fiddled with this outfit whenever Luther Challis professed innocence of any manly passions that might lead him to associate with less-than-reputable ladies. Had Challis known any ladies at the French Ball, for example? No, Challis had perhaps seen some of them on the street before, perhaps he had spoken to them, but known, no. Howe had glanced down at his belly and jerked his waistcoat to straighten its wrinkles.

Have you ever met any of those ladies in Twenty-Sixth Street?

No.

In Thirteenth?

No, sir.

In Thirtieth or Thirty-First or Thirty-Fourth? Had Challis been in any houses along those streets?

Challis sneered distastefully at the imputation that he visited brothels. Howe queried again in a manner too blunt for the assistant district attorney prosecuting the case to keep his seat. Nor was that question the only time the man jumped up to object "in the name of the decency of judicial proceedings." Ultimately Challis admitted to attending the ball with his friend James Maxwell, to joining Tennie Claflin in a box, and yes, to two young ladies having been present. They had shared a tiny quantity of wine, he said, and he had later seen one of the ladies on Broadway—several times, in fact. But he denied any impropriety at the French Ball or later on or, for that matter, ever, with those ladies or any others.

Today's proceedings promised to be yet more entertaining. Howe chose an outfit of a richly hued Scotch plaid. He attached a brilliant diamond to his breast that would twinkle so incessantly as to befuddle any prosecution witness about to utter words objectionable to the defense. A perfect taunt for that holier-than-thou prig Anthony Comstock, who would testify.

About half past two, Howe pranced into the Jefferson Market police court, playing a courteous gallant defending the fortunes of innocent damsels. Three knights followed in his wake, Abe Hummel and two junior attorneys. Howe greeted Woodhull and Claflin. The sisters had risen late, exempt from the rules of Warden Tracy's Hotel. After breakfast, Woodhull read news from across the country to visiting friends. Whether from the camaraderie of the morning, this respite from the walls of Ludlow, or the opportunity to tell their story on the stand, she and Claflin appeared jolly. The *Sunday Mercury* described Claflin as ready "for a thousand years of earthly free-love," Woodhull with "a spiritual glow on her cheeks as if ready to be transported like the Prophet Elijah right up through the clouds."

Officers escorted Colonel Blood in. He looked haggard from his less-desirable accommodations in the local holding tank. Only he was the subject of today's hearing. Since the ladies' federal confinement had prevented them being served in the libel case, they appeared only in defense of Blood, specifically to tell the court he played no role beyond employee at *Woodhull & Claflin's Weekly*. The two names on the masthead were solely responsible for its content.

Colonel James H. Blood, Victoria Woodhull's husband, whom Anthony Comstock could not identify as the defendant in court.
Missouri History Museum

The paper wetter involved in the printing of the alleged libel of Challis was the first witness. Comstock was the second, identified by reporters as the obscene literature prosecutor and agent of the Young Men's Christian Association. During his examination by the assistant district attorney, Comstock described himself simply as a resident of Brooklyn who did business in Manhattan. He had gone to the office of Woodhull, Claflin & Company on Friday, November 1, where he had seen the sisters who published the paper bearing their names. He'd seen Colonel Blood too. Three hundred copies of the *Weekly* lay in the window. He bought one.

Are you an amateur? Howe asked him during the cross-examination.

An amateur? What would that be in a case like this? Comstock wondered. He didn't know the meaning of the word. His role in cases of this sort was simply as a witness in court in regard to the selling of obscene literature.

Howe was skeptical. *Haven't you prosecuted certain persons for selling obscene literature? Haven't you filed complaints against many persons for doing so? And earned money from it?*

Comstock admitted he had visited the district attorney regarding such prosecutions. As complainant he was in some cases entitled to half the fines upon conviction. But never once had he asked for or received his share. He had made arrests but always under whatever law was surest to procure conviction, never because a law promised him the greatest financial reward.

And did you not file a complaint that led to the indictment of the two ladies Victoria Woodhull and Tennie Claflin for sending obscene literature through the mail, and did you not coordinate that action with Henry Ward Beecher and his associates, and did you not also communicate with Luther Challis regarding his libel suit against those two ladies and Colonel Blood?

Never had he been before the grand jury that indicted the ladies, Comstock swore. Never had he seen Beecher in reference to the case, nor had he consulted with any of Beecher's friends, nor ever spoken with Challis about his libel suit. Left unsaid was his appearance before Commissioner Osborn armed with an affidavit signed by a clerk of the *Independent* and another describing a package marked M. Hamilton, the initial and maiden name of his wife. Howe let that go and moved on to Comstock's visit to Woodhull, Claflin & Company.

Where was Colonel Blood during your visit? Howe asked.

On a sofa in front of the door, Comstock recalled.

Could the witness please identify Colonel Blood in court?

Comstock looked around. Howe asked again. And again, and again. *I cannot do so,* Comstock admitted.

Who did you buy the paper from? Howe asked.

From Miss Claflin.

Please point to her.

"She is the individual at your left, sir."

"What?" Howe said, expressing considerable irritation at Comstock referring to his client as "the individual."

"The individual at your left."

Howe turned to the judge. "Your Honor, when I represent a lady in a court of law I would like to have her treated as such."

Hissing erupted. The judge pounded his gavel. When order was restored, Howe asked one more question.

Can you point to a line in the copy of the Weekly *that can be taken as obscene?*

Out of order, the judge ruled. The proceedings before this court related not to whether any content was obscene but whether any libeled Luther Challis. Howe held his fire. He had damaged Comstock's credibility enough for one day. Now he would enjoy another crack at the purity of the life Challis claimed to lead.

When Challis took the stand, Howe asked, "Do you know a Mr. Cutler in Eighth Street?"

Yes, Challis said, he was a tailor, and yes, he furnished undergarments. Challis had gotten some there himself.

"Did you ever order any undergarments for Miss Claflin?"

No, never.

Howe addressed the court. "I propose to show that the complainant ordered a pair of drawers for Miss Claflin, and had them made for and sent home to her."

"Not a word of truth in that thing from beginning to end," Challis said. "False as hell."

The judge chastised Howe. "That question must be struck out. Further examination in that line is excluded."

"That is to say, Miss Claflin's drawers are to be struck," Howe said, and then continued in the same vein. "Did you ever order a bedstead for Miss Claflin?"

After that question was struck, "Did you ever kiss Miss Claflin?" Again, struck.

"Did you ever say to any person at the Hoffman House that what you disclosed on your finger was ink and not blood?"

Before judge or prosecutor could intervene, Challis spit out a lengthy denial of ever exhibiting his finger as the libelous article claimed. It was a lie beginning to end, fabricated by enemies with a vendetta against him. Howe had no more questions for this witness. He would revive his theme with another waiting in the wings.

That witness would have to wait until Woodhull and Claflin took their turns. The purpose of their testimony was to convince the court that Colonel Blood had not acted as their agent. He had no more role in the paper's production than any of their servants about the office, they testified. Like others, he received a salary—nominal, in his case. But he shared none of the profits. As such, Blood was not responsible if the paper contained a libel. Only the sisters could be held to account.

Once on the stand, Woodhull seized the opportunity to attack. After the French Ball, Challis became a frequent visitor to their home in Murray Hill, she said. He boasted of seducing young girls. Though the judge interrupted her description of the ball as indecent, he allowed her to relate her later conversation with Challis regarding it. She had witnessed terrible debauchery that night at the Academy of Music, she had said to Challis. The men attending debauched society, damned women, and sent them into the world as prostitutes. So he had seduced a young girl at the ball, Challis had responded. What Woodhull had seen was an everyday occurrence at the academy involving the most prominent men in the city, he had told her. Every brothel had standing orders for "spring chickens," girls as young as twelve. He himself preferred to seduce maidens, he had said, and he was doing society a good when he did. Never had he seduced a maid but that she wanted it. "You may say what you like about the women," Challis had told her, "but you must not make war on the men on this subject. If you do, they'll crush you."

The sisters' friend and fellow suffragist Laura Cuppy Smith added to the story as the next witness. She had visited Murray Hill to find Tennie Claflin dressed for an evening out with Challis. When that gentleman arrived, he said, *Tennie, you look charming*, and kissed her. The couple sat together "very familiarly"—so familiarly that he greeted Annie Claflin with "Good evening, Mother."

With Challis's reputation suffering, Howe at last called his witness from the wings. James Maxwell was the man with Challis at the French Ball. Today he had little to say about that evening. But he recalled another when he and his friend had visited a house on Thirty-Fourth Street. There they met two girls from Baltimore.

"Did you ever hear Mr. Challis say anything about a red trophy?" Howe asked him.

Yes, a few days after that evening on Thirty-Fourth Street, Maxwell testified. He was at the Hoffman House with a few others. Challis bragged about a maid he had seduced. He held up his finger. He called the stain upon it "the red trophy of her virginity."

The next day's papers had a field day with Challis's sexual exploits—Claflin's underwear, debauchery at the French Ball, deflowering maidens for the good of society. But none of the papers would quote the offensive words Challis allegedly used to describe his finger, the ones the federal obscenity charge would ultimately come down to. The *Herald* came closest, saying Maxwell repeated "words that were imputed to [Challis] in the libel." That paper's restraint came a bit late. Several days before, it had printed the complaint Challis filed to commence his libel suit. That filing included the allegedly libelous article in full. Any tender readers who would object to words about a red trophy and a girl's virginity had already seen them.

Unfortunately for Colonel Blood, the evidence that the article was true rather than libelous did no good. In this hearing, the only question was whether Blood was a principle in *Woodhull & Claflin's Weekly* and therefore responsible for what it published.

Determination of libel would occur at trial. Within the week, the judge ruled the case would go forward. He committed Blood to Jefferson Market until such time as the prisoner could produce $5,000 bail.

As November waned, Woodhull grew antsy in the confines of Ludlow Street jail—the American Bastille, as she called it. The hospitality was startlingly pleasant. Tennie and her daughter, Zulu Maude, were loving companions. Friends like Laura Cuppy Smith visited often. She made new ones, too, like George Francis Train, the eccentric who had offered bail the day of her arrest. His anecdotes enlivened their stay several times a week. Several other gentlemen offered solidarity along with financial and legal aid. Three weeks in, her husband, Colonel Blood, bailed from Jefferson Market but immediately rearrested, joined them at Ludlow.

Kind notes poured in from around the country. True, many formerly loyal friends had slinked away, fearing an association would blacken their reputations. But strangers wrote of the courage she and Claflin showed, of their certainty that the *Weekly* contained not a word of obscenity, of how the *Weekly* was the finest advocate of reform ever issued. *Use our names, publish our letters, if they are any help*, writers urged.

In the month since it went to press, "The Beecher-Tilton Scandal" had swept across the country in a firestorm. Newspapers ran hundreds of stories, riveting the public from the largest cities to one-horse towns. Though many writers hurled every epithet at the sisters, from *harlot* and *prostitute* to *degraded brute*, defenders appeared in unexpected quarters. The *Hartford Times* decried US marshals putting irons around people they wanted to crush, like Woodhull and Claflin for their remarkable article on Beecher, rarely matched in the history of journalism. Syracuse's *Sunday Morning Herald* shouted shame on the headlines that rained calumny on Woodhull for ostensibly mailing obscene literature but really for telling the truth about a famous divine. Beecher's hometown paper the *Brooklyn Eagle* called the incarceration of Woodhull and Claflin a gross blunder. Beecher must deny the charges or sue for libel—or expect the public to believe him guilty, the editors said.

Beecher had uttered only one word to protest his innocence, and that only when a reporter caught up with him and asked, "Mr. Beecher, this thing is a fraud from beginning to end?" "Entirely," Beecher said. The single word carried little weight outside of Plymouth Church. He couldn't brush the scandal off with a wave of the hand.

And what of the sources Woodhull had named—Tilton, Moulton, Paulina Davis, Elizabeth Cady Stanton, Beecher's sister Isabella? many papers asked. Each could refute what Woodhull attributed to them. Their silence spoke volumes.

So fellowship wasn't lacking within Ludlow. Its walls chafed because martyrdom was not enough. In refusing to post bail, Woodhull had kept her persecution in the limelight. The glare of injustice shined brighter and brighter as the weeks passed. But sitting within prison walls and speaking through reporters was hardly carrying the battle forward. Early on, Woodhull wrote a letter to the *Herald*. She was sick in body, mind, and heart, locked away with no justice because she was a woman, unable to reach the public. It came across as self-pity. Halfway through the month, she tried a second letter. Gone were cries of unjust treatment. Woodhull argued her case for social revolution. She reminded readers that for centuries the world had resisted revolutionary figures but now embraced their preaching—Christ and his apostles, Luther and Calvin, and more recently slavery opponents Frederick Douglass and William Lloyd Garrison. She challenged the public to assess her ideas against their own experiences, to question whether immorality arose from herself, who exposed acts of indecency, or from those who committed them. *Answer these questions*, Woodhull insisted, *then condemn me if you will. But be warned.* If she were crushed as a martyr, it would not be in a jail cell. She would mount the ramparts and fight to her last breath, and then from the ashes of her body a thousand Victorias would spring to carry her banner to victory.

William Howe needed the rest of November to bail the sisters out of Ludlow. Assistant US Attorney Davies resisted any reduction in the amount, then declined to accept residents of Brooklyn as sureties. After Howe relented on the amount and Davies on the sureties, Howe negotiated on the state criminal libel case pending in Jefferson Market and then on a civil libel suit Luther Challis also filed. Finally, on December 3, Woodhull and Claflin posted bail before the US commissioner. Jefferson Market police immediately rearrested them. A state judge standing by took more bail. Then officers marched the women across the street to the sheriff's office, where they posted a third round in the civil suit. With their sureties guaranteeing over $50,000, the sisters walked free.

With the district attorney throwing up roadblocks, Howe needed another two weeks to free Colonel Blood. Meanwhile Woodhull and Claflin began work on the next issue of the *Weekly*. The supposedly obscene issue was "red hot," Woodhull said before her release. "Their next shall be at white heat."

23 | "THEY TREAT ME THERE LIKE A DOG"

WILLIAM HOWE NEVER GAVE UP ON A CLIENT, not even if the client gave up on him. Jacob Rosenzweig was a case in point. The Fiend of Second Avenue, who had stuffed Alice Bowlsby into a trunk when his botched abortion killed her, had been in Auburn Prison two months when he turned on his attorney. Back in January a reporter from the *Sun* found him dishing slop onto plates in the dining room. "How do you like it here?" he asked.

Rosenzweig liked it fine at Auburn, much more than Sing Sing, where he had first gone. "They treat me there like a dog," he said. "But, oh, my family, I cannot hear from them." He had left his wife and children with his hated stepmother in a hovel on Bayard Street. His wife visited once, but the guards took her away after fifteen minutes. He could say hardly anything. And "Oh! Seven year—seven year—seven year! Mein Gott!" If his attorney Howe was worth anything, he'd get a new trial. Rosenzweig knew nothing about the death of that girl and ought to have been acquitted.

"Don't you think Mr. Howe has been doing you justice?"

Rosenzweig sneered. "Justice! I'm damn sorry I had a lawyer at all. The Court was bound to furnish one for me, and there my wife went and give Howe $500 when she needed the money. He didn't do a damn thing for me."

Yet a full year after Rosenzweig's conviction, Howe was still earning that $500. While Victoria Woodhull sat in Ludlow Street jail, the attorney she and Rosenzweig shared appeared in the New York Supreme Court to argue his client in Auburn Prison deserved a new trial.

With Howe's friends Judges Cardozo and Barnard chased off the court, two other judges had joined his old colleague Judge Ingraham. Point one, Howe told them, no evidence showed that Bowlsby was with child. Points two and three, the charge to the jury erred in stating that they could not convict of a lesser crime, nor was the onus on the defendant to prove that the malpractice was necessary to preserve the life of the mother, as the judge had ruled. Finally, the witness Nettie Willis, who had testified that Rosenzweig performed an abortion on her two years earlier, was inadmissible. Under cross-examination, Rosenzweig had previously denied knowing Willis, and as her claim was disconnected to the facts of the case, she could not be introduced to impeach the defendant's prior testimony.

The court bought only the last point. The admission of such testimony was "an error, upon well-established authority," the judges concluded. Once again, Howe had worked his magic. Rosenzweig would get a new trial. Howe immediately dispatched Rosenzweig's wife with the sheriff to retrieve his client from Auburn Prison. When Rosenzweig appeared a few days later in the Court of General Sessions, his wife and daughter clutched his manacled hands. Judge Bedford committed him to the Tombs to await a trial, expected in January.

Howe had other plans for his client, however ungrateful the man might be.

When Ned Stokes read about William Howe's machinations to free Woodhull and Rosenzweig, he must have wondered whether he would ever see the light of day. He had great hopes when his jury hung, if not to go free without retrial, at least to post bail. In his dreamier moments, he pictured himself recuperating in Europe. Day after day the papers reported his attorneys almost ready to apply for bail. Day after day those attorneys dawdled. Stokes watched from the Tombs as the hallboys testifying against him were bailed from the House of Detention, the handiwork of Howe. Then Howe's partner, Hummel, secured the discharge of a witness in Stokes's favor, the boy who testified that eyewitness Thomas Hart had lied for a bribe. Yet still, Stokes's team did not act.

Three weeks after Stokes's trial had ended, his attorneys delivered the bad news. If Stokes sought bail, the district attorney would request a change of venue for the second trial. They vehemently opposed a change. Stokes must stay locked up.

His cell felt like a tomb. In its dampness, wallpaper peeled, mildew grew. Asthma and bronchitis attacked him. His family physician and two other doctors agreed he was neither healthy nor safe. Attaching their affidavits, his attorneys requested a move to a drier place as was available in the wing for boys. In the name of humanity, they pleaded, only to have the Tombs physician accuse Stokes of faking his sickness. All his life Stokes had enjoyed vigorous activity in the open air. Here the warden didn't permit him so much as the prison yard, nothing but a stroll in the corridor outside his cell. Finally he was allowed a cold plunge bath each morning. It alone kept him alive as his confinement lengthened to almost a year.

Stokes turned to poetry and literature to get through the days. Walt Whitman's *Leaves of Grass* was a favorite, and Sir Walter Scott's *Marmion*. Slippers, suits, and silk scarves, a few items of toilet, were among his few luxuries. A diamond to wear on his bosom when visitors called. Friends, reporters, anyone to talk to lifted his spirits.

In darker moments he railed against the injustice of his situation. He had begged for a new trial since July. The district attorney promised early fall. His attorneys demanded a date. Maybe in the October term of the Court of Oyer and Terminer, the DA agreed, but when that month ended even the judge was so frustrated that he considered extending the term. But he didn't, and the DA ginned up some excuse for November. The delays were an outrage upon the public laws. It was no surprise, though. Fisk and Gould and their cronies had plundered $50 million from the Erie Railroad. Stokes could name every man implicated in the theft. That's why Fisk had come after him, like he had attacked all his enemies, doing them in with his cold and clammy touch. The man's hatred had nothing to do with Josie Mansfield. Stokes hardly knew the woman. Now Gould and the other cronies were keeping Stokes behind bars for fear he'd tell all to the legislature. Why shouldn't the DA go along? He had no case, especially not since a new witness emerged, a *Times* reporter who may not have seen everything start to finish but had heard the shots and seen Fisk staggering with a pistol in his hand. Yes, the shooting was self-defense, and the DA knew it. But if he could delay until the end of the year, his newly elected replacement would inherit the problem.

And what about Stokes's family? This ordeal was driving his father to penury. Rich uncles and cousins helped with legal expenses, but how could they alleviate the emotional toll?

Then, in November, another tragedy. His brother Clinton, an exemplary youth, a Sunday school teacher at his Baptist church, an officer of the Young Men's Christian Association, died at age twenty-six. As Clinton neared the end, the sheriff consented to let Stokes go and speak with his brother a last time, if only the DA agreed. The DA agreed, but he refused to sign the document that would open the prison doors. Ned could exchange no final goodbyes nor mourn with his family nor whisper comforting words to his dear mother, who surely felt she was losing a second son.

24 | "A GROSS SCANDAL ... HELPED BY A GROSS BLUNDER"

THE *BROOKLYN EAGLE* proclaimed itself the largest circulation evening newspaper in the United States. It was a staple for the four hundred thousand people living in the country's third-largest city. One of those reading the Friday edition in the middle of November was Anthony Comstock. The more he read, the angrier he grew.

The serious news began on page 2. In its upper left corner, the headline ran How a Gross Scandal Has Been Helped by a Gross Blunder. The scandal referred to the charges "two women of bad reputation" published against Henry Ward Beecher, Theodore Tilton, and others. With proper reaction, the scandal would have died a quick death, the editors concluded. Had the parties simply paid no attention, the public would have disbelieved it on the basis of its principal target's character during his twenty-five years as Brooklyn's leading pastor. A robust denial would have accomplished the same. Or if the affected parties desired an airing of the facts, a libel case could demonstrate the falsity of the claims.

The gross blunder was the federal action against the women that precluded those options. The arrest of Woodhull and Claflin for mailing obscene literature turned scornful inattention to the matter into a national spectacle. The case no longer centered on whether the journal published lies but on the language it used. An obscenity charge neither required the ladies to substantiate their assertions nor allowed those named to refute them. Their jailing and denial of a timely trial instilled a perception of persecution in the mind of the public.

Furthermore, the federal government had no more business in this case than in feeding and clothing all its citizens. The article held nothing obscene. The US prosecutor offered a grossly ignorant statement in asserting the government should protect the reputation of a citizen. The whole affair amounted to a menacing usurpation of federal authority. Today the oppressed was a free lover. Tomorrow it could be an honorable man or woman.

Comstock was reading an indictment not of the ladies' criminal actions but of himself. What was worse, the editors hadn't so much as named him. He had hardly appeared in the New York papers beyond descriptions of his cross-examination by the "Tombs shyster" William Howe. Even Comstock could see the papers treated that testimony with ridicule, not praise.

Comstock wasn't standing for it. He drafted a letter setting the record straight. He instigated the charges, he told the *Eagle*. The case was one of forty or fifty obscenity prosecutions he had instituted to protect public morals. He had no ties to Plymouth Church or to any people connected to it. A friend gave him the *Weekly*. After investigating, he contacted the New York district attorney, who promised to get a warrant. The DA failed to do so by the end of the week. In the meantime, Comstock read the *Weekly* and learned the publisher had issued it through the US mail. He gathered proof and secured a warrant from the federal authorities.

The charge did not involve the story about Beecher. The rest of the paper was so palpably obscene no one could doubt the ladies' guilt. Their trial's delay arose solely because no court was in session for taking up the case. Comstock hoped the *Eagle* would reconsider its views. The law under which the ladies were charged had suppressed a large class of the vilest literature and effected great benefit so far.

The *Eagle* printed Comstock's letter on Tuesday. The editors did not reconsider their views, concluding that the authorities "cannot too soon withdraw themselves from the false position in which the irresponsible action of the more zealous than sensible Comstock has placed them."

Despite the refutation of everything he argued, Comstock could take heart. His name appeared seven times. He was no longer an anonymous figure in the case, and his letter instigated a controversy that raged for days. The *Eagle* printed dueling letters to the editor, along with an editorial that the mail overwhelmingly opposed the sisters' prosecution. The *New York Witness* asserted the *Eagle* "ranged itself" on the side of obscene literature and against Comstock and the public prosecutors. The *Eagle* responded that if money could impart brains to the *Witness*, two cents for a copy of that paper might be justifiable. As for Comstock, the *Eagle* never heard of the man until he "ranged himself" with Woodhull and Claflin as their prosecutor and worldwide advertiser. Even then the paper had not referred to him just as it did not refer to last year's flies.

Beyond a few lines buried in the *World*, none of the major New York newspapers picked up the story. Still, it was a start, and Comstock was cooking up another trick to keep his name in the public eye.

Anthony Comstock kept meticulous records. For each arrest, he documented biographical information from birth and marriage to occupation and religion. He named everyone involved, from victims and accomplices to police officers, marshals, and court officials. He inventoried confiscations. Throughout a case, he noted witnesses, bail, indictments, sentences, and, more times than he liked, culprits going free. He offset those setbacks with others he drove out of business without an arrest, or into an early grave.

As 1872 waned, he combed through his records. Despite the resistance from the fainthearts at the Young Men's Christian Association, his plans for a stronger federal law to fight obscene literature were progressing. An attorney Jesup knew had worked on his draft bill. Now Jesup was introducing him to William Strong, associate justice of the US Supreme Court. Strong was a man of like mind with Comstock when it came to God. Before his appointment to the court, Strong had been president of the National Reform Association and led the fight to write the Almighty into the Constitution. Strong agreed to revamp the bill before its presentation to Congress.

Through an editor he knew, Comstock lined up the support of Connecticut senator William Buckingham. Justice Strong brought on Senator William Windom of Minnesota. New York congressman Clinton Merriam took on the effort in the House of Representatives. Merriam asked Comstock to build a picture of the traffic in obscene literature. What better measured its volume than his successes, Comstock decided.

He wrote to Merriam, explaining that a year earlier he had known only one place carrying on the business. He told the story of William Simpson and how a policeman's betrayal foiled that dealer's arrest. Protesting when Comstock instigated that officer's dismissal, the *Sunday Mercury* clued him in to the smut community around Nassau Street. His crusade started in earnest. He had now seized 180,000 pictures, five tons of books, two tons of unbound sheets, two tons of handbills, catalogs and sheet music, 5,000 microscopic watches, charms and finger rings, 625 negatives, 350 steel and copper plates, 6,000 playing cards, 30,000 immoral rubber articles, names of 6,000 dealers throughout the country, 15,000 letters ordering through the mail. . . . The list went on and on, finally noting Comstock's arrests of more than fifty dealers and culminating with "publishers, manufacturers, and dealers dead since March last, 6."

Comstock had accomplished the work almost single-handedly. *So I know whereof I speak*, he assured Merriam.

The record was too good not to broadcast. Comstock distributed his list to the newspapers. By now the major New York papers were wary and ignored it. But from Connecticut through the Midwest to Arkansas, editors praised his handiwork. One called him "the exterminator of obscene publications . . . a Hercules [battling] the many-headed monster of lasciviousness." Another prayed Comstock could make the fight his life's work.

The fainthearts lined up, or at least fell silent. In mid-December the *New York Times* reported the YMCA was pressing for new legislation to suppress obscene publications in the US mail. Comstock traveled to Washington with Robert McBurney to meet with lawmakers.

25 | "STOP THEIR PRESS, PERHAPS; BUT THEIR TONGUES, NEVER!"

WHEN VICTORIA WOODHULL LEFT THE AMERICAN BASTILLE, Henry Ward Beecher and his scandal were no longer the top story. She was. Newspapers feasted on her. Many vilified, some sympathized, a few praised, she didn't much care which. The exposure of Beecher had ignited the revolution she sought, a war to upend sexual relations and bring about a new social order. That's the banner she hoisted now, and if the press and the public wanted to continue to feed, she would serve up another dish—at white heat.

In little more than two weeks, the next issue of the *Weekly* was ready to come off the boil. Woodhull held no doubt it would race off the stands. Its articles didn't disrobe any more gentlemen, infamous or divine. Instead it presented a story of her revolution that was theatrical in scope. The story encompassed her experiences from the moment she entered business to her persecution for printing the truth. It lauded the forces fighting beside her and berated the enemies rallying against her. It praised heroes and demonized villains, and the grudges seething within, old and new, added to the drama. She called the centerpiece "Moral Cowardice and Modern Hypocrisy; Or Four Weeks in Ludlow-Street Jail."

Woodhull indicted the obvious suspects—the cabal that ran Plymouth Church, the federal prosecutors and justices lumped together as US Government & Co., the press who adjudged her and her conspirators guilty without so much as an examination, the power and money wielding its weight to crush them. She built her most savage ire against a new target, a private citizen of whom she had probably not previously heard and certainly considered beneath her notice.

Woodhull described him as the most sanctimonious individual as could be found in New York. He deceived by his saintlike face. He carried conviction in his very look. He ventured into Broadway concert saloons undercover, ostensibly to find obscene pictures and drink beer served by pretty waiter girls. But always his bearing revealed a desire to unite in prayer.

He had appointed himself generalissimo in the campaign against her and Claflin. He dispatched his stool pigeon to secure their villainous publication and deposit it in the US mail. With his evidence, he repaired to the US court and consummated his plan to capture the offenders.

This special agent of Christ was also the agent of the Young Men's Christian Association to suppress obscene literature, Woodhull wrote. After mocking his actions, she taunted him with his holy book. *Oh, Christian Comstock, can you really prosecute the editors of the* Weekly *for language that is chasteness itself compared to passages in the Bible? Look at Deuteronomy, where father and mother bring forth the token of the damsel's virginity and spread the cloth displaying that token before the elders of the city. Or consider David, who, spying the beautiful Bathsheba, daughter of Eliam, wife of Uriah, lay with her and when she conceived sent her husband to die on the front lines of the hottest battle so that David could take Bathsheba into his house. Or Solomon, who kept seven hundred wives and three hundred concubines. Are these passages and thousands of others in the Bible not more obscene, indecent, and vulgar than anything the* Weekly *printed?*

All the latter-day Christians were shams who had stolen the livery of Christ to serve the devil, Woodhull charged. She challenged them with a wager. She would bet that all the volumes of *Woodhull & Claflin's Weekly* showed more of the teachings of Christ than all the sermons of Henry Ward Beecher. None would take the bet, she predicted. The whole so-called Christian civilization was a fraud.

This is war, she swore to the agent of the Young Men's Christian Association. It would be fought from the pine forests of Maine to the gold mountains of California, from the wheat fields along the Mississippi to the rice plantations of Florida until the despots were swept from their thrones!

As the *Weekly* went to press, Woodhull carried the battle into the heartland of her long-standing enemies, New England's suffragists. The Boston papers ran advertisements for her lecture scheduled for three days before Christmas, with Claflin sharing the platform. "The Distinguished Lady Bankers of Wall street, New York, backed by Commodore Vanderbilt, his Money, his Influence and his advice," would speak on "Moral Cowardice, or Four Weeks in Ludlow-street Jail." As further enticement, the copy added "The United States Court says: 'It is the duty of the Government to protect the reputation of its Revered Citizens.' How about those WHO ARE NOT SO REVERED? Let the people answer. FREEDOM OR DESPOTISM—Which?"

Woodhull caught the train as Claflin and Blood put the *Weekly* to bed. She was giving a solo preview in Springfield three days before Boston. Her agent was finalizing arrangements at Boston Music Hall. Tickets at forty and seventy-five cents brought in hundreds of dollars the day sales began.

As Woodhull checked in to Springfield's Haynes House, the Music Hall's representative informed her agent he could not carry out their contract. The trustees forbade its rental to Woodhull and Claflin. While they discussed the matter in the Music Hall's office, former Massachusetts governor William Claflin, no relation to the sisters, arrived to enforce the decision. "We have bad women enough in Boston now, without permitting this one to come here to further demoralize us," he said. "Why, she might repeat the vile stories about Mr. Beecher, or even attack some of us in Boston. No, sir! . . . This prostitute shall not disgrace this hall or insult this city by speaking in it."

That evening, Woodhull waited in the wings at Springfield's opera house. The gentleman introducing her announced the news she had just learned. Boston had banned the speaker about to come onstage.

The spirits didn't possess Woodhull this evening. She ranged from sarcastic to scornful, occasionally rising to magnetic, but never gripped the audience. The events in Boston had sapped her confidence. Nearing the end though, she singled out the forces trying to crush her: Comstock, Plymouth Church, Government & Co., and now Boston. Her anger burst out with a defiance that saved the night. *We are an indomitable pair, Tennie and I*, she ended. *The* Weekly *shall live, or if it be crushed, we will travel over the country from extreme to extreme, speaking in the street if debarred from halls, but speaking nonetheless.* "Stop their press, perhaps; but their tongues, never!"

Woodhull meant to keep that promise when she traveled to Boston the next day. While she protested to city officials, her agent secured the St. James Theater. But when he applied for the license required for a public lecture, the board of aldermen voted it down. Woodhull offered a printed copy of her speech as proof she would say nothing untoward. With apologies, the chief of police told her if she appeared upon any platform in Boston, he would, under orders, arrest her. Cambridge and Charlestown offered venues. She said no; she would bide her time until the people of Boston rose up and demanded the first and greatest principle of American liberty. As her train for New York pulled out, she promised to return and lecture to one of the largest audiences ever convened in Boston. Free speech demanded it.

Within days, the foregone lecture proved a magnificent triumph. The story of Victoria Woodhull banned in Boston burst across the country. The speech alone would never have spread her name to so many far-off corners.

26 | "THEN IS OUR COUNTRY A DESPOTISM"

TWO DAYS BEFORE CHRISTMAS, Susan B. Anthony went to court for the third time. A deputy marshal had called at her Rochester home a month earlier. He had asked her to accompany him to see Commissioner William C. Storrs of US circuit court.

What for? she asked.

To arrest you, he stammered out.

Anthony wasn't going to resist. She was not, however, going to allow the marshal to treat her with kid gloves because she was a woman. "Is this your usual method of serving a warrant?" she asked.

The marshal pulled out the warrant. While state law governed who could vote, the warrant charged Anthony with a federal crime. Anyone voting "without having a lawful right to vote" violated the Enforcement Act of 1870.

When Anthony asked to change her dress, the marshal said she could come to the courthouse when ready. No, she was not going on her own, she said. He must wait. When she reappeared, she reiterated that she expected a normal arrest—in other words, where were the handcuffs? The marshal put his foot down. He would not manacle a woman. Together they rode a streetcar downtown. After her attorney Henry Selden arrived, Anthony refused to plead. Commissioner Storrs scheduled an examination to determine whether he should detain her pending an indictment.

At the examination several days later, the prosecutor called two election inspectors, a clerk, and the poll watcher Sylvester Lewis, whose complaint had resulted in the warrant. These witnesses confirmed the facts of the case. Anthony was a woman and had dressed as such on Election Day. She had cast ballots. Upon being challenged, she had taken the oaths. The defense said *so what?* No evidence indicated that Anthony had knowingly violated the law, as the Enforcement Act required. When asked whether she held any doubt about her right to vote, Anthony replied, "Not a particle." The commissioner didn't buy it. But he acknowledged the defense's right to argue the point and gave Selden until today's Christmas week hearing to prepare. The other Rochester women who voted were in court too, charged but awaiting the outcome of Anthony's case before being examined.

Selden pursued a three-pronged defense. First, voting was a privilege guaranteed to all citizens by the Fourteenth Amendment. Therefore Anthony was entitled. Second, even if she did not have the right, the law could not convict any person without "the indispensable ingredient of all crime, a corrupt intention." Third, since Anthony believed she had the right, whether correctly or not, she had no corrupt intention to break the law.

The argument for Anthony was straight out of Victoria Woodhull's playbook when she'd spoken before the House Judiciary Committee two years prior. The prosecutor seized on that point. Congress, in the form of reports by Representative John Bingham and Senator Matthew Carpenter, had overtly refuted that argument. Anthony was surely aware. She could not claim ignorance of the law.

The commissioner ruled Anthony and the other women must give bail to appear if the grand jury returned indictments. The others posted $500 apiece. Anthony refused. Commissioner Storrs signed a record of commitment sending her to Albany County jail. He handed her into the custody of a federal marshal, who promptly did not deliver her there. She remained free. This time she did not protest the special treatment.

The sympathetic *Rochester Express* reported that many regarded Anthony as destined for state prison or a heavy fine. Anthony would eagerly risk either punishment to prove whether her rights as a citizen were inherent in the country's democratic institutions or subject to legislative restrictions. "If the former, then is our country free indeed," the paper quoted her. "If the latter, then is our country a despotism, and we women its victims!"

Early in the new year, the grand jury ruled for legislative restrictions and despotism. Its indictment stated that Susan B. Anthony did knowingly, wrongfully, and unlawfully vote for a representative in the Congress of the United States, without having a lawful right to vote, the said Susan B. Anthony being then and there a person of the female sex.

27 | "PARADISE FOR MURDERERS"

NEW YORK was becoming a "paradise for murderers." In no other city on the habitable globe had life ever been so insecure. Every week a villain pulled a knife or cocked a revolver with almost no provocation. A victim screeched, his body jerked, he crumpled. Some people rushed up—had a friend fallen? Others shook their heads and walked on. The more squeamish made for the nearest saloon to wash away the taste of blood. Veteran officers kept their distance. On rare occasions, a greenhorn copper might haul the villain to jail, where he would lodge and board at the expense of honest laborers. A sharp attorney would meet a corrupt judge. A writ of habeas corpus or other invention would release the villain. He would escape the meshes of the law, adding to the criminal recklessness and disregard of human life infesting the city.

Pomeroy's Democrat delivered this damning assessment of the state of New York justice in mid-November. The city's other papers stampeded through the gate *Pomeroy's* opened. "Down with the Assassins!" cried the *Commercial Advertiser.* Murderers must be promptly tried and executed. The blood of many an Abel dripped on the ground, and the city must avenge it. "Reign of Murder!" echoed the *Herald.* Pistol, knife, and bludgeon arbitrated every quarrel, remedied every wrong. "Is hanging for murder played out?" asked the *Tribune.* The murderers were convinced. Even if convicted, who suffered more than a few years in prison before a technicality or pardon freed him? When blood is not avenged, society disintegrates. Hang the murderers!

In less than three years, 130 murderers had killed in the city. Twelve eluded capture. Coroners discharged ten. Sixteen were never indicted. Fourteen were indicted and never tried. After referral to the district attorney, sixteen or seventeen cases simply disappeared. Of five murderers sentenced to prison, only one was for life. Another earned fifteen years, three more not even seven. Yes, some died—one of his wounds, six by their own hands. The number hanged in the last twelve months? One. True, four more were sentenced to the noose, but with appeals pending, would any mount the gallows? The *Evening Post* crunched the numbers to conclude the average punishment for killing a man was three years imprisonment. *Pomeroy's* calculated the chances of a murderer facing death at one in three hundred.

The culprits for this dismal record were many—district attorneys who failed to prosecute, shady lawyers who pettifogged the law, corrupt or incompetent judges who so managed their courts that convictions fell apart on appeal, jurors who could not agree, governors who pardoned after a short stay in Sing Sing. The public, too, was responsible, with its rising sentiment against executing a man.

Whoever deserved blame, the only remedy was swift and certain punishment. Without it, violent men would estimate the consequences of their atrocious misdeeds and conclude the odds favored no punishment at all. With this record, the community just might rise up in self-defense and redress in an hour the accumulated injustices of a decade. A few doses of lamppost hanging administered by indignant citizens might have a good effect, suggested the *Journal of Commerce*.

For the twenty-odd murderers locked in the Tombs during November, the papers made interesting reading. For some, the city's lax administration of justice might raise hopes of walking free with little more than a slap on the wrist. Others might fear that the vengeful sentiments expressed foreshadowed a backlash raining hell upon them.

Whichever way he leaned, Ned Stokes, his trial at last scheduled, could not enjoy reading his name over and over. The papers made him the poster boy of murderers who settled into jail life with cheerful hopes of ultimate release. It shouldn't be, chided the *Herald*. The death penalty was still on the statute books. The hanging of a convicted murderer, rich or poor, was simple justice. The law tried not the purse but the crime. Still, the paper acknowledged an axiom much believed in New York. It was harder to pass a rich man's neck through a hangman's noose than for a camel to pass through the eye of a needle.

The prosecution opened its case against Ned Stokes two days before Christmas. Jury selection had consumed a short four days despite a dustup when a prospect identified himself as an undertaker. Three attorneys for the defense leaped up. The gentleman had a pecuniary interest in the conviction of the prisoner, they charged. Spectators laughed, as did the counsel, the jurors so far selected, and Stokes himself. Judge Douglass Boardman manfully maintained his gravity. Most of the city didn't think the jury mattered anyway. Attorneys on both sides were so skilled in the art of legal humbuggery that twelve men of ordinary mental caliber would be too confused to ever agree.

Stokes had grown stout and gray during his incarceration. An awareness of the ordeal before him displaced his jaunty air of the first trial. He instructed his attorneys to drop the strategy of throwing everything against the wall and to argue that his shooting of Fisk was justifiable homicide. The *World* printed his statement laying out that case. "As God shall judge me," he began, "I did not expect to meet James Fisk that Saturday afternoon." He had been rambling around when they'd come face to face, when Fisk had pulled a pistol. Stokes had seen it plain as day in Fisk's hand, by God, so he'd raised his own pistol, and then Fisk had fired, and he'd fired back. Even then he had no idea he had wounded Fisk, not even when the police later took him for Fisk to identify. He felt almost like making friends with the man. He knew Fisk as well as anyone, the faults and the good stuff. But Fisk had pointed a gun at him, and Stokes would prove it to the world.

William Fullerton, again assisting the prosecution, opened with a brief narration of facts, then launched into a diatribe straight out of the press. *We live in perilous times*, he told the jury. *Scarcely a week goes by without some horrible crime. Bad men congregate here to ply their trades of wickedness and mischief, fearing no retribution. They know death as punishment for murder is a dead letter, or as an assassin recently said, hanging is played out here.* If the situation continued, anarchy and bloodletting would engulf the city. Bad men must pay. He who took a life must yield his own. Only with death as its cost would the bloodletting stop. Fullerton then laid the entire responsibility on the twelve men in the jury box. If they listened to flimsy excuses or threadbare stories of insanity or self-defense, bad men would turn to the gun or the knife with impunity, jails would fill, laws would be nullified, the city would be disgraced. *You must take courage and perform your duty*, he told the gentlemen who would decide Stokes's fate.

The statement had nothing to do with the innocence or guilt of the man on trial. Still, it was inflammatory enough to be more interesting than the rest of the prosecution's case. Witness after witness trooped to the stand to recite the same testimony as in the first trial. After a couple of days, the papers described the trial as barren of dramatic interest, scarcely enlivened by a single interesting incident. Half the usual spectators showed up. Little improved when the defense took its turn. At least the attorneys exchanged the first trial's tedious medical testimony for new witnesses swearing Fisk had carried a gun. After rebuttal by the prosecution, the Fisk gun debate was tied four witnesses to four. No physical evidence decided the issue.

Not even Josie Mansfield stirred things up. She had slipped off to Paris to study for the French stage. The most excitement in the closing summations was the defense claiming that Fisk had been such a despicable character, perhaps a Higher Power took control of Stokes and the pistol did a justifiable act. Stokes's counsel stopped short of asking the jury to acquit God or the pistol.

When the case wrapped up, the New Year had passed. The day was Saturday, January 5, 364 days since Stokes had shot Fisk. The *Tribune* breathed a sigh of relief. The trial would be forever ended, for whether the verdict be acquittal or disagreement of the jury, the case would never be tried again. The editors discounted any possibility of conviction.

At 8:10 that evening, the jury retired to deliberate. Over the next three hours, reporters scribbled. Spectators slept on the benches. The judge dined at Delmonico's, reportedly with attorneys from both sides. Walking to and fro with his cousins, Stokes seemed sanguine, believing the jury would set him free with acquittal or win him release on bail if unable to agree. He ate a plate of oysters. Afterward, his cousin Henry prepared a bail bond to file should the jury hang. Stokes didn't want to spend a moment longer in a Tombs cell.

At 11:09, the jury filed back in. The judge asked, "Gentlemen, have you agreed upon a verdict?"

"We have," said the foreman.

The clerk asked the jurors to rise and look upon the prisoner, and the prisoner to rise and look upon the jury. "What say you, gentlemen of the jury? Do you find the prisoner at the bar, Edward S. Stokes, guilty or not guilty?" he asked.

"Guilty of murder in the first degree," said the foreman.

Monday morning, Stokes stood again before Judge Boardman. *The court orders you taken to the Tombs until February 28*, Boardman told Stokes, and "upon that day, between the hours of 11 o'clock in the morning and 3 o'clock in the afternoon, you be hanged by the neck until you are dead, and may God have mercy on your soul."

28 | "WHAT CAN I DO, WHAT CAN I DO?"

THE REVEREND HENRY WARD Beecher told his flock to have no fear if troubles come, not to worry when it is just as easy to be happy and trust in God. But when his own trials became too much to bear, he turned to Frank Moulton. This friend was the only man on the globe he could talk to at times—not his wife nor children nor brothers and sisters nor members of his church—not another human being. Without Moulton's trust and love, the preacher would have been totally alone and that would have killed him.

Two years earlier Moulton came to Beecher's home at a time of crisis. "What can I do, what can I do?" Beecher asked. Moulton said, "Mr. Beecher, I am not a Christian, but if you wish I will show you how well a heathen can serve you." The crisis was a lot of foolishness—Theodore Tilton had told Beecher his wife had confessed their adultery, threatening to expose the preacher unless he resigned from his church. Henry Bowen had egged Tilton on, carrying an accusatory letter to Beecher's home, then turning on Tilton and threatening to fire him from the editorships of Bowen's papers if he pursued the matter. Beecher had snuck into Lib Tilton's bedroom to demand she deny any impropriety. Moulton negotiated an armistice between the parties lest the scandal erupt before the public. That's the kind of man he was, stepping up to prevent what he considered a national calamity, one that would wipe out Beecher's beneficent power for good in the country, blast the prospects of the brilliant young Tilton and blight his family, and indeed undermine the very foundations of the social order.

When the truce broke down a year later, Moulton again brought the parties together. He convinced each how much he had to lose, laid out the mechanism through which each could immunize himself from the others. His arbitration resulted in the "tripartite covenant," signed by Tilton, Bowen, and Beecher, removing "all causes of offense existing between us, real or fancied." Whenever grievances resurfaced, Moulton threatened and wheedled to keep the scandal under wraps.

God looked down from Heaven and sent this man to serve me, Beecher wrote. Was it not an intimation of God's intent of mercy that he had such a tried and proven friend?

Mr. Beecher at Different Ages.
(1) At 23 years of age. (2) At 32. (3) At 40. (4) At 52. (5) At 65.

Henry Ward Beecher at Different Ages.
Lyman Abbott, DD, Henry Ward Beecher,
A Sketch of His Career, *1883*

So when a man from the *Brooklyn Eagle* told Beecher that *Woodhull & Claflin's Weekly* had broken the scandal open, Beecher sought his friend. He had an inkling the story was coming out, Beecher told Moulton. A distressed gentleman had called on him days before wondering whether its publication could be stopped. Beecher had guessed the man was just nosing around and put it out of his mind. Now he despaired. *Keep silent,* Moulton advised. *Silence will kill it.* They debated it, just the two of them, and at the end of a week could find no better approach. Let Beecher's past life answer for him. It would overcome any evil effect among the public. To people asking privately, Moulton would say that if the story was true, it was infamous to tell, and if false, it was diabolical to have told it. A judicious reply, Beecher agreed. The strategy worked with several people, and when a few pressed him, Moulton denied outright that Beecher was an impure man.

Tilton, lecturing in New Hampshire, heard nothing until he returned to Brooklyn on Election Day. His wife shoved the *Weekly* under his nose. He rushed off to Moulton's house. Moulton summoned Beecher. The two of them explained how the story had circulated up and down the streets for days now. Their best judgment was to kill it with silence. A denial would provoke Woodhull and Claflin into reiterating the story in other forms. They meant mischief, Beecher said, and the first denial would have to be followed by a second and a third and countless more denials. Did Tilton concur? He did.

Beecher got nervous. After several more meetings, he changed his mind. Tilton should publish a card denying the story, he proposed. He presented a draft, in which Tilton admitted that in his "unguarded enthusiasm," Woodhull had sucked him into her circle and proven "utterly untrue." Tilton was repudiating her and her story entirely. Tilton objected. The public would never accept such a denial from him. *Simply protecting his wife's reputation,* everyone would say, *and making excuses for falling under Woodhull's spell.*

The more Tilton thought about the proposal, the more indignant he grew. To think Beecher was trying to blame him and his "unguarded enthusiasm" for getting involved with Woodhull. *You understand full well,* Tilton told Beecher. Tilton had sought out Woodhull to protect his wife and Beecher himself, and Beecher had been party to it from the outset, Moulton too. *You involved Mrs. Tilton in this,* Theodore said, *and if you were a brave man, the denial would come from you at whatever cost.* Beecher dissolved into tears.

So the policy of silence endured. As Thanksgiving arrived, Beecher's sister Isabella Beecher Hooker threatened to blow it apart. When the scandal broke, she had written brother Henry a long letter. Though laying out stories she heard from many people, she did not directly accuse him of adultery with Lib Tilton. Nonetheless she believed it true, and if so, his only honorable path was to come clean. "Confide to me the whole truth," she wrote. "Then I can help you as no one else in the world can." Beecher blew her off. He would tread the falsehoods into the dirt and go on his way rejoicing, he replied. Now in another letter, Isabella wrote she could endure no longer. She would be in New York Friday. Together they would write a confessional paper that she would read from his pulpit Sunday morning. "Do not fail me, I pray you . . . as you hope to meet your own mother in heaven. In her name I beseech you, and will take no denial."

Appalled, Beecher bolted for Moulton's house. Moulton summoned Tilton. He arrived with Beecher ranting that his sister intended to invade his pulpit to read a confession of his relations with Lib Tilton to the congregation. "What is to be done?" Beecher cried. "Is there no end of the trouble?"

Tilton mulled the problem over before saying, "Give me the letters, and I will go and see Mrs. Hooker. I will stop this mischief."

Desperate times called for desperate measures. Tilton found Hooker at the home of Elizabeth Phelps. Phelps assured him her guest would bring her brother "to the pillory or down from his pulpit." Tilton wanted to hear it firsthand. Alone with Hooker he asked her intentions. To charge her brother with adultery with Lib Tilton, she acknowledged.

And I, Tilton replied, *am accusing you of adultery in Washington*. He named a prominent senator with whom he understood she was criminally intimate.

Beecher was delighted when Tilton reported back the next day. Though Moulton turned away in disgust, the problem was solved. Lest it resurface unexpectedly, Beecher invited sister Harriet Beecher Stowe to sit in the front pew Sunday morning, a position from which she could intercept Hooker should she carry out her invasion. A sympathetic brother might have decided that was enough. But Beecher was taking no chances. He enlisted other siblings to see that Hooker was shunned in her hometown of Hartford. One prominent member of the community, author Mark Twain, forbade his wife to cross Hooker's threshold and vowed to tell the lady why, should he run across her. Word spread that the Beecher family feared the satanic influence of Victoria Woodhull signaled insanity in Hooker. The doctor they consulted diagnosed a monomania induced by overexcitement, citing Woodhull's influence on a too susceptible mind. He recommended temporary confinement in an asylum for the insane.

Still, the larger danger had not passed. Mark Twain predicted privately that Beecher's silence would prove a hundredfold more obscene than Woodhull's *Weekly* and a thousandfold more potent in convincing people the scandal was true. Though cartoonist Thomas Nast, who had so brutally portrayed Woodhull as Mrs. Satan, did not caricature the preacher, he foretold tragedy in a letter: "The people were fooled with Greeley, as they are fooled with Beecher, and he will tumble further than Greeley yet. . . . A terrible downfall surely awaits the one who has erred and conceals it."

Hardly a day went by that some newspaper didn't tie Beecher's name to Tilton or Woodhull and the scandal. And the ridicule—in a clip about another evangelist caught "in the embraces of the wrong females, and drunk too," *Pomeroy's Democrat* commented that at least Beecher did not get drunk. As if all that press were not bad enough, newspapers piled onto the *Brooklyn Eagle*'s demand that Beecher deny the scandal.

The clamor fueled demands from Beecher's friends and talk of an investigation within Plymouth Church. The pressure had become unbearable, Beecher told Moulton and Tilton. They must abandon their policy of silence. Instead they should find a reputable paper like the *Tribune* to blame Henry Bowen for inspiring Woodhull's story. No one would argue. Over two years, Bowen had circulated rumors of Beecher's adultery and was intimating similar stories now. But as part of the "tripartite covenant" signed in April, Bowen had retracted all charges. Reading of the rumors with the retraction, Beecher predicted, the public would say, "Well, we always knew there must be something in the Woodhull story, and now we know what it is, a collection of stories which Bowen has told and which Bowen has retracted."

A fatal policy, Tilton said. Bowen had told friends he signed the covenant under duress, and it was so loosely drawn any lawyer could drive a coach and four through it. The retraction would not stand up. But the real risk lay in Bowen's nature. *If you drive Bowen to the wall and he has got any evidence against you*, Tilton warned, *he may strike you a death blow before you are aware.* Further discussion concluded Bowen had such evidence and it extended farther back than Beecher's relationship with Lib Tilton.

Beecher would regret ever raising this idea. It got Tilton thinking maybe he should publish something else—the "True Story" of the scandal on which he had been working for some time and which he admitted was anything but true. Moulton asked him to read it aloud. Tilton quickly got to the meat, a letter Lib Tilton had composed days ago to another Brooklyn clergyman. Lib Tilton indicated Beecher had solicited her to become a wife to him, together with all that implied. Left unsaid but clearly intimated was that she had not complied.

This will kill me, Beecher burst out. *You might as well state the facts outright.* He caught himself there. Only later would he admit to Moulton that he considered such a statement by Lib Tilton worse than the reality. It would not only expose him as seeking favors from the woman but also put him in the position of being rejected by her.

Tilton conceded. He would not publish his "True Story." But with the community hounding them all to make some public explanation, he felt a weight beyond the power of language to describe. The last week of December, he broke with Beecher and Moulton. With no warning he published a letter to "A Complaining Friend" in the *Eagle*. The letter gave a litany of excuses why a simple denial of the scandal, no matter how false, was impossible. "You urge me to speak," he wrote his unnamed friend, "but when the truth is a sword, God's mercy sometimes commands it sheathed."

When confronted the next day, Tilton insisted he expected the letter to bring peace between him and Beecher and to protect his wife. Beecher said hardly, it would stir up the hornet's nest. Based on the *Eagle*'s accompanying editorial that the "vague, fast and loose letter" was neither a denial nor a confession and that Beecher must speak on the subject, the preacher appeared on target. Lib Tilton also was furious. Her husband had exposed her before the world. The only solution was for her and Beecher to coordinate denials to send the papers. With Moulton absent at work, Beecher leaned toward the idea and drafted a card. But he had one objection, he told Theodore Tilton. If, after he published it, Tilton ever turned on him and published the letter of contrition Beecher had sent him two years ago, a virtual confession, the public would convict him not only of his original crime with Lib Tilton but also of lying about it now. On his word of honor, Tilton promised never to lift a hand against him, short of Beecher striking him unjustly.

Beecher pocketed his draft to mull over. Whether he couldn't bring himself to trust Tilton or Moulton talked him out of it or he couldn't voice the words, he abandoned it.

The year ended with the pressures greater than ever. Feeling a prisoner in his house, Tilton relived the scandal in his dreams each night. Lib Tilton, suffering "blow after blow ceaseless and unrelenting," was revolted at the sight of her husband. Beecher could imagine no horror worse than the great darkness that had descended upon him. Anxiety, remorse, fear, despair—they consumed him like the tortures of the damned.

VI

THE NEW YEAR, 1873

THE TOMBS - INTERIOR.

Inside the Tombs.
George W. Walling, Recollections of a New York
Chief of Police, *1887*

29 | "THE NAKED TRUTH"

ON NEW YEAR'S DAY 1873, Anthony Comstock confided his resolution to his diary. On every day of this year he aimed to do "something for Jesus." He immediately targeted his zeal at the sisters who closed the prior year calling him the sanctimonious, self-appointed agent of Christ and generalissimo of the campaign against them. Besides that accusation, the *Woodhull & Claflin's Weekly* dated December 28 contained two notices to inflame Comstock. A new edition of the suppressed issue exposing the Beecher scandal was available at 48 Broad Street. And in early January, Victoria C. Woodhull would lecture at the Cooper Institute on the "Present Situation." For Jesus, Comstock would stop both.

Four days into January, he caught a train to Greenwich, Connecticut. There he deposited a letter in registered mail ordering copies of the suppressed *Weekly* under the alias J. Beardsley, payment enclosed. He returned home and took to bed with an ulcerated throat, so weak he could hardly record the event in his diary.

Three days later he received word a bundle of papers had arrived. Illness and sharp winter weather notwithstanding, he climbed out of bed to catch another train. After picking up the papers in Greenwich, he went by sleigh to Norwalk to collect a bundle a friend ordered. The next day he hauled himself to the US circuit court of a Commissioner Davenport and secured warrants against Woodhull, Claflin, and Colonel Blood for sending obscene literature through the US mail. Too sick to walk, he went by carriage to Broad Street with marshals. They found only Colonel Blood, along with several of the hardest kind of free lovers, or so Comstock judged by their looks. Blood was the lesser of his concerns, as Woodhull and Claflin were speaking that evening at the Cooper Institute. The papers advertised the event under the title "The Naked Truth," itself an abomination which the newspapers should never have printed. Few seats remained available.

Officers scoured the city to no avail. No matter that the sisters escaped Comstock's net for the time being, however. With outstanding warrants against them, they wouldn't dare show their faces near the Cooper Institute. If they did, marshals would collar them.

Comstock was pleased. Good men all seemed to appreciate his intervention, not that he cared. "In my heart," he wrote in his diary that night, "I feel God approves and what care I more. If Jesus be pleased, I care for nothing else."

––––––––––––

When Anthony Higgins of New Jersey saw the advertisement for Victoria Woodhull's lecture at the Cooper Institute, he thought "The Naked Truth" was a strange title. It would surely shock the sensibilities of fashionable society. But look at it another way, as fact without fiction, God Almighty's truth without a fig leaf. Could the insignificant little woman with the terribly significant soul expose the social corruption undergirded by fraud, ignorance, and humbuggery? Higgins decided to find out.

When Higgins arrived, a crowd surged toward the institute's doors. Some entered, others retreated. Were the latter "lily-livered loons" suddenly afraid to hear the woman's ideas? he wondered. No, turning them away was Uncle Sam in the form of US marshals. They watched with lynx eyes for the woman of the hour. "There will be no lecture tonight," Higgins heard them say. "Mrs. Woodhull is to be again arrested and flung into prison." Hundreds pushed inside anyway. Policemen arrayed to the left and right, equal in number to those surrounding the building, one hundred in all.

The clock ticked past the eight o'clock start. The crowd murmured, *Shame! Outrage! Persecution!* Feet stamped. Stragglers came in. A marshal helped an old Quaker lady. She tottered down the aisle in a gray dress and coal-scuttle bonnet to a front seat where she might hear. Distracted only a moment by this eccentric figure out of "Rip Van Winkle," the crowd grew angrier, stamped louder, patience exhausted.

Laura Cuppy Smith glided onto the stage. The noise died down enough to hear her apology that Woodhull could not appear lest she be flung again into the American Bastille, to hear her berate this violation of free speech, of a free press. Meanwhile the Quaker woman climbed the stairs and disappeared behind a pillar on the platform.

Smith said that despite the injustice, the speech would be heard. Woodhull had deputized her to read it. Sudden as a flash of lightning, the Quaker woman appeared before her. The coal-scuttle bonnet disappeared, the gray dress coiled upon the floor. Struck by this thunderbolt, the audience stared upon Victoria Woodhull, an inspirational fire scintillating in her eyes. Higgins saw before him "the personification of Liberty in Arms."

––––––––––––

Confident that Beecher's friends in the YMCA had instigated her banning in Boston, Woodhull held no doubt they would disrupt her appearance at the Cooper Institute. So when word reached her that Comstock had put up another job to arrest her, she was prepared. She arranged for Laura Cuppy Smith to represent her at the institute and went into hiding. The *Sun* reported she decamped for Taylor's Hotel in Jersey City, a long-used hideout by the likes of Jay Gould and Jim Fisk when they were under indictment for their Erie Railroad caper. Tennie Claflin hid under the washerwoman's tub when officers called at the house, rumors asserted.

Whatever she told friends, Woodhull would not let Comstock thwart her. As the hour approached eight, she drove down Third Avenue disguised as a Quaker woman. Her carriage stopped short of the Cooper Institute while scouts reconnoitered. With marshals at every entrance, she could not avoid them. With the densest crowd around the main entrance, it seemed the best bet for slipping by. The strategy went off without a hitch. Seeing a deaf and hobbling woman, one marshal offered a hand. The most attention she got was chuckles from a few people in the audience at her appearance—until her costume fell to the floor and she exclaimed, "Yes, I am here," that is. A deafening cheer welcomed her. The marshals were too astounded to move. Had they tried, a barrier of feet and bodies blocked the rail surrounding the platform.

Woodhull opened angry and defiant. She cursed the cowards fighting her and her sister. Had she and Claflin murdered anyone? Robbed? Blackmailed? Not a living soul, she declared. They had simply tried to earn their bread and butter in New York City, yet their persecutors had robbed them, broken up their business, suppressed their newspaper. Launching into her prepared speech, she called out Anthony Comstock, the YMCA, Henry Ward Beecher, the members of Plymouth Church, prosecutors, and judges. All tried to run them to earth. But what had those enemies achieved? Their hate, stupidity, and ignorance had only raised her social revolution to a vantage it could never have achieved otherwise.

The harangue continued for an hour and a half, punctuated with bursts of applause and occasional catcalls. By the end, she declared the *Weekly* would come out every week she was not locked up and begged pardon for not removing her heavy overshoes, as she needed them for her forthcoming journey to Ludlow Street jail. She then retired to the rear of the platform, received congratulations, and surrendered to the waiting marshals. After a short carriage ride to Ludlow Street, she joined her husband in cell 12.

She was well satisfied with the evening. Marshals turning people away had halved her expected lecture receipts. But she would never barter the effect her actions produced on the community for a few more dollars. She hoped Comstock and his Jesuit friends were satisfied as well, though she doubted it would turn out so. "You are filling up for yourselves a measure of iniquity," she advised them, "the consequences of which you will some day be under the necessity of accepting; and which you will then, too late, bitterly bewail."

The courtroom being his natural habitat, William Howe was probably the only person involved who enjoyed the next month. After one night in Ludlow, Woodhull and Blood appeared before Commissioner Davenport on the latest obscenity charge. Bondsmen put up another five grand to get them released. Despite bail in all her cases exceeding $60,000, Woodhull was immediately, and mistakenly, re-arrested on one of the Challis libel charges. She endured another night in Ludlow before that mix-up was straightened out.

Though she was freed, this latest episode of their legal nightmare would extend into the coming months. The examination in US circuit court continued through the week, with Comstock testifying, Challis watching, Tennie Claflin surrendering, and Commissioner Davenport refusing to allow Woodhull and Blood to speak on their own behalf. Howe started his fun over this last matter. He charged Davenport with violating the practice of every other commissioner, not to mention the explicit ruling of a superior district court judge. Would he forbid Howe's clients the opportunity to deny they deposited the supposedly obscene publication in the mail? But Davenport didn't care what other commissioners did in their courts; he wouldn't allow the defendants to speak in his.

Howe interrogated Comstock. He read the Challis article aloud, stopping frequently to ask whether particular lines were obscene. Comstock finally pointed to one sentence that qualified in his mind, that containing the reference to a finger stained red. Howe read similar discussions of virginity from Shakespeare, Byron, and the Bible, querying whether they, too, were obscene. Over several days, he called Comstock a "male prostitute," alleged his actions were a "malignancy unprecedented in the annals of criminal prosecution," and insisted that no matter his efforts, these ladies could not be driven out of the city at "the point of a bayonet."

Davenport finally ruled the Challis article was obscene and left indictment with the grand jury. Meanwhile, Luther Challis filed another libel complaint in the Court of General Sessions. That led to another arrest of Woodhull, Claflin, and Blood, too late in the day to make bail. They spent that night in the Tombs before putting up another $1,000 apiece. By the beginning of February, cases against them were pending in US circuit court before two different commissioners, in the Court of Oyer and Terminer, and in the Court of General Sessions. Despite Howe's pleas for quick trials, commissioners, judges, and prosecutors refused to set dates.

The government would never dare bring them to trial, Woodhull had predicted at the Cooper Institute. Nor would it enter a nolle prosequi, an end to their prosecution. Rather, she expected the authorities to hold the charges over their heads, delaying time after time while pretending a trial was forthcoming, hoping the defendants' death, poverty, or virtual surrender would offer a way to escape giving them their day in court. Woodhull couldn't take much satisfaction in being proved right.

But she, Claflin, and Blood could get on with their lives. They resumed regular publication of *Woodhull & Claflin's Weekly*, hardly missing an issue for the rest of the year. Woodhull launched a lecture tour in Delaware. With help from the New England Labor Reform League, she evaded authorities in Boston and spoke there. She traveled to Ohio, Illinois, Wisconsin, and upstate New York. Newspapers labeled her talks filthy, vulgar, and obscene. But when the public saw advertisements for "The Fearless and Irrepressible Victoria C. Woodhull" speaking the "Naked Truth," they came in droves. As an extra enticement, attendees could acquire the celebrated suppressed issue of the *Weekly* and photographs of Woodhull.

Between lecture receipts and sales of the *Weekly*, money flowed in, albeit barely enough to stay afloat. Every *Weekly* reminded readers of the persecution and financial distress Woodhull and Claflin suffered, begged them not to delay their remittances, and thanked those who contributed. Even those purchasing photographs helped meet the bills, the paper noted.

Woodhull had her voice back, and it erupted on the *Weekly*'s pages. She "took a scalpel" to Commissioner Davenport's tortured logic in concluding the Challis article obscene while admitting Congress never contemplated its law applied to such a case. She accused Comstock of playing dictator to public thought and censor of morals. She dubbed the Young Men's Christian Association the American Inquisition, though she would no more compare Comstock to Torquemada than contrast a living skunk with a dead lion. She berated federal authorities for assuming the right to pounce on any newspaper, suppress its publication, shutter its offices, and march its proprietor off to prison. As if that wasn't precedent enough for tyranny, she wrote, criminal lawyers assured her of worse if her case ever went to trial. When the prosecution ended, the judge would order the jury to find her guilty of obscene libel. The defense would get no opportunity to prove the truth in what she published.

Well, if she was as good as convicted, why not go down taunting? In February the *Weekly* reprinted "a bouquet of advertisements" from the medical section of the *Herald*. The enticements included "Unfortunate Ladies in Trouble . . . safely relieved" and "Modest and Delicate Ladies in Trouble . . . honorably treated." Though the *Weekly* omitted the advertisers' names, one need only look at the *Herald* to see Dr. and Mrs. Grindle and Madame Van Buskirk among them, three abortionists arrested over the past year but getting off scot-free. And what if Comstock considered the reprinted advertisements obscene and arrested the sisters again? Woodhull would cite the *New York Times*. Its January 30 editorial criticizing the *Herald* itemized a dozen such advertisements. The Grindles topped the list, followed by Van Buskirk and the most notorious of all, Madame Restell. Let Comstock go after the *Times*. Or was he too much of a coward to hunt big game, as so many editors were charging?

30 | "SPECIAL AGENT, P. O. DEPT."

THE FIRST WEEK OF FEBRUARY, Anthony Comstock climbed the stairs of the US Capitol lugging a satchel. In the office set aside for the vice president, he spread out his exhibits. A Connecticut newspaper editor introduced him to Vice President Schuyler Colfax and a half dozen or so senators. Over the next hour, the senators examined contraband he had acquired—books and pamphlets, photographs and stereoscopic pictures, wood cuts, rubber goods—and heard his tales about the nefarious business of obscenity. The senators declared they were ready to give him any bill he asked for so long as it was constitutional. They could pass it before the current session closed for President Grant's second inauguration, not a month away.

This reception pleased Comstock immensely. The past month had tried his patience. He told himself the belittling by the Tombs' "shyster" William Howe didn't matter, that Howe was injuring his clients Woodhull and Claflin and Blood more than himself. Still, Howe's accusations stung. Comstock took solace when a friend told him, "Blessed are they who are persecuted for righteousness' sake." Comstock didn't consider himself worthy of that homily, but it reminded him that sometimes a man best serves the Master by bearing patiently.

The drumbeat in the press pounded out sympathy for the sisters and harangued him for doing what was right. Whether editors applauded or abhorred Woodhull's doctrines didn't matter. From states throughout the country, they echoed an Ohio paper arguing that whatever despicable ideas she spouted, she had a right to advocate them with her tongue and pen. No sooner had they cried free speech for free love than they accused Comstock of inciting a mob against the woman, debauching the courts, garroting liberty. When one paper extended that list to rotting the church, well, that was too much.

Fed up with the whole affair, Comstock turned to getting a stronger obscenity law through Congress. After Justice William Strong of the US Supreme Court finished working on it, "my bill," as Comstock thought of the law, outlawed obscene literature plus advertising for it and rubber goods or anything else used to prevent conception. New

York congressman Clinton L. Merriam introduced it in the House, and Connecticut senator William Buckingham in the Senate. On Tuesday next, Merriam expected to pass it under a suspension of the rules.

On Saturday Comstock got a head start on enforcement. He dropped by the Washington YMCA. On Treasury Department letterhead, he drafted letters to nine doctors advertising in the *New York Herald*. "I am an employee of the Treasury," he wrote under the pseudonym Anna M. Ray, "and I have got myself into trouble. I was seduced about four months ago, and I am now three months gone in the family way." After chronicling her abandonment by her lover and the widowed mother and crippled sister she supported on the sixty dollars she earned as a clerk, "Anna" begged each doctor to send something to relieve her condition. "For God's sake do not disappoint a poor ruined and forsaken girl whose only relief will be suicide if you fail me," the letters closed.

Comstock's wife, Maggie, arrived that afternoon. The couple attended church and a temperance meeting Sunday, and in the evening Anthony spoke at a service of song. He felt invigorated for the coming week, only to run straight into disappointment. Congressman Benjamin Butler insisted on changes to the bill, necessitating a reprinting. Another congressman insisted on the regular order of rules in the House, preventing his bill from coming up Tuesday. The Senate referred the bill to the Committee on Post Offices and Post Roads. Despite the delays, Comstock's allies promised quick passage. He consoled himself by attending a reception at the White House, where he shook the hand of President Grant—a hand he would need to sign his bill. He was not impressed with the event. The ladies present caricatured everything a modest one ought not to be—brazen, with enameled faces, powdered hair, and low-cut dresses, altogether disgusting to every lover of pure, noble, modest woman.

Prospects improved when the Post Office Committee unanimously approved the bill. And the Senate Committee on Appropriations authorized over $3,000 as salary for a special postal agent after the postmaster general promised to appoint Comstock. A kind Heavenly Father had blessed him with facilities to so much better enable his great work, Comstock mused about his commission as "Special Agent, P. O. Dept."

The joy didn't last. A Vermont senator so stubborn he would object to the Lord's Prayer forced the bill back to committee. The man wanted to shield his friends in the smut business, Comstock concluded. His heart sank.

With several prosecutions pending, court appearances called him to New York. While there, the YMCA's Committee for the Suppression of Vice passed a resolution approving his actions in the capital. But several of its members could not have been pleased by publicity for their support in the *Woodhull & Claflin's Weekly* then on the newsstands. The leaders of the YMCA were fighting for legislation that would "subvert the people to their control and compel them to their religion," the *Weekly* charged. Motivating them was "fear of detection" that some practiced what they pretended to abhor. The paper named James Patterson and William Dodge, two "Associated Brothers" of the YMCA whose financial scandals were raging in the press. Even the postmaster general considered it unwise "to put the United States Mail Service under the espionage" of these gentlemen, the *Weekly* reported. As for the YMCA's agent Comstock, he was inventing new aliases to cover his tracks.

So Comstock was "cheerless leaving home and wifey" when he returned to Washington. A week and a day remained before Congress adjourned and his bill would have to start over. The *Herald* tolled the bill's death knell, headlining COMSTOCK'S CHRISTIANITY REFUSED BY THE SENATE. Despite Comstock's exhibition of indecent engravings and immoral articles, the senators had cruelly ended his hopes and left him out in the cold with his indecent stock in trade.

But no, the senators told him, the Senate had passed the bill. For any other man, sorrow would have turned to joy—for Comstock, one might guess, to rapture. But no sooner had he heard the news than he learned the bill did not include a saving clause. Unless amended, the bill's passage would quash all prosecutions for crimes committed while the prior obscenity law was in effect. *Ignore it*, his congressional allies told him. With only a week and a day before Congress adjourned, the time was too tight and the risk too great to send an amended bill back to the Senate. His enemies were attacking, the press was hostile, and even friends of the bill were having second thoughts. *Let the House pass it and the president sign it. The fight will be won*, they advised.

Comstock contemplated the cases he had pending, close to twenty. He pictured the culprits who would go free, the smut dealer Charles Mackay, the free lover Victoria Woodhull. He said no, the bill must be amended.

By the end of the week, he was spewing venom to his diary: "The exhibitions of today in the Halls of legislation has been one that outrages all decency. Men assailing one another's character while legislation goes begging. Malice fills the air. Party bitterness and venom. Loud talk of constitution, law, justice. It seems a burlesque on our Forefathers. . . . They tear out all principle and leave the skeleton, and where then is the Constitution." He vented at his sponsor, Congressman Merriam, at Speaker of the House James Blaine, who was ignoring pleas by the YMCA leaders.

On Saturday, March 1, Blaine promised to put the amended bill through. Comstock sat in the House chamber that evening. Blaine had his bill in hand, but others were called up and passed. Time and again, Merriam could have called out "Mr. Speaker" to get the floor. Instead he sat mute.

Comstock despaired. At midnight, a voice called to him. "Remember the Sabbath day, to keep it holy." *No, you must stay and watch your bill*, he thought, picturing the savage attacks, the sneering exultation in the newspapers should he fail. But could he expect God to answer his prayers if he did not obey His commands?

He left the Capitol and walked up Pennsylvania Avenue. Reaching his room, he tried to pray. He could not bring himself to accept God's will if it crushed his own.

His heart rebelled, his trust evaporated. He would disobey. He spent a sleepless night beset by the devil.

Early in the morning, he walked to the YMCA. The doors were locked. He passed churches, their bells ringing. He did not turn in. He ended up back in his room. He picked up a paper to forget himself. Within it was a sermon, "Christian Life." Reading it he broke down. He dropped to his knees, unburdening his troubles to Jesus and asking God's forgiveness.

"Thy will, not mine, be done," he prayed. If his bill did not pass, let him go back to New York submissive to God's will, feeling it was for the best. His burden lifted. He had won a victory greater than forcing any bill through Congress.

Uplifted, he returned to the YMCA, where he had promised to speak to prisoners from the penitentiary. He found the Senate's chaplain, who asked, "Well, how is it?"

"It is in God's hands; it's all right," Comstock answered.

"Your bill passed the House at 2 o'clock this morning," the chaplain said. It had immediately been sent to the Senate and passed and was awaiting the president.

The next day President Grant signed the bill into law. "Thy will be done!" Comstock cried.

31 | "GOD KNOWS I AM NOT THE MAN"

ON VALENTINE'S DAY, the *Times* published a letter from Tombs cell 61. "I am a Polander," Jacob Rosenzweig wrote. "I have no friends. I am poor. God knows I am not the man who committed the terrible deed. The press are doing all they can to prejudice people against me. [Will you] let these few lines appear in your great paper from a countryman of Pulaski and Koscuski [*sic*]?"

Printing the lines was the most pity the editors would show the abortionist who had stuffed Alice Bowlsby's body into a trunk. To discourage the Polander from writing again, they added they should be very glad to see him brought to the gallows.

Pretty much everyone agreed Rosenzweig deserved hanging but for the wife and comely eighteen-year-old daughter who sat near him in court the past week. His guilt was not in doubt, nor the horror of his actions. Even his counsel understood the enormity of his crime and the howl of indignation at the prospect he might get off. But William Howe recognized the sanctity of the law and gave it precedence, no matter if justice was miscarried in the process.

Howe had been cooking up Rosenzweig's defense long before he'd won his client a new trial in November. He tried the recipe out the prior summer in the case of Dr. Gyles, another abortion gone bad though under more benign circumstances. When the jury acquitted Gyles on the evidence, Howe filed the recipe away for another day.

That day came in February in the Court of General Sessions, where Recorder John Hackett was ready to retry Rosenzweig's case and Assistant District Attorney H. Russell to prosecute. Howe informed the court that the defendant wished to withdraw his plea of not guilty. Instead he wished to enter a special plea on two points. First was that this second trial would place the defendant in double jeopardy and so could not proceed. That was nonsense, since the court had thrown out his first trial on appeal and ordered a new one. The second was that in the intervening period, the New York legislature had passed the abortion act of 1872. Section 5 specifically stated that "all acts and parts of acts inconsistent with this act are hereby repealed." No part contained a saving clause allowing prior crimes to be prosecuted under the old law. With the old law invalidated and the new law enacted after the supposed crime, New York State had no statute on which to try the defendant.

After a few days' postponement, Recorder Hackett outlined a solution to prevent Rosenzweig going free. Should the defense argument thwart a retrial under the abortion laws, Hackett would instruct the district attorney to have the grand jury indict Rosenzweig for murder in the first degree. Howe was surely amused by the *Commercial Advertiser*'s description of how this "broadside" by Hackett staggered a defense "counsel more familiar with tricks than with principles." No one was better versed in the murder laws and how to elude them than William Howe. An indictment Thursday, as the papers predicted, three days from now? On a charge that the doctor had planned with forethought to kill the woman he was trying to help? Seriously?

Thursday came and went. Over the next week, rumors swirled. Several papers reported the grand jury had delivered. An Albany paper speculated Rosenzweig would regret not serving out his original seven-year sentence instead of facing a first-degree murder charge. The *Commercial Advertiser* contradicted—the first-degree charge wasn't holding up. The *Herald* investigated, sending a reporter to the district attorney's office. When cornered, the newly elected district attorney said he didn't know about the indictment. He delegated the matter to an assistant. The assistant said yes, the indictment was for willful murder. The grand jury wanted the man to hang. The arraignment would be in two days. Leaving, the reporter noticed that claim astonished others in the office. And when the grand jury delivered a batch of indictments the next week, none related to Rosenzweig.

As February ended, the prosecutor finally cleared things up. Though the grand jury had acted, he had not brought the indictment to the court. He doubted the evidence could sustain a charge of murder in the first degree. He intended to try the case on the old indictment. The trial would begin the first week of March.

Seriously? By now, the papers were asking that question.

32 | "THE AWFUL TOILET FOR THE GALLOWS"

THE TOMBS CONTAINED TWO HUNDRED CELLS. Though planned for a single prisoner each, they held 517 inmates on New Year's Eve. The men's section rose in four tiers. The uppermost housed minor criminals charged with crimes like petty larceny. Offenders accused of committing grand larceny and burglary occupied one level down. Murderers' Row filled the second tier.

The ground floor contained a handful of cells. They were the largest in the prison thanks to the tiers losing two feet of depth with each level up. The extra space didn't make these cells desirable. Built on a shallow lake filled with dirt and rubbish, the prison was slowly sinking. Damp and cold permeated the ground level. Water flowed up through the drain pipes, flooding the floor. Its inhabitants were forbidden the luxuries a prisoner's wealth could buy on the higher tiers—furnishings, clothes, a barber and valet, meals from the city's finer restaurants.

The ground floor inmates shared one thing besides location. They were condemned to death. A typical stay would be the few weeks before a man's march to the gallows. Halfway through February, men occupied two of the cells. In a drunken rage, William Foster had smashed a horse car hook into a stranger's skull. His hanging was three weeks away. Ned Stokes had shot Jim Fisk. His noose was two weeks off.

With a death sentence hanging over Stokes, the sheriff rather than the warden had responsibility for him. He allowed minor additions to the cell's bare walls, stone floor, and cot—a table and two chairs, a narrow strip of carpet, books. Stokes huddled in his overcoat to keep warm. He ate meals from the prison's matron, read the newspapers, took short walks in the yard, and stewed over the injustices that had landed him here. He blamed Jay Gould and the Erie Ring, the private attorneys they hired for the prosecution, witnesses who perjured, a jury determined to convict, the money paid to make Fisk's pistol disappear, the authorities seeking to prove wealth and respectability couldn't turn the iron hand of the law to velvet.

Hordes came to see him—the prison keepers would estimate fifteen thousand people during his stay in the Tombs. Most sought to satisfy morbid curiosity. Others were well-dressed women seeking a handsome gentleman. These gazed from an upper gallery as he paced the corridor below, calling *Ed, Ed*, to attract his eye. Stokes ignored them. He refused to visit with anyone but family and intimate friends, his counsel, and an occasional clergyman. Reporters granted an interview spoke through the iron grate of the cell door, its holes so small Stokes could extend only two fingers for a handshake. Guards watched that no one slipped in an instrument with which he might do himself in.

Stokes maintained the cool demeanor he had presented in court. His dress was scrupulously neat. His counsel bolstered his spirits with talk of a reprieve. But to the keepers who saw him daily, he wore a poorly concealed dejection behind his smile.

His brother Horace brought news to the Tombs one afternoon, and suddenly whatever fortitude remaining in Stokes fled. Judge Douglass Boardman in the Court of Oyer and Terminer had rejected every item in the bill of exceptions his counsel had filed. Misbehavior by jurors, objectionable language by the prosecution, the trial judge's momentary absence from the courtroom, error in the instructions to the jury—none warranted a new trial. Judge Boardman refused to stay the execution.

His counsel had cued an appeal to Judge Noah Davis, newly installed on the New York Supreme Court. The next day Davis issued a ruling essentially agreeing. The points in the bill of exceptions were by and large frivolous or of such slight importance they did not prejudice the defendant. On only one point could he question this conclusion—the instruction to the jurors that they should presume malice in the shooting of Fisk unless the defense proved otherwise. His duty was not to rule on that matter, only to determine whether it carried enough weight to warrant consideration by a panel of New York Supreme Court justices. It did, and "with regret," Davis issued a stay until a panel could hear the appeal. Ned Stokes would not hang on the last day of February.

Hearing this news, Stokes staggered. Blood rushed to his face. The ruling was a thin thread on which to hang his hopes. But his hopes were better than William Foster's, his neighbor on death row. Foster had exhausted every appeal. Only clemency from the governor could save him.

The stay allowed Stokes to leave death row. He returned to his old cell with the appurtenances a gentleman should enjoy. Foster, too, had good news. His mother and wife had begged the governor to commute his sentence to life. Clergymen petitioned too. Leading citizens joined the effort, noting how a criminal laboring for decades would do more service to the state than one hanged by the neck like a dog. Now the widow of Foster's victim chimed in. Foster's execution would not assuage her sorrow over the loss of her husband, her letter read. Let his life be spared to afford him time for repentance. Rumors spread that the governor would act.

"Poor fellow," said Stokes. "I hope he will get a commutation. His fate is a very hard one."

At 6:00 AM on the third Friday of March, a crowd gathered outside the Tombs. Men and women cast their eyes at the prison's grim and frowning walls. Groups debated the mournful fate of the man destined to die today. The governor had granted the car hook murderer William Foster a two-week respite. But he found no circumstances to justify annulling the determination of the jury. The good order of society demanded that he maintain the supremacy of the law so every man who struck a murderous blow would feel his own life in peril.

Shortly after eight, the tramp of three hundred feet echoed up the granite walls of the yard as police filed in. The pounding burned into the brain of the condemned man. He vomited up his breakfast, then fell back, his cheeks whitening, his bluish lips quivering.

In the tier above, the tramping rang in the ears of other men as they finished breakfast—William Sharkey, another liquored-up killer; Ned Stokes, shooter of his former friend; Jacob Rosenzweig, the abortionist threatened with a first-degree murder charge; twenty-odd others incarcerated for capital crimes. The sound was not their first reminder of the fate they might face. Yesterday hammers had pounded on wood as the scaffold rose. The prisoners could look out their narrow windows at its shadow on the wall across the yard, at the hundreds of people holding tickets for the spectacle shoving through the gates, at the press heading for benches with a close-up view.

Clergymen comforted the condemned man in his cell. The sheriff and deputies entered. Within black-gloved hands they carried wands of their authority draped in mourning. The deputies pinioned Foster's arms. They circled the noose around his neck, its knot positioned under his left ear. They placed a black cap loosely on his head, completing "the awful toilet for the gallows."

The prisoners above could not see the tremors that ran through Foster's body, the color draining from his skin, his strength so feeble he could take no step without deputies sharing his weight. But those men on Murderers' Row could imagine how he looked, for during their daily exercise pacing the gallery, many stared down. In the corridor below, Foster had spent his last days receiving his family and friends. He had perused photos of his children but refused to allow them in the prison lest its gray gloom mar the memory of their father.

Only prisoners with strong stomachs or completely void of feeling peered out their windows as Foster approached the gibbet. Silence overtook the yard but for pigeons cooing. Foster shivered. A clergyman read the Episcopal service for the condemned. After five minutes, the sheriff whispered, "It's too long." The reverend shut up and hurried away. The executioner reached for the rope running over the scaffold to three iron weights, their three hundred pounds held aloft by a cord. He clamped it to the noose. He lowered the black cap over the prisoner's eyes. A handkerchief waved. The executioner felled his ax on the cord. The weights crashed to earth. Foster's body shot up. His legs jerked into him. His heels clicked sharply. For half a minute, the body writhed, then struggled no more.

After five minutes, doctors requested it be lowered enough to examine. The wrist trilled with a pulse for another four minutes. The heart beat for another three. At last the executioner lowered the body into a rosewood coffin and removed the cap and noose. The neck had broken. The left eye stood open on an orange-colored face. Foster's relatives took custody of his body. Tomorrow they would bury it in Brooklyn's Green-Wood Cemetery.

As to the men listening on Murderers' Row, what sentiments filled their minds could not be told, concluded the *Herald*. But as Foster's steps to the gallows rang on the flagstones, all surely felt the heels were tramping on their hearts and crushing out the hopes to which they clung.

Perhaps. But Ned Stokes gave no sign of it. As the New York Supreme Court considered his appeal over the next several weeks, his demeanor was the coolest of any prisoner in the Tombs. He smiled and chatted with friends as jocularly as if he were whiling away his leisure in an abode of pleasure. "Stokes downcast?" responded the warden to a reporter's question. "Whoever saw him downcast?" And when the New York Supreme Court unanimously denied him a new trial the first week of May, Stokes said so what. The case was going to the Court of Appeals, he told a reporter. He liked his chances there. As for clemency from the governor, he would accept nothing of the sort. If he had to forfeit his life for defending himself when another man drew a pistol on him, so be it. It was preferable to pining away in a state prison for an imaginary crime.

33 | "TODAY IS A GOOD DAY TO TALK ABOUT HEAVEN"

WITH 1873 ALMOST FIVE MONTHS OVER, Henry Ward Beecher had stuck to his policy of silence. The closest he came to referring publicly to Victoria Woodhull or the scandal was when Plymouth Church offered him a $10,000 raise. He refused it, saying his congregation needn't cover him with bank notes to protect him from being "assailed by a nameless animal." The annual pew auction in January further signaled the scandal had not diminished Beecher's popularity. Proceeds topped $60,000, a bump up from the prior year.

The downside to the auction was Henry Bowen bidding for a pew right below the pulpit. Beecher couldn't escape the man's glare on Sundays. Worse were the slanders Bowen was again spreading. Throughout the spring, the *Eagle* headlined stories with the likes of BEECHER VS. BOWEN and THE BOWEN-BEECHER SCANDAL. The paper took Beecher's side, labeling Bowen a libeler and a Judas. Nonetheless, with every story the editors called for Beecher to deny the allegations.

Tilton at least kept his mouth shut. But too many people blamed him for spreading the scandal, what with him cozying up to the Woodhull woman before she published the story—at least that's what Tilton heard traveling around the country. So he dug out an old letter he had written when he was angry at Bowen for firing him from the *Independent*. The letter related all the stories Bowen had told Tilton about Beecher's debauchery. The preacher went beyond adultery, Bowen claimed, reciting one incident in which Beecher had taken a woman into his arms by force, thrown her onto a sofa, and accomplished his devilry upon her. Tilton sent the letter to the *Eagle*, which published it late in April. He didn't accuse Beecher of any crime. He simply aimed to shift responsibility for circulating the rumors from himself to Bowen.

Nonsense, Beecher concluded. Publishing that letter was outright treachery.

Why couldn't Tilton have done the right thing and disappeared with his family to Europe? Beecher would have footed the bill. Already he had paid thousands of dollars to hush people who observed what went on in the Tilton household—Lib Tilton's mother, whose ingratiating letters asked for $1,500 so she could pay the rent; the Tiltons' servant Bessie Turner, shipped off to school in Ohio. Thank God for Moulton handling these transactions. Now Beecher had mortgaged his home to pay off Tilton himself. Five $1,000 bills he counted into Moulton's hand. *Feed it out as if from you when Tilton needs capital to keep the* Golden Age *alive*, he instructed, referring to the journal Tilton published. The man would never take charity, especially not from Beecher. But if he was earning a living from his paper, he might not do something rash.

That was how May began. It would only get worse. As the month neared its end, Beecher learned that a paper had gotten hold of the tripartite covenant resolving the differences between Beecher, Tilton, and Bowen. Bowen's piece of the agreement, a year old now, retracted all charges he had made against the preacher. Hence the paper's anonymous source conjectured its publication would counteract the slanderous rumors against Beecher. Hardly, Beecher guessed. It would ignite a firestorm.

Before the paper published, Beecher had to make Bowen stand by his word. The retraction was weak to start with—while Bowen took his statements back, he never denied they were true. And in recent months he had said privately that his arm had been twisted to sign the covenant. If Bowen repeated that when the covenant came out, the heavens might fall.

Brooklyn didn't have enough horses to pull Beecher into a meeting with Bowen. But he sent his carriage as far as Manhattan to collect a group to confront the man. When those gentlemen appeared at his home, Bowen admitted his private retraction of the covenant. He swore Beecher had dropped to his knees before him and confessed. *Bring the preacher here and we'll get the truth*, he said. It wasn't a promising start.

On May 30, the *Times* published the covenant in the morning. The *Brooklyn Eagle* picked it up in the evening edition. Bowen, his mouth shut, had left on a short trip west to "benefit his health." The general opinion, the *Eagle* reported, was that publication of the covenant sealed Bowen's doom. But the document itself satisfied no one. Bowen retracted whatever charges he had made without denying them. Tilton promised only never to repeat innuendo or allegations against Beecher or Bowen growing out of what Bowen told him. Beecher merely revoked anything he had said injurious to Bowen or Tilton or that detracted from their standing as Christian gentlemen and members of Plymouth Church. None of the three contested the truth of the scandal itself, that Beecher had engaged in adultery. Almost everyone agreed Beecher's good name now required that he speak in his own defense.

Beecher was long practiced at ignoring such calls. The evening of the publication he opened Plymouth Church's Friday night prayer meeting with a hymn:

From every stormy wind that blows,
From every swelling tide of woes
There is a calm, a sure retreat,
'Tis found beneath the mercy seat.

It was as close as he would come to acknowledging the earthquake shaking his church.

The next morning, Moulton summoned Beecher to his house. Tilton waited there. He had read that the public was drawing erroneous conclusions from the covenant—namely, that Tilton was admitting to an unspecified wrong against Beecher, that he was regretting it, and that Beecher was forgiving him for it. "This I will not stand," Tilton raged. "I will not, after having suffered this wrong, after having had my family destroyed, my wife debauched, I will not be held up to public odium as having committed a crime against you, and been magnanimously forgiven by you. Relieve me of this or I will relieve myself."

Tilton laid out the relief he planned if Beecher did nothing. He would send the *Eagle* the letter he had received from Beecher on New Year's Day 1871, when the scandal was first about to erupt. "I will die before anyone but myself is implicated," Beecher had written. "All my thoughts are running towards . . . the poor child lying there and praying with her folded hands. She"—Lib Tilton—"is guiltless—sinned against; bearing the transgression of another. Her forgiveness I have. I humbly pray to God that He may put it into the heart of her husband to forgive me."

Beecher's confession—the public would read either it or another card Tilton had drafted, an exoneration signed by Henry Ward Beecher absolving Tilton of any responsibility for slanders or injurious statements against him. The preacher's choice, Tilton said.

Moulton persuaded Tilton to hold off until Monday. Beecher returned home. He felt as if a fetid flood of scandal was overwhelming him—and not just him, but also Tilton and his family, who he had tried so long to protect, and the community of Plymouth Church. Tilton would precipitate it. Or if not him, the deacons of the church, who talked of forming an investigative committee. He wanted desperately to prevent it. It would likely lead to the expulsion of Tilton from the church, and Beecher could not bear the harm that would inflict on the family he had pledged to save. He could see only one solution. He would resign his pulpit. He began to write to the trustees of Plymouth Church: "For two years I have stood with great sorrow amongst you, in order to shield from shame a certain household. Since a recent publication makes this no longer possible, I resign my ministry and retire to private life."

That evening Beecher carried his resignation to Moulton's study. *This will not do*, Moulton told him. It amounted to a confession of his crime with Lib Tilton, and on top of that a cowardly act simply to walk away when they could clearly satisfy Tilton's demand for exoneration. Tilton arrived downstairs. Moulton went down alone. He told Tilton of Beecher's plan and recited the letter. When Tilton heard the words "shield from shame a certain household," he pictured the stain those words would brand on his wife, and he exploded: "If he publishes that with such a reason, I will shoot him on the spot."

So Beecher returned home alone, and as the clock ticked toward midnight, he wondered how the mess would ever end. No sooner had he gotten out of one complication than another arose. On top of the pressures of his church, of thousands of men pulling at him for one thing or another, of always building a facade of serenity to hide his torments, it was too much, grinding him into nervous debilitation. In moods like this he contemplated death. A hundred times he had entered his pulpit fearing he would not come out alive. On this night he could see no other end to the accumulation of troubles. Death could come easily; he could reach for the poison he kept in his study, a photographer's concoction easily mistaken for water. He had before contemplated drinking it if his crime with Lib Tilton came out. He once confessed the plan to Moulton.

But no, no matter how clouded his mind tonight, he would not go there. So often he had carried on, and he would carry on now.

The next morning, Sunday, Beecher awoke early. A sound sleep had chased the clouds from his mind. He pictured the earth tranquil, the heavens serene, an atmosphere "as befits one who has about finished this world-life." With the clarity of crystal, a path unfolded before him. He laid it out in a letter to Moulton.

He would resist no more. No matter how hard he tried, Tilton would never let him escape. Any respite Beecher won would bring another demand. Tilton was destined to self-destruct, if not from this threat to publish Beecher's confession, then from another rash act.

So instead of fighting, Beecher would issue a statement to the public that would bear the light of the Judgment Day. God would care for him. *Frank*, he wrote, *you need waste no more energy on a hopeless task. No one can depend on salvation coming from such a man as Tilton. No good comes from trying further.*

A great peace had come over him, Beecher wrote his friend, a feeling he was spending his last Sunday and preaching his final sermon. He could see rest and triumph ahead, and the glory of everlasting emancipation.

"Your loving, H. W. B.," he signed the letter and sent it on its way. Then he turned to the sermon he would give this morning—"For the Former Things Are Passed Away." At half past ten, the organ filled Plymouth Church with music, and its preacher stepped onto the stage. He looked upward. "Today is a good day to talk about heaven," he began.

Not being a churchgoing man, Frank Moulton slept in on Sundays. He was still in bed when his wife brought a letter from Beecher. As he read the first sentence—"as befits one who has about finished this world-life"—a dark cold settled over him. Once again a cowardly hopelessness had overtaken the preacher. How could a man who preached about the fragrance of morning flowers and other wonders of life be so fixated on death? He had the means within reach, Moulton knew. "It would be simply reported that Beecher died of apoplexy," the preacher had once remarked about swallowing the poison. "But God, and you, and I will know."

Evidently Beecher had not taken that final step to emancipate himself from what his letter called "the pain of life." His patience exhausted, Moulton did not mince words in his reply. *Your mood is a reservoir of mildew. It shows only a selfish faith in God to go whining into heaven because you are not courageous enough to live on earth. You don't begin to be in the danger today that you faced many times before, and it is not impossible to find a way out of this impasse. You know I love you so I shall try and try as in the past.*

Moulton sent the letter off for the preacher to find when Plymouth Church ended its morning service. Soon Tilton arrived to see what Beecher had decided about his resignation. He had also redrafted the card he proposed Beecher issue to the *Eagle* absolving Tilton of all responsibility for spreading slanders. After Tilton read Beecher's letter of this morning, both men agreed his own to the *Eagle* offered the only solution. Now Moulton had to convince Beecher.

"I don't believe there is a soul on earth, in whom there is some indication that God's grace has not entirely died out, who will not find an entrance into heaven." With that lesson, Beecher closed his sermon. After parishioners headed home, Beecher found Moulton's reply. If his friend's harsh words upset him, Beecher showed no sign when he returned to Plymouth Church for the evening service.

Lingering after the close, Beecher called to Frank Carpenter, one of the gentlemen he'd sent to confront Henry Bowen several days ago. "Have you seen Theodore?" he asked.

No, he had not seen Tilton, Carpenter replied.

"He is going to publish my letter. . . . It will be my ruin and his too." Whatever composure Beecher had maintained since awakening crumbled.

Carpenter walked Beecher to Moulton's house. Beecher ranted: "I can bear anything but the suffering of others for my fault. If Theodore will not do this thing, publish that letter, if he will withhold it, I will divide my fame and my fortune with him."

In Beecher's agitated state, Moulton easily convinced him to sign the card he and Tilton had agreed on. The next evening's *Eagle* carried it. Theodore Tilton was not the author of any of the calumnies or slander against him, declared Henry Ward Beecher, and it would be a great injustice for the public to think so. "Mr. Tilton's course towards me has been that of a man of honor and integrity."

Another crisis averted, by all appearances. But earlier that day, Beecher showed up at Moulton's, this time to see Frank's wife, Emma, with whom he also had a confidence. He remained despondently preoccupied with death. This was probably his last conversation with her, he said, for it was useless to live after Tilton published the confession he had signed.

Emma Moulton was as blunt as her husband. That would be a cowardly thing, she told Beecher. She offered an alternative: "Go down to your church and confess your crime. They will forgive you."

He couldn't. His children would despise him, his congregation would not listen, and if he lost his position as a spiritual and moral leader, nothing would be left. He had a powder he could take. He could sink quietly off as if falling asleep and be released from all his trials and troubles. So much better than publishing the card in the *Eagle*; its respite would be temporary. Trouble would break out again.

He raved for hours, tears streaming. He ignored her insistence that all was not lost, that Frank would stand by him no matter what, that she would always be his friend. She spotted a glimmer of solace when he promised to return tomorrow. He would bring little mementos to give different people. He came as promised, and the next day too, and though he remained depressed, he held out hope.

After several days, Beecher realized he needed help. He called in a doctor. His general health, his vigor, had come through the winter well, he said, but he wished to consult on his mental state. He was experiencing a peculiar state that he recognized as illusion but that seemed real. After sleeping soundly, he would be startled awake hearing his name. Voices called. He felt no terror—on the contrary, it was blissful, as though he were on the borders of heaven. He lay fully aware it was hallucination. Yet he seemed to have another self beside him in the bed, a self swayed that the illusionary perceptions truly existed.

The doctor prescribed *Cannabis indica*—hashish, as it was called in the East. The medicine soothed Beecher enough to get through the rest of the month. In July he left for his farm up the Hudson, the sanctuary where he spent his summers. His depression lifted among the forests and hills, the piping of birds, raspberries ripe for the picking, grapes on the vine. "I am a little heart-hungry to see you," he wrote Moulton, "not now because I am pressed, but because I love you."

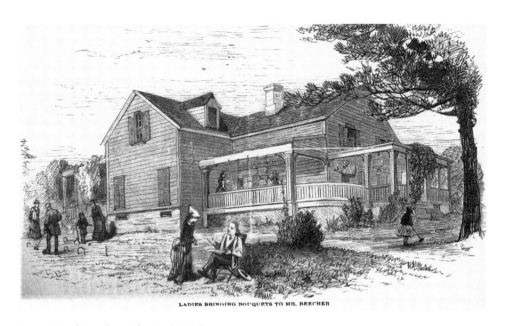

LADIES BRINGING BOUQUETS TO MR. BEECHER

Henry Ward Beecher at his Peekskill farm.
J. E. P. Doyle, Plymouth Church and Its Pastor, or Henry Ward Beecher and His Accusers, *1875*

34 | "PRONOUNCED DEAD"

THE FIRST MONDAY OF JUNE, Victoria Woodhull and Tennie Claflin appeared in the Court of Oyer and Terminer. The district attorney had at last scheduled their trial for libeling Luther Challis. Though the sisters were anxious for their day in court, their attorney, William Howe, protested that the trial could not proceed. Newly elected judge Noah Davis sat on the bench, the same man who had indicted the sisters while he was US Attorney. He could not preside. Though assuring Howe he could try the case impartially, Davis gave way, immediately calling in another judge.

Back in court the next morning, the defense team argued that material witnesses were unavailable. Most critical was Challis's companion James Maxwell. He would describe evenings when the two of them caroused, including the eventful one when Challis exhibited the red trophy of his seduction. Since the DA had indicted Maxwell for perjury, his trial must precede the sisters' lest the jury hearing their case be prejudiced against his testimony. After much wrangling, the DA agreed to postpone.

On Wednesday the sisters' obscenity case came up in US district court. The defense had insisted the case be moved there to escape US circuit court judge Charles Benedict. The excuse was that Benedict was a member of Plymouth Church and therefore an interested party in the outcome. The reality was that he had presided over several obscenity convictions based on testimony of Anthony Comstock, who would be the chief prosecution witness against Woodhull and Claflin. As the case opened, Howe petitioned to quash the indictments. The US Attorney argued back, only to discover he had brought the wrong indictments into court. The proceeding ended amid considerable embarrassment, only to be replayed Thursday morning.

By the end of the week, the city's horrible heat and her apprehension of impending imprisonment had worked Woodhull up to a pitch of intensity beyond endurance, or so judged the editors of the *New York Star* when she arrived at their offices Friday afternoon. She handed over a letter for publication decrying how the courts were being used as vehicles for spite, malice, and revenge.

Woodhull returned to the Broad Street office feeling ill. Catching a stage home with Claflin, she confided a fear that the week's pressures might kill her. She fiddled with food over dinner, then headed upstairs with Colonel Blood. Still at table, Claflin and her mother heard a crash. They found Woodhull crumpled on the stairs. With Blood, they laid her on her bed. After sending for doctors, they sought signs of life. A looking glass under her nose detected no breath. Tickling with a feather spurred no movement. The doctors applied restoratives to no avail.

She is dead, they told the family.

A half hour later, blood oozed from Woodhull's mouth. Her lips moved. A doctor whispered in her ear, "You must not speak, do not move. Your life depends on your remaining quiet." They put her hands and feet into hot water, applied mustard plasters to her body. The doctors consulted. *Apply restoratives without cessation*, they told the family. *Permit no one to see her. Even these efforts will be fruitless*, they counseled. *She could die before morning.*

VICTORIA WOODHULL DYING, headlined Saturday morning's *New York Sun*; PRONOUNCED DEAD BY HER TWO ATTENDING PHYSICIANS. The news rocketed across the country.

Over the next few days, Woodhull moved in and out of danger. Early Saturday morning she regained consciousness. By afternoon, she was suffering palpitations of the heart. Her lungs hemorrhaged until nightfall. Fever set in. On Sunday her life hung by a thread. As visitors descended on her house, doctors warned the slightest excitement could bring death.

Her condition won her little respite in the courts. Five days after her collapse, the proper obscenity indictments were delivered to the US district court, naming Woodhull, Claflin, and Blood as defendants. When informed that Woodhull would be unable to leave her house for at least ten days, the judge set the trial for Claflin and Blood anyway, three days hence.

Like all women, the defense protested, *Woodhull insists on having her own way. She will probably disregard her doctors' advice and appear, and likely suffer a relapse.*

"Well," said the judge, "if she wants to be willful and come, she can come for all I care." Under that ruling, the obscenity trial would begin nine days after the doctors had mistakenly pronounced her dead.

As Victoria Woodhull lay near death, Susan B. Anthony entered US circuit court in Canandaigua, a picturesque village among New York's Finger Lakes. The prior evening she had delivered her lecture "Is It a Crime for a United States Citizen to Vote?" for the fiftieth time. The first twenty-nine had been in Monroe County, where she had voted the past November and where her trial for that crime had been scheduled for mid-May. When the date arrived, the district attorney prosecuting her obtained a postponement and a change of venue. Her speeches had prejudiced potential jurors, he argued. Anthony said, fine, she would cover the new venue, Ontario County, as thoroughly as Monroe, and she did, twenty-one speeches in twenty-two days leading to the opening of her trial today.

Entering the courtroom, Anthony saw the more important reason the DA had sought to move the trial. Judge Ward Hunt, recently confirmed as associate justice of the US Supreme Court, was presiding. He was not a friendly face.

The trial opened with the DA describing Anthony casting ballots. "At that time she was a woman," he told the jury. The defense conceded that point. That was as exciting as things got except for the moment when Henry Selden, leading the defense, called Anthony to the stand. "She is not competent as a witness in her own behalf," the DA told the court. Judge Hunt agreed, prohibiting Anthony from uttering a word during her trial, at least within earshot of the twelve men presumably about to pass judgment. Selden's only choice was to stress that the jury must weigh three questions. First, was Anthony legally entitled to vote? Second, if she was not so entitled but believed in good faith she was, did Anthony's voting constitute a crime? Third, did Anthony in fact believe in good faith that she was so entitled? On the basis of those questions, the jury must acquit the defendant, he said.

The jurors need not have listened. When Selden concluded, Judge Hunt pulled out an opinion he had written earlier. Never leaving the bench, he informed the jury that the Fourteenth Amendment gives no right to a woman to vote. Anthony had voluntarily cast a vote, which was illegal and thus was subject to the penalty of the law. There was no question for the jury. Hunt directed the twelve men to find a verdict of guilty.

Selden objected: "It is for the jury to determine whether the defendant is guilty of a crime or not." He demanded the clerk poll the jury on the verdict.

No, Hunt said. The question was wholly one of law, and he had decided as a question of law that the Fourteenth Amendment did not give Anthony a right to vote. Hunt turned to the jury. "I therefore direct that you find a verdict of guilty."

"That is a direction no Court has power to make in a criminal case," Selden said. He demanded the clerk poll the jury on the verdict.

"No," Hunt said. "Gentlemen of the jury, you are discharged."

Susan B. Anthony was convicted without a second of deliberation, without even one of the twelve voicing an opinion—an opinion in court, that is. Freed from their duty, several of the jurors spoke freely. They would never have returned a guilty verdict.

The next day, Anthony got her voice back. Hunt ordered her to stand, and asked, "Has the prisoner anything to say why sentence shall not be pronounced?"

"Yes, your honor, I have many things to say; for in your ordered verdict of guilty you have trampled under foot every vital principle of our government. My natural rights, my civil rights, my political rights, my judicial rights, are all alike ignored.... I am degraded from the status of a citizen to that of a subject; and not only myself individually but all of my sex are."

Five times Hunt told her to sit down and shut up. Five times Anthony continued her harangue. He could deny her citizen's right to vote, her right of consent as one of the taxed, her right to a trial by a jury of her peers, even her right to life, liberty, and property. But she would not let him deny her the poor privilege of protest against his high-handed outrage, not after she hadn't been allowed a single word of defense since the day she was arrested. As for her sentence, after failing to get any justice, she wasn't going to ask for any leniency at his hands. He could sentence her to the full penalty the law allowed. Then she sat down, forcing Hunt to ask her to stand again for the sentence.

"The sentence is that you pay a fine of $100 and the costs of the prosecution," he said.

"May it please your honor," Anthony said, "I will never pay a dollar of your unjust penalty.... Not a penny shall go this unjust claim. And I shall earnestly and persistently continue to urge all women to ... the old Revolutionary maxim. 'Resistance to tyranny is obedience to God.'"

As the papers debated the injustice of Susan B. Anthony's conviction, Victoria Woodhull heard the gavel bang down to open her trial. She had already endured days of jury selection in a wretchedly ventilated courtroom. The man whose efforts had dragged her here sat gazing from the prosecution's table, his hands fidgeting with his necktie. The bundle of papers Comstock considered obscene rested before him. The man she relied on to fend off his accusations was absent. William Howe had taken sick, and though a few days' postponement would have brought him to her side, the judge refused. True, she had able substitutes well coached in Howe's tricks, and her sister and husband to share her plight. Neither was enough to wipe away the strain showing on her haggard face, no more than fanning with her bonnet relieved the oppressive heat.

"I am feeling very ill," Woodhull had confessed to a reporter after Henry Bowen and several gentlemen had called at her home a few days ago. They sought letters she possessed from Henry Ward Beecher. The spat between Bowen and Beecher had again burst open, and such letters might prove the preacher's crimes. She refused them. Heaven knows she had suffered enough abuse already, a great deal for one weak woman to bear. She would not get involved. But of course, the papers now bandied her name about with those two blackguards.

The prosecutor, a Mr. Purdy, began his opening statement. He lauded Anthony J. Comstock. The federal legislation forbidding obscene literature in the US mail had been a dead letter until Comstock began organizing prosecutions under it.

Nothing to do with the case, objected C. W. Brooke, substituting for Howe.

Judge Samuel Blatchford agreed. "Stick to the case," he said.

Thrown off his game, Purdy fumbled around until saved by the court adjourning.

When he called Comstock the next morning, the witness reminded everyone; he wanted it distinctly understood that his name had no *J*, Comstock said. It was simply Anthony Comstock, no initial. He was special agent of the Post Office Department of the General Government engaged in suppression of obscene literature.

It was not an auspicious start for the prosecution. After repeated defense objections that the judge sustained, Purdy managed to introduce as evidence the letter Comstock had sent under the alias J. Beardsly requesting the Beecher-Tilton scandal issue of *Woodhull & Claflin's Weekly*. Then he introduced the bundle of papers Comstock received in reply.

Objection, snapped J. Parker Jordan, a junior attorney at Howe & Hummel. He proceeded into a nearly incomprehensible explanation of the point he wished to make.

The judge got the essence, though. "I want to get down to hard rock," he said. "Do you mean that the words of the statute under which the defendants are indicted, 'other obscene publications,' are too vague to describe an offense?"

Jordan fumbled around some more before the judge made the argument for him. The original federal obscenity law passed in 1865 prohibited indecent books, pamphlets, prints, or other publications from the US mail. Congress passed a second obscenity law in 1872, explicitly adding to the prohibitions letters and envelopes with scurrilous epithets written on them. Finally, earlier this year, Congress had passed a third law explicitly adding more items, including papers, physical devices intended for indecent uses, and circulars related to those devices. If Congress added explicit items in 1872, the judge decided, it couldn't have intended those items to be covered under "other" in the 1865 act, and by extension, if Congress added "papers" in the 1873 act, it couldn't have intended that papers be covered under "other" in the 1872 act. Congressman Benjamin Butler, instrumental in passage of these acts, had said as much. Since the defendants were indicted for sending an obscene "paper" under the 1872 act, the judge ruled, the prosecution could not be maintained.

Anthony Comstock, still on the stand, watched. At some point it dawned on him that the obscenity law for which he secured passage three months ago was the reason Woodhull, Claflin, and Blood were about to go free. Prosecutor Purdy recognized it and called to enter a nolle prosequi on the indictment—a nonprosecution—leaving the defendants at risk of new charges. The defense would have none of it. "We want a verdict," defense attorney Brooke insisted.

The judge agreed the defendants were so entitled. "I state to the jury that the government has offered no evidence to support the indictment."

When the jury acquitted the defendants, no applause burst out. Several women surrounded Woodhull, Claflin, and Blood, many embracing, some kissing. But in five minutes "the court room was as empty and silent as if its echoes had never been disturbed with the story of the Woodhull & Claflin prosecution."

The next issue of *Woodhull & Claflin's Weekly* was neither empty nor silent. "And thus ends the most infamous series of persecutions that were ever instituted against any persons in the world," reported the *Weekly* with an exaggeration even the sisters on the masthead must have recognized. "Judge Blatchford informs the persecutors that they have caused us to be arrested and imprisoned, and held in an unheard-of amount of bail, without even a shadow of law for so doing."

The *Weekly* framed the whole ordeal as an "unholy war against two women," and identified its perpetrators: the YMCA and its great jackal Comstock, US prosecutors and New York district attorneys, federal judges and commissioners, and above all, the "revered citizen" the great scheme was designed to vindicate—Henry Ward Beecher. And the result? "No sane person will for an instant doubt that had there been no truth in what had been related, Mr. Beecher would have instantly pronounced the whole statement false. Instead . . . he did not dare to deny anything."

This attack on their persecutors differed little from other stories the *Weekly* had run since their original arrest. But they doubled down in two pieces. The first served as a sort of footnote to Woodhull's Beecher story, assuring readers that she knew of what she spoke. It reprinted an interview Woodhull gave the *Brooklyn Eagle*. The reporter asked about Henry Bowen seeking letters Beecher wrote her that would corroborate his adultery. Yes, she told him, she had letters from the preacher. She would keep them to herself. But any sensible person would realize from her "several month's intimacy with Mr. Beecher, being with him frequently and alone, that our correspondence was not one of mere platonic affection." Citing an evening in the Tiltons' front parlor bedroom upstairs, she confirmed "from intimate acquaintance that Mr. Beecher is a Free Lover . . . as he at different times proclaimed himself to be."

The second piece was an advertisement on the last page:

Published in Pamphlet Form,
THE
BEECHER-TILTON SCANDAL,
With numerous Extracts from
THE PRESS OF THE COUNTRY
ON THE

Prosecution and Illegal Arrest of the brave defenders
of freedom,
VICTORIA C. WOODHULL,
TENNIE CLAFLIN,
AND
COLONEL BLOOD.
Price of pamphlet reduced to $15 per hundred.

Woodhull and Claflin understood they had been acquitted on a technicality. Lest anyone pursue them under the new obscenity law that Comstock had pushed through Congress in March, they were announcing they would combat their prosecutors as tenaciously as heretofore.

35 | "THE GALLOWS IS ACCORDINGLY CHEATED"

A FEW WEEKS AFTER Susan B. Anthony's conviction and Victoria Woodhull's acquittal, the *Herald* sent a reporter to Murderers' Row in the Tombs. He found the most famous murderer enjoying an afternoon promenade with three other aristocratic inmates. A policeman delivering a drunken woman into the prison's safekeeping could hardly believe his eyes. "That gentleman without his hat, in white pants, light coat, and vest, with slippers on," he asked the reporter, "ain't that Stokes?"

Indeed it was, the reporter said. All four men had purchased luxuries poorer prisoners could never command, dressing as fashionably as if they were strolling along Broadway, dining together on meals served from the city's finer restaurants. Their appearance was like Milton's representation of Satan, the *Herald* noted the next morning—"In shape and gesture proudly eminent."

The noose that hung over Stokes's head had disappeared when the New York State Court of Appeals ordered a new trial. The unanimous decision cited errors Judge Boardman had made. "Law good enough to satisfy society fastens the halter around the criminal's neck," the *Herald* editorialized, "the Judge makes a mistake in knotting the rope, and the gallows is accordingly cheated. . . . The man who shot down Fisk is alone in the position to laugh at the law's delay."

Stokes did not laugh. Hearing the news, he was coolly complacent. How could the court have ruled otherwise, he asked, when his last trial was so notoriously unfair? Judge Boardman had acted more as an advocate for the prosecution than a judge. Now Stokes was hoping for a speedy retrial. He felt assured of acquittal.

The second most famous man on Murderers' Row occupied a more plebeian station, observed the *Herald* reporter. The "wretch Rosenzweig" also was awaiting his new trial. While the *Herald* guessed the people would in all probability rejoice at the abortionist's punishment by death, confusion in the district attorney's office was delaying that moment. When the *Herald* last checked, the office indicated Rosenzweig was Assistant District Attorney H. Russell's "pet case." As that gentleman was enjoying his vacation at Saratoga, the reporter asked another assistant DA about rumors the abortionist would be discharged. "Not that I know of," he said, and attributed the trial's delay to the heat. "In this Summer weather we want to take up and dispose of as many small cases as possible, so as to empty the City Prison. We don't want to have them all huddled together there in a cell." And no, he added, the new law against abortion passed since Rosenzweig's crime did not pose difficulties.

The reporter found the summer heat as the reason for delay hard to swallow, particularly as the prisoner had yet to be indicted. And for not the first time, he noted a general skepticism as he passed through the DA's office.

Would either man ever leave the Tombs? And if so, would he walk into the street a free man, be carted up the river in chains, or be carried out in a box? Whatever one's sympathies, one had to wonder.

One answer came November 1, twenty-two months after the crime. Deputy sheriffs unlocked the door of Tombs cell 4. *Prepare to depart*, they told Ned Stokes. Surprised the moment had come so quickly, Stokes gathered his papers and stepped into the corridor. He lit a cigar and stood with his back to the stove. Stoical to the end, he held out his hands. One of the deputies snapped on handcuffs with a sharp click. A shock like that from an electric battery shook Stokes's body. He bid a hasty goodbye to other prisoners standing on the tier above, then walked across the yard, where the deputy cuffed him to another prisoner headed up the river.

His trial had ended three nights earlier. It rehashed all that had gone on before— the defense had returned to the first trial's strategy, throwing everything against the wall to see what stuck. Witnesses had been coached and bribed, Stokes had fired in self-defense when Fisk drew first, Fisk's threats had driven Stokes insane, the doctors, not the bullet, had killed Fisk. The prosecution rebutted every such argument. The judge, too, got in on the act, addressing each point in a three-hour charge to the jury.

Who could be surprised that a confused jury came up with a verdict that satisfied no one? Guilty of manslaughter in the third degree, the foreman told the court.

The judge, New York Supreme Court Justice Noah Davis, expressed his outrage during the sentencing: "In rendering this verdict, Stokes, the jury have exhausted, and more than exhausted, all mercy in your case. No appeal to this court can diminish the sentence beyond the highest penalty . . . and that is apparently trifling as compared to the great crime you have committed. . . . [I] impose upon you all that the law confers upon me power to give, only regretting that that sentence cannot be more adequate to the awful crime that rests upon your guilty head." He ordered Stokes confined in Sing Sing at hard labor for the maximum four years.

The *Times* expressed the general opinion of the press, sharing Judge Davis's regret that he could award a sentence of only four years and lamenting the encouragement the lawless classes would take from this conclusion to the trial. The verdict satisfied Stokes no more than the papers, despite congratulations from his friends and attorneys at exchanging the noose for four years. Anyone of intelligence who heard the evidence and set aside petty prejudices, he told a reporter, could come to no conclusion but full acquittal. And after two years in the Tombs, he should not have to suffer a further four in Sing Sing. Instead of being incarcerated, he should be congratulated for his actions.

As for the public's mood, Harry Hill polled the patrons at his dance hall, one of the city's most notable if not respectable. As the hour waxed late, Hill interrupted the fiddlers drawing on their bows and announced the sentence: "Guilty of manslaughter, and he's got four years in State prison. . . . What do you think of it?"

"I say it's a shame," remarked a woman by the piano.

Agreement echoed from across the room. "He ought to be hung," said another.

"Here's another gal that says Ed Stokes ought to be hung," Hill said. "Anybody else think that?" Hearing the response, he declared hanging as the unanimous opinion of the crowd.

Outside the Tombs gate, the deputy flagged a horsecar headed for the Grand Central Depot. Stokes climbed aboard, ignoring passengers who crowded on for a closer look. The crowd followed as he boarded the train. Reaching the prison, he donned the striped uniform of the inmates.

That wardrobe was as onerous as his term was likely to get. Upon meeting the new prisoner, the warden assured Stokes that the "misery" of his confinement would be mitigated as much as possible. Rather than a dank cell, the prisoner would occupy comfortable quarters in the hospital, where he would soon receive anonymous female callers. Nor would he spend his days breaking stones or making shoes. Instead he would perform the light duties of a bookkeeper in the prison's cigar manufactory.

Young dandies with homicidal inclinations might note how serenely a murder could culminate in a trip up the river, observed the *Herald*.

Dr. Rosenzweig got his decision days later. Over a month had passed since William Howe had argued the case before Judge Sutherland. His grounds were simple. The abortion law the state legislature passed last year invalidated the 1869 law, which had been in effect when Rosenzweig committed his crime. No law existed on which to retry the doctor.

In his ruling, Judge Sutherland agreed. The conclusion inevitably followed from the repealing words in the fifth section of the 1872 act. Strike out that section and the prisoner would not go free. He couldn't do it, Sutherland said. A judge had no right to strike that part or any other. The prisoner must be discharged.

Assistant DA Russell asked for a twenty-four-hour delay to consider his case. Rosenzweig would endure another night in the Tombs. The next morning Russell requested a writ of error to hold the prisoner until a higher court could rule. Judge Sutherland said no. It was as plain to him as two and two make four. The law didn't care that Rosenzweig was a notorious criminal. The judge must discharge him.

Rosenzweig's wife and daughter surrounded him. Other friends—Rosenzweig still had some—congratulated him on his good fortune. Howe barged in to vigorously shake the hand of the client who had berated his efforts in the papers. Though he would later call the case "a manifest miscarriage of justice effected by a wise change in the laws," the law was sacred. Howe had done his duty to uphold it.

The doctor dubbed the Fiend of Second Avenue left the courtroom a free man. After two Thanksgivings imprisoned, he had much to be thankful for on the upcoming holiday.

36 | "DENOMINATIONAL ARGUMENT"

ON HALLOWEEN, the lecture hall at Plymouth Church filled to capacity. It was an intimate place compared to the church, seating only a thousand. Crimson-cushioned settees substituted for pews, and a simple cane chair awaited the preacher. The crowd was unusual for the Friday night prayer meeting. The attraction tonight was the business meeting to follow.

Promptly at eight, Henry Ward Beecher sat in the chair. He called out a number. The audience rustled through their hymnals, the organist tapped the keys of a grand piano, and Beecher led his congregation in song. He enjoyed a full chorus, he would remind the singers if they lagged.

Beecher was hopeful tonight. He had returned from his summer vacation early in the month. The fresh air and recreation of the country had invigorated him. Work had too. He had preached on every Sabbath but two—so much better than idleness. He even escaped his usual attack of hay asthma. As he began another year of labor at Plymouth Church, he announced on his first Friday back, he would work as the birds sing—for joy's sake. His was a labor of love, and he aimed "to avoid any manner of preaching that would incite contention or denominational argument."

So far he had not found his church cooperating much with this aim. The first week, one member filed charges against Theodore Tilton with Plymouth Church's Examining Committee. William West accused Tilton of circulating scandalous reports about Beecher. For months he had lobbied for an investigation, aiming to have Plymouth Church expel Tilton. In August he had told Tilton as much. Not necessary, Tilton responded, he was no longer a member of the church. He hadn't set foot in the place since he'd withdrawn years ago. Nor would he go back for any purpose, investigation or otherwise. Nonetheless West wanted the whole Beecher-Tilton affair aired. When he found Tilton's name still on the church's membership roll, he pushed forward.

Beecher desperately sought to avoid any investigation that would revive the scandal. *It is no matter for the church*, he repeated over and over to the brethren who approached him. *It will accomplish nothing.* With the Examining Committee looking into it, Beecher and Frank Moulton called Tilton to Moulton's house. They agreed on a solution—Tilton would send a letter declining to accept a copy of West's charges on the ground he had ceased his membership four years ago. The church would then pass a simple resolution that whereas Tilton had terminated his membership, be it resolved that the roll be amended with that fact. No mention of the scandal or differences between Beecher and Tilton was necessary.

That resolution would be taken up at the business meeting tonight. Its approval would drive the final nail into the coffin of the scandal Beecher thought long since buried.

After the opening hymns, Beecher delivered a short address on dealing with trouble. If man knew but how to lean back upon the strength of God and say He will not lay on a burden that cannot be borne, adversity would be shorn of its terrors, Beecher told his flock. "God is a present help in time of need. We may trust implicitly in that." He then called another hymn to close the prayer meeting.

Midway through the song, Theodore Tilton strode up the main aisle and sat near the platform. His face was flushed, his demeanor excited. A decided sensation rolled through the crowd.

———

Four days earlier, Tilton had discovered a short piece about himself in the *Sun*. According to the paper, he had written a letter to the Plymouth Church Examining Committee saying that inasmuch as he had not been a member for the past four years, he did not feel duty bound to obey the committee's citation to appear and answer charges against him. Tilton was not pleased to find the *Sun* announcing he was accused of "charges." Everyone would know they referred to slandering Beecher. The agreement he had struck with Beecher and Moulton specifically avoided mention of any animosity between himself and the preacher.

In an interview published that evening in the *Brooklyn Eagle*, Tilton disputed the *Sun*'s account. He had written no letter to Plymouth Church. Nor had he refused to answer any charges. The church had made none. It had not even contemplated an investigation. The Beecher scandal was dead, and any effort to resurrect it was only less contemptible than the course of lying and equivocation that created it. Beecher agreed, stating that Tilton had never slandered him and the effort to make that gentleman appear in such a light was no less annoying to him, Beecher, than it was grossly unjust to Tilton.

The presumed instigator of the *Sun*'s story responded in a letter the *Eagle* published two days later. As a member of Plymouth Church and interested in its welfare, William West wrote, he could not let Tilton's statements pass uncorrected. For three years Tilton had circulated scandalous reports about Beecher. The only way for Plymouth Church to meet these accusations was to call Tilton to account. Accordingly, West had filed charges with the church's Examining Committee, which had sent them to Tilton two weeks past with a request to answer. Tilton had refused, claiming he was no longer a member of the church. West was prepared to prove the charges at any time and expected the committee to thoroughly investigate.

Tilton could not abide people thinking he was pleading nonmembership in Plymouth Church to evade answering the charges. By the morning of Halloween, he learned the report the Examining Committee would present at the business meeting tonight cited such evasion as reason to expel him from Plymouth Church. He would attend in person to defend himself.

As the business meeting got underway, the assistant pastor read the Examining Committee's report. It was exactly as Tilton feared but for the words "dropped from the rolls" substituted for "expel." That change did not soften the blow.

His accuser, William West, was no more satisfied. Rule number seven did not allow Tilton's removal in such a manner, he insisted. It required the accused member be duly served with the time and place of a hearing and have the opportunity to defend himself. West proposed the Examining Committee appoint a time and place for hearing the case against Tilton.

As the debate degenerated into confusion, Tilton stood up, scorn on his face. Fending off dissent, the moderator of the meeting let him speak. After defending his withdrawal from membership and denying any slander of Beecher, Tilton got to the point. He was here tonight of his own free will to say in Beecher's presence that "if I have slandered him I am ready to answer for it to the man whom I have slandered. If, therefore, the minister of this church has anything whereof to accuse me let him speak now, and I shall answer, as God is my judge."

As another uproar threatened, Beecher stepped forward. A member had every right to withdraw as Tilton had, he said. Then he addressed Tilton: "He asks if I have any charge to make against him. I have none. Whatever differences have been between us have been amicably adjusted and, so far as I am concerned, buried."

Applause burst out. The assistant pastor said the time had come to put the matter to bed. "Isn't it possible," he asked, "to put the question into so simple a shape that we may all understand it?"

"Are we to understand," asked a member, "that the simple dropping of Mr. Tilton's name settles the whole of what is called the scandal without even a censure of anybody?"

That simple approach would not prevail. The Examining Committee's original resolution was resurrected for a vote. With 201 ayes against 13 nays, Tilton's name was "dropped from the role of membership."

Beecher disappeared to the right of the stage. Tilton stood on the opposite side while the congregation exited by him. Many shook his hand warmly. Others conspicuously avoided any contact.

Since the resolution passed cited his evasion of charges, Tilton might have blown up. But Beecher had publicly validated his withdrawal from Plymouth Church four years ago and absolutely denied any differences between them. It was enough to mollify Tilton. When a reporter asked him the next day whether Plymouth Church had expelled him, Tilton responded emphatically no. Saying that would be false and defamatory. He had gone to Plymouth Church last night prepared to meet any accusation. Beecher had none to make.

Like Beecher, Tilton was ready to bury the scandal. Surely their public declarations to each other would allow it. But no, the "denominational argument" Beecher sought to avoid was too powerful. Other men would keep it alive.

37 | "REFORMATION OR REVOLUTION— WHICH?"

IN MID-OCTOBER, four thousand people filled the Cooper Institute, paying fifty cents for the privilege. Not an inch of space was vacant, not an aisle, stairway, or ante-room. Thousands more were turned away at the door. The night's lecturer was Victoria Woodhull, speaking on "Reformation or Revolution—Which? Or, Behind the Political Scenes." So eager was the crowd that howls chased the gentleman introducing her from the stage. They wanted Woodhull and they wanted her now.

Woodhull needed the support of eager audiences this autumn. The season had started badly. Leaving work in September, she had climbed aboard a horsecar going uptown. Gentlemen headed home from their labors filled most seats. Not paying much attention, she took one beside an elegantly dressed lady. The lady immediately hid behind her fan and whispered, "For heaven's sake, Mrs. Woodhull, don't recognize me here. It would ruin my business." Woodhull remembered the lady as the keeper of a house of assignation she had once called upon, as she was wont to do on mis-sions of mercy for fallen women. How could she ruin this lady's business? She puzzled before the understanding hit her. Gentlemen aboard the stage frequented the house for their assignations. They might never return if Victoria Woodhull was associated with the place. Even women whom the world called prostitute, women whom Woodhull defended with every breath, dared not be seen with her. The realization had made Woodhull feel like the most ostracized person in the world.

And over the past two weeks, she had been arrested twice. Despite her acquittal in June, three obscenity indictments were still outstanding. Since the US commissioner hearing her case understood none of those indictments would come to trial, he released her on her own recognizance. But the US Attorney's office was considering new indict-ments. The stress continued to undermine Woodhull's health. The audience tonight could see it in her flushed face, hear it in her voice occasionally breaking up like a dilapidated flute. They welcomed her with turbulent applause and when she faltered urged her on, calling out "Go in, old gal" and "Wet your whistle." She took heart, at times laying aside her speech and prancing about the platform.

Woodhull could have played the martyr, could have reprised her well-known ideas on women's rights and social freedom. She touched upon those elements. But overall, she embraced a new theme driven by the tumult that had rocked the country over the past month. In mid-September, Jay Cooke & Company, the leading financier of railroads, collapsed. A "mad terror" took over Wall Street. Hordes of men rushed to dump their stocks, almost begging people to take them at any price. The day was the most tempestuous since the collapse of Jim Fisk and Jay Gould's gold corner four years before. The next day opened with fresh calamities. Depositors launched a run on the banks. The Fourth National shuttered first, leading to a cascade of failures. By the close of business, at least twenty leading financial firms had failed. The stock exchange shut down for the next ten days. Across the country, business went into a tailspin. Railroads, the driving engines of the economy, became as worthless as so much old iron left to rust in the sand. Men worth millions found themselves penniless. Tens of thousands became destitute in New York alone. As what became known as the Panic of 1873 rolled across the country, businesses failed by the thousands.

"We are on the verge, if not already in the flood of a financial convulsion that will shake this country from centre to circumference," Woodhull told the Cooper Institute crowd. The wealthy and powerful who were losing enormous amounts did not win her sympathy, not the "Upper Ten" who devoted their time and talent to securing the gains from what others produced. Woodhull spoke for the "Lower Millions" whom they subjugated, those who toiled for sustenance, who faced "hunger with its long, bony fingers, pinched cheeks and fiery eye," the men, women, and children eking out a miserable life upon what a "sport" would disdain to feed his dogs. Already thousands of New York fathers had lost their jobs. Would their wives and children be left to beg, steal, or starve?

Woodhull blamed many culprits for the calamity—business enterprises outstripping their regulators, politicians selling themselves to retain power, railroads charging farmers two bushels of wheat to deliver one to market, monopolies of land and industry, the God-in-the-Constitution movement pushing a national religion, and on and on.

But this night she tempered her voice. The lecture's title, "Reformation or Revolution—Which?" reflected the change. Whereas she had long called for revolution, she now pushed for reformation. "On every hand, the murmurings of discontent among the masses are breaking out into rebellion," she told the crowd. Only through overhauling political institutions could revolution be avoided. Woodhull cited a trinity that reform required: freedom to choose how to live one's life, justice in how society treats people, and equality in enjoying the comforts and wealth the country produces. The time was ripe to build this trinity, riper than she had before imagined, she said. Society was embracing an intellectual and moral awakening that might bring this reform without the bloody strife she had long anticipated, a strife from which she shrunk with horror.

And she got personal. She came tonight in a new spirit, she told the crowd, not so much to trumpet her truths as to feel the pulse of the public. To learn as much as to instruct. She had done the best she could, she was proud to say, had been true to the convictions she held. Now the public must pass judgment. She expressed her newfound confidence that the people would give the principles she advocated a fair consideration based on their merit.

"We still have before us an immense work," she said, "the greater work than all that have preceded it." She would continue to push for what she believed. But she looked forward to a day when her duties as an agitator would end: "I am tired of fighting."

When Woodhull concluded, applause in the hall was deafening. Several gentlemen stepped forward to address the crowd. The roar drowned them out. Even when Woodhull returned to adjourn the meeting, the crowd clamored for more, and if Woodhull could speak no longer, they demanded Tennie Claflin take the stage.

Despite the conciliatory elements in her speech, Woodhull had predicted the morning papers would abuse her. She was right. The *Herald* called her listeners a "Black Crook" audience attending to hear her utter obscenities. The unusually large portion of women occupying seats exposed that lie. Nor did anything she said signal surrender, or even truce.

The overflow crowd at the Cooper Institute foreshadowed how Woodhull's career would thrive in the years ahead. Over the next three, she filled halls from the largest cities to one-horse towns, from New England through the Midwest to the Deep South and on to the west coast. A lecture in St. Paul, Minnesota, in February 1874, demonstrated the enthusiasm and diversity of her audiences. An hour beforehand, "the crowd began to swarm over the entrances and into the body of the Opera House. The more anxious few made a dash for seats . . . beardless young men, closely followed by a few members of the Legislature . . . Ex-governors and grave-looking Senators stalked in . . . church dignitaries elbowed their way past the habitues of Eight and Nash-street brothels . . . It was an irruption of all classes and conditions of people, from banker to apple peddler, from military hero to night scavenger—all mixed in democratic confusion," noted the *St. Paul Daily Press*. In Atlanta, Woodhull herself greeted attendees as they arrived— "members of the senate and house of representatives were present in force and were flanked on all sides by some of the first gentlemen of the city in every department of commercial, literary and professional life." Ladies too filed into an event they previously would have shunned. They filled a quarter of the opera house in Cincinnati, "ladies who were not too cowardly to come out to a public place and listen to a lecture which in their hearts they long since had a desire to hear, [who] went away well pleased with themselves at having had the 'grit' to go," the *Cincinnati Daily Enquirer* ventured to say.

How did a woman so vilified become one of America's top attractions on the lecture circuit? Certainly controversy contributed mightily. Whether they agreed with or abhorred what Woodhull advocated, people wanted to "hear exactly how terrible were the doctrines which had lifted this woman to such prominence and brought upon herself and her sister such an avalanche of abuse and vituperation," observed the *Atlanta Constitution*. Woodhull did not disappoint them. She applied "the scalpel of her oratory to the pustular tumors of the social system with an unrelenting purpose and a pitiless hand," said the *Reading Times* of Pennsylvania. The *Standard* of Northfield, Minnesota, wrote she exposed "the diseases that have made society little better than 'rotten at the core,' and with a bold unflinching hand [held] up the hypocritical canters of the day to the public gaze in all their hideous deformity."

Whether people agreed with Woodhull or not, she succeeded "in impressing the most of her hearers with the idea that she is honest and mightily convinced of the theories which she so ably advocates," noted the *Waterton Daily Times* in upstate New York. "That she tells much truth is not to be denied," echoed Wisconsin's *Monroe County Republican*. Woodhull herself proclaimed the power of truth: "If you want to put me down you must prove that I have not told the truth, otherwise you will only fill my houses."

More than controversy, more than Woodhull's ideas and conviction, the woman herself filled the halls. She mesmerized her audience. The press described her as "one of the two or three most eloquent and forcible speakers among the women who have appeared on the American platform . . . the boldest of them all." As a woman who "seems to speak in the very glow of inspiration . . . [who] can borrow at pleasure the thunderbolts of the gods and hurl them with unerring precision." As "launch[ing] forth in a perfect torrent of eloquent and impassioned words." Or as one member of her audience said within earshot of a reporter, "They do say as how she's lightnin' when she really do get warmed up."

Had all the talk and all the controversy accomplished anything? Woodhull told her audiences yes, and she invoked the exposure of Henry Ward Beecher as a huge contributor. "People's ideas now are very different from what they were two years ago," she said in Cincinnati. "The Brooklyn scandal has helped open the eyes of the multitude." The *Waterton Dispatch* agreed, calling the exposure of Beecher a "masterpiece." "On the wings of this, her name and her theories, though misunderstood, have been wafted over the inhabited world," the paper said. "A mind endowed by extraordinary talent in so many directions is a rare occurrence in the world," it continued, "and if she lives she will doubtless leave an impress upon the race which in extent at least will compare favorably with that of any who have lived before her."

It was a remarkable tribute, but only one of many superlatives during these years of lecturing. Through her exposure of the most famous man in America, Victoria Woodhull had become "the best known woman in America" and "the most remarkable woman of the age," or so the press said. One paper compared her renown to another Victoria—she was probably "more talked and written about than any other woman living, save perhaps her namesake, the Queen of England."

Said another: "Victoria came; Victoria conquered!"

EPILOGUE

THE SECOND WEEK OF JANUARY 1875, crowds thronged around the City Court of Brooklyn. Only the lucky few with tickets held any hope of getting inside. Even then, likely as not a policeman would forbid entrance to courtroom number 2, its floor and galleries too packed to squeeze another soul into the opening days of the trial Theodore Tilton versus Henry Ward Beecher. Inside the rail, the participants crammed around tables, the legal teams jostling among themselves, the principals involved in this drama—Henry Ward Beecher, Theodore Tilton, Lib Tilton, Frank Moulton—so tight together they could hardly avert their gazes from one another. Only the press seemed to enjoy sufficient space, perhaps in recognition that the public's fascination over the past six months had not abated.

In a sense, this was the third trial, though the prior two had not played out in court. A rival Congregational minister to Beecher had instigated the first, charging that Plymouth Church had violated Congregational doctrine when it dropped Theodore Tilton from its rolls without an investigation. Though Plymouth told him to mind his own business, a council of Congregational churches convened to look into Plymouth's action, along with Beecher's and Tilton's that had led to that point. In reporting the results, the council chairman lauded Beecher to the skies. Never had he known a man of larger and more generous mind. He denounced Tilton as a dog and a knave.

Tilton couldn't abide it and responded with a review of the scandal published in his journal the *Golden Age*. This new airing built enormous pressure on Beecher. Desperate for relief, he asked Plymouth Church to investigate "the rumors, insinuations, or charges made respecting my conduct, as compromised" by Tilton's publication. Over the summer of 1874, Beecher's handpicked committee interviewed scores of witnesses and compiled reams of evidence. The details leaked daily and were reported across the country by hundreds of reporters staked out in Brooklyn. In late August it delivered its conclusions. Henry Ward Beecher had not committed adultery with Elizabeth Tilton; nor committed any unchaste or improper acts with her; nor made any unchaste or improper remark, proffer, or solicitation to her of any kind or description whatever. Nothing whatever in the evidence should impair the perfect confidence of Plymouth Church or the world in the Christian character and integrity of Henry Ward Beecher.

The investigation was a whitewash. The *Herald* called it an inquiry into whether a man was guilty only in order to declare its support of him, whether guilty or not. In exonerating Beecher, it condemned Theodore Tilton as the instigator of the scandal, by implication if not words. Again, Tilton refused to accept that judgment. He sued Beecher for "contriving and willfully intending to injure the plaintiff and deprive him of the comfort, society, aid and assistance of [his wife] . . . and to alienate and destroy her affection for him."

So the scandal would play out once again over the next six months. The key evidence against Beecher would be the testimony of Theodore Tilton, Frank Moulton, and Moulton's wife, Emma, plus all the letters and other documents generated during the years the parties had conspired to cover up the scandal. Emma Moulton's statement would be cited as the most damning. She described how both Beecher and Lib Tilton confessed their intimacy to her, and she backed up her story by relating how Beecher had tearfully threatened suicide.

Beecher's defense boiled down to simplistic arguments. On April 1, he took the stand sniffing a nosegay of violets and refusing to swear on the Bible. He flatly denied what witnesses Tilton and the Moultons had said. Lib Tilton had "thrust her affections upon [him] unsought," he said, and had concocted the affair in retaliation for her husband's philandering. His mistake was only in trying to help the couple through their difficulties, thereby creating dissent within the household. His letters, such as the confessional one known as the "letter of contrition," were no more than apologies for that interference.

His attorneys added two twists. Accusing Emma Moulton of using an unladylike expression, they impeached her testimony by telling the jury, "Gentlemen, you have seen for yourselves that Mrs. Moulton is naturally a lady. She could no more have made that coarse and vulgar speech to her pastor at that time than she could have cut off her hand." Or as a Beecher biographer expressed it, she was such a respectable lady that she must be a liar to testify she had said such things to Beecher. As for Beecher himself, his attorneys argued he was such a great man that Tilton's charges were not against Beecher but against society and civilization. Said one in his opening statement, "It is a miracle if he was guilty." The prosecution must "produce sufficient evidence to convince the jury that a miracle has happened."

Six months after the trial began, the jury went into deliberations. Through eight days of unbearable heat and nearly sleepless nights, the twelve men cast fifty-two ballots. Then they gave up. They disagreed on the facts of the case, they told the judge, on the veracity of the witnesses. The judge put them through one more miserable evening before he declared the jury hung. The twelve limped away, three of them ill from the ordeal.

The diverging opinions of the jury reflected the world, observed the *Times*. For months the public had been divided over Beecher's innocence or guilt. No verdict would change one in a hundred's belief.

The reaction of Plymouth Church bore the paper out. The congregation welcomed Beecher back to a church filled to the rafters, with hordes more turned away at the door. One member summed up the feeling: "No voice uttered from the press or pulpit could make them leave Mr. Beecher, and ten thousand juries could not make them doubt his word. They would go through with him to the end, whatever that might be." Others complained of the injustice of forged documents and altered evidence wielded against the Reverend Beecher. Throughout the service, many watched one of their brethren sitting in a front pew, one of the just-released jurors from the trial. They had looked on him as an unrelenting adherent of their preacher throughout the trial. Days later the church expressed their devotion by quadrupling Beecher's annual salary to $100,000, recompense for legal bills he had incurred.

Though not surprised, the *Times* concluded the evidence could not support such blind loyalty. Irrespective of the verdict, all sensible men would acknowledge in their hearts that Beecher's management of his private friendships and affairs was unworthy of his name, position, and sacred calling. A survey of attorneys across the country concurred with that assessment, with a sizable majority concluding that the evidence supported full conviction. As for the public's thoughts, who could tell from the blizzard of opinions?

In the years ahead, Beecher's partisans unflaggingly supported him. But as his loyal brother William predicted, the majority of the world would accept his guilt. Beecher could write his friends that "the old scandal is hardly thought of anymore." Yet lecturing across the country, he fought his way through screaming, spitting crowds at train stations, hotels, and halls where he spoke. At one stop in Iowa, a mob attacked the private railcar he rode in. Only another man grabbing a hot poker and slashing a rioter barreling through the door saved Beecher from a savage beating.

Beecher remained the pastor of Plymouth Church until its bells tolled his death twelve years later.

In 1877 Victoria Woodhull turned to a new chapter in her life. She was exhausted from lecturing and the halls weren't filling anymore. With health and money troubles dogging her, *Woodhull & Claflin's Weekly* had closed the prior June. And she had divorced Colonel Blood. The divorce papers charged him with adultery, a legal necessity. Blood summed up the more honest cause. Work had bound him and Woodhull together. Now that work—the *Weekly*, the brokerage, the political campaigning—had run its course. Still, he called her "the grandest woman in the world."

So in the summer of 1877, Woodhull sailed for England with her children, mother, and Tennie. Rumors claimed Cornelius Vanderbilt's son William footed the bill with a $100,000 payment. His father had died in January, leaving almost his entire estate to

William. The rumors supposed William didn't want Woodhull or Claflin subpoenaed as his siblings contested the old man's competence. Woodhull denied it. She was leaving for the sake of her daughter, who was just budding into womanhood. "I wish to leave [her] an untarnished name," she said.

Her father, another sister, and nieces soon joined the family in London. Woodhull resumed her lecturing. Her topic was sex education, a subject no man would touch, observed one reporter, but one that much pleased her audience. Another praised her as unquestionably a great orator, with language impassioned and fearless. Nonetheless her notoriety had followed her across the pond. Hisses mingled with applause. The London suffragists rebuffed her after Susan B. Anthony wrote that the sisters were lewd and indecent and advised to leave them alone.

A prominent banker attended one of the lectures. John Biddulph Martin had developed an interest in women's rights through his late sister and had been following Woodhull in the press. He hoped to find something of his lost Penelope in the speaker. He found much more. "I was charmed by her high intellect, and fascinated by her manner," he recalled, "and left the lecture hall that night with the determination that if Mrs. Woodhull would marry me, I would certainly make her my wife."

Martin called at Woodhull's home and enjoyed a talk with her daughter, now going by Zula. Not until a year later, after ending another relationship, did he meet Woodhull. "She was more alive than anyone I have ever met," he wrote. "When you were with her . . . you saw miracles all around you."

Several months later, he rented a house next door, where they could be together privately.

They began talking of marriage. Her antecedents and his aristocratic family were obstacles that would take years to overcome. She reinvented herself, essentially disavowing much of her prior life. He brought her to the family seat, going back five generations, and introduced her to the family. The estate and Martin's family overawed her. Though she won his parents over, a brother investigating Woodhull's background disrupted a planned wedding. Woodhull enlisted Francis Cook, Tennie's friend who would eventually make her Lady Cook, to press her case. Almost three years would pass, the couple's bond growing ever stronger, before they wed in October 1883. A year later Martin wrote, "The happiest year of very many that passed, my love and esteem for Victoria grew every day." The affection was evident in the notes they exchanged until his death ended their fourteen-year marriage.

During the marriage, Woodhull relaunched her career. She began a new journal, the *Humanitarian, a Monthly Magazine of Sociology*. In 1892 she returned to the United States with Martin. That September, a national convention of woman suffragists meeting in Washington, DC, nominated her for president. She admitted this campaign was educational but predicted that before many years a woman would win the White House.

Woodhull lived to see American women win the vote in 1920, dying seven years later at age eighty-eight. As a wealthy widow and philanthropist, she had supported causes from children's education and health care to the International Peace Society. She enjoyed visits from her old suffrage friends Elizabeth Cady Stanton and Isabella Beecher Hooker.

In her sixties, Woodhull had discovered a new joy, the automobile. She was the first woman to drive through London's Hyde Park and to motor through the English countryside. Her first car was an electric Victoria. When a neighbor spotted her driving it, he told her it wasn't ladylike. "It will be," she said, ever the prophetess.

In 1912 Anthony Comstock celebrated his fortieth anniversary as a crime fighter for the New York Society for the Suppression of Vice and its predecessor YMCA committee. "We hope that you will find endless satisfaction in the measureless good you have done," the society wrote in a letter of appreciation. "We thank you for the heroic services you have rendered to our country and to humanity."

Comstock claimed to have destroyed fifty tons of vile books, seventeen tons of stereotype plates, and four million obscene pictures. He totaled his arrests at 3,646 and convictions at 2,682. The goods would fill sixteen freight cars and the collared criminals sixty-one passenger cars, by his count. The criminals collectively had been sentenced to 565 years, 11 months, and 20 days, and had paid $237,140.40 in fines. Surprisingly his statistics did not include the culprits he had driven to death. Decades earlier he reputedly had boasted that the one who would become the most notorious was number fifteen. In 1878 he had entrapped Madame Restell, the abortionist known as the wickedest woman in New York. The night before her trial was to begin, she filled her bathtub, stepped in, and slit her throat.

Despite the antivice society's praise, by the turn of the century Comstock was overplaying his hand. During the 1893 World's Columbian Exposition in Chicago, he got a taste of how time was passing him by. Like a new Columbus, he undertook a voyage of discovery to the exposition's Midway Plaisance in search of something to offend his moral sensibilities, wrote the *New York Evening World*. He found it at "The Street in Cairo," where Little Egypt was dancing the hoochie-coochie. The dancer's shimmying was "distinctly and disgustingly obscene," Comstock told the reporter. In demonstration, he wreathed his shirt-sleeved arms over his head and made his ginger-colored whiskers shiver in the air. "Not at all libidinous," concluded the reporter.

The episode was an early warning of the laughingstock he would become. In the years ahead, he attacked New York's Art Students' League for a study of nudes in its catalog. He endured withering parodies from the artists and almost lost his commission as US postal inspector. He insisted garment makers remove unclad mannequins from public view. He protested nudes in art gallery windows, only to have dealers draw enormous crowds by defying him. Others learned from that experience. After he arrested the promoters of the Mammoth Physical Exhibition, an athletic contest in which the men appeared bare chested and the women wore white union suits, twenty thousand rushed to Madison Square Garden. When he publicly threatened the producer of a play by George Bernard Shaw, the man answered. Two exchanges of letters printed in the press guaranteed the play's success. Shaw got into the act, calling Comstockery "the world's standing joke at the expense of the United States."

In 1915 Comstock testified in his final case. He had arrested Margaret Sanger, at the time a little-known advocate of birth control, for her pamphlet *Family Limitation*. She fled to England, leaving behind her husband, William, an artist and architect. Comstock sent an agent to his studio. The agent portrayed himself as a friend of Margaret who had all her works but that one. He sought it to distribute to the poor. William dug up a copy. Comstock secured a warrant and arrested him. Upon conviction, the judge said if the women advocating for suffrage would tell women to have more children, they would do a greater service. When he sentenced William Sanger to a $150 fine or thirty days in jail, the defendant shouted, "It is indeed the law that is on trial here today. I will never pay that fine." As officers seized him, Sanger supporters who had packed the court launched a storm of protest. The judge pounded and pounded his gavel until police arrived to clear the room.

Comstock had won his verdict, but he would lose this war. The uproar over the case catapulted Margaret Sanger's fame and ideas. She returned to New York and opened a birth control clinic in Brooklyn. After World War I, she founded the American Birth Control League, which lives on as Planned Parenthood.

ACKNOWLEDGMENTS

I WANT TO EXTEND A SPECIAL THANKS TO MY AGENT, Amy Bishop at Dystel, Goderich & Bourret, and to my editor, Jerry Pohlen at Chicago Review Press. Without them this story would never have made it on to a bookshelf. Nor would it have gotten there without Ben Krapohl and the rest of the staff at Chicago Review Press.

Over two decades, I've worked with many writers, both established and aspiring. My work has improved greatly with their help and encouragement. I want to mention especially Jacob Miller at Jacob's Studio in Manhattan and the workshop leaders at Sackett Street Writers' Workshop in Brooklyn: founder Julia Fierro, Ted Thompson, Will Boast, and Aria Sloss. They go all the way back to my novel-writing days and may remember that is how this story started.

My friends who read drafts of this book are too numerous to list, but they too deserve a huge amount of credit.

Most due my thanks is Diane, who persevered through this adventure and has shared all the others hiking the world.

A NOTE ON SOURCES

IN WRITING ABOUT 1872 NEW YORK, I am most indebted to the city's journalists. Their pieces in the *Times, Herald, Tribune, Evening Post, Commercial Advertiser, Sun,* and other papers I reference fueled my understanding not only of the characters and their stories but also of the city itself. With the rest of the country entranced by events in the city, papers coast to coast contributed as well.

I also relied on the city's chroniclers of this era. James McCabe, Matthew Hale Smith, Junius Hale Browne, and Gustav Lening painted broad portraits of New York. Others focused on particular segments: Thomas Byrnes and Charles Sutton on criminals; Marshall Stafford, Willoughby Jones, and J. W. Goodspeed on the life and death of Jim Fisk; Lyman Abbott, J. E. P. Doyle, and Joseph Howard on Plymouth Church and its pastor, to name a few.

The characters themselves told their own stories: Victoria Woodhull through *Woodhull & Claflin's Weekly,* her speeches, and her letters; Anthony Comstock through his diary, now disappeared but quoted heavily by Heywood Broun and Margaret Leech, plus his books, his criminal records, and his official biographer, Charles Trumbull; Susan B. Anthony also worked with her biographer Ida Husted Harper, and the Elizabeth Cady Stanton and Susan B. Anthony Papers Project published her diary and letters. Thanks to the voluminous records of the Plymouth Church investigation and the subsequent trial, the players in the Beecher-Tilton scandal reprised their roles through letters, statements, and testimony.

Finally, memoirs by contemporaries like financier Henry Clews and lawyer Theron Strong added to the tapestry.

The endnotes are limited to quotations. For readers interested in detailed sourcing for facts, descriptions, and so forth, I have a more comprehensive set of notes available for download at my website, www.BillsBrownstone.com.

NOTES

Abbreviations Used in Endnotes

CA—Commercial Advertiser
NYEP—New York Evening Post
NYH—New York Herald
NYT—New York Times
NYTrib—New York Tribune
WCW—Woodhull & Claflin's Weekly
NYS—New York Sun

Chapter 1

"the grand entrée" and *"the Woodhull and Claflin wing"*: NYT, Jan. 8, 1872.
"throw the Negro": NYT, May 14, 1869.
"fatherly care": Lois Beachy Underhill, *The Woman Who Ran for President: The Many Lives of Victoria Woodhull* (Bridgehampton, NY: Bridge Works, 1995), 44.
"the open sesame": Underhill, *Woman Who Ran*, 62.
VANDERBILT'S PROTÉGÉS: NYH, Jan. 22, 1870.
"A thorough-bred": CA, Feb. 5, 1870.
"We are so deafened": NYTrib, Jan. 24, 1870.
"While others": NYH, Apr. 2, 1870.
"This journal will support": WCW, May 14, 1870.
OBSCENE LITERATURE: NYT, Jan. 15, 1872.
"the moon lavishing": Heywood Broun and Margaret Leech, *Anthony Comstock: Roundsman of the Lord* (New York: Albert & Charles Boni, 1927), 57.
"A new victim": NYT, Aug. 22, 1871.
"The Evil of the Age": NYT, Aug. 23, 1871.
"You screech": WCW, Sept. 16, 1871.
"put a head on": NYH, Nov. 10, 1870.
"gambling hells": Gustav Lening, *The Dark Side of New York Life and Its Criminal Classes from Fifth Avenue down to the Five Points: A Complete Narrative of the Mysteries of New York.* (New York: Fred'k Gerhard, Ag't., 1873), 285.

Chapter 2

"friend of the family": NYTrib, Jan. 13, 1871.
"takes well" [and subsequent quotes from burlesque story]: NYH, Jan. 18, 1871.
"I've got you now" through *"Yes, and there goes"*: NYH, June 28, 1872.
"Will anyone protect me" and *"Is that you"*: Albany (NY) Argus, June 28, 1872.

"I am shot" through *"By Jove, if things"*: NYH, Jan. 7, 1872.

"Let's go to the Station-house": NYT, Jan. 6, 1872.

"Do you believe" through *"He is the gamest"*: NYH, Jan. 7, 1872.

"Is there even" and *"Keep up a good"*: NYH, Jan. 8, 1872.

"What do you think": NYH, Jan. 7, 1872.

"Is Miss Mansfield" through *"I want it distinctly"*: NYH, Jan. 7, 1872.

"Doing nicely": NYT, Jan. 8, 1872.

"Ah, they may" through *"It is not only the personal"*: NYH, Jan. 8, 1872.

"I shot him" through *"I merely wished"*: NYT, Jan. 8, 1872.

"I can only die": NYH, Jan. 8, 1871.

"That as an expression": NYT, Jan. 8, 1871.

"I am the resurrection": NYH, Jan. 6, 1871.

Chapter 3

"It is an error": Victoria Woodhull to Isabella Beecher Hooker, Oct. 19, 1871, quoted in Underhill, *Woman Who Ran*, 188.

"a good share": Edward Winslow Martin, *Behind the Scenes in Washington* (Continental Publishing, 1873), 207.

"third house": Underhill, *Woman Who Ran*, 94.

"feast his eyes": Underhill, 97.

"a shyster": Underhill, 101.

"It would ill become": WCW, Nov. 2, 1872.

"a frisky lad" and *"jerky movement"*: *Washington, DC, Evening Star*, Jan. 11, 1871.

"anthems to Woodhull": NYT, Jan. 12, 1871.

"Some day you will occupy": Barbara Goldsmith, *Other Powers: The Age of Suffrage, Spiritualism, and the Scandalous Victoria Woodhull* (London: Granta Books, 1998), 252.

THE COSMO-POLITICAL PARTY: WCW, Jan. 28, 1871.

"her guardian spirit" and *"her first discourse"*: Theodore Tilton, "Victoria C. Woodhull, A Biographical Sketch," (New York: Golden Age, 1871), 12.

"fire and freedom": *Washington Chronicle*, reprinted in WCW, Mar. 4, 1871.

"Though I may be on the far": Paulina Kellogg Wright Davis, quoted in Underhill, *Woman Who Ran*, 119.

"the grand work": WCW, Mar. 4, 1871.

"seiz[ing] the bull": WCW, Mar. 11, 1871.

"the ablest woman's journal": WCW, Mar. 4, 1871.

"Bravo! My Dear Woodhull" and *"Go Ahead!"*: WCW, Feb. 25, 1871.

"ahead of anything": Susan B. Anthony to Victoria Woodhull, Feb. 28, 1871, quoted in Mary Gabriel, *Notorious Victoria: The Uncensored Life of Victoria Woodhull—Visionary, Suffragist, and First Woman to Run for President* (Chapel Hill, NC: Algonquin Books of Chapel Hill, 1998), 87.

"who bring[s] brains": Susan B. Anthony to Isabella Beecher Hooker, Mar. 21, 1871, quoted in Goldsmith, *Other Powers*, 256.

"To show men": WCW, Oct. 18, 1873.

"That a woman had political rights": WCW, Feb. 10, 1872.

"the ability to earn" and *"the glorious freedom"*: WCW, Sep. 17, 1870.

"the gilded palaces" and *"the lowest purlieus"*: Victoria C. Woodhull, "And the Truth Shall Make You Free: A Speech on the Principles of Social Freedom," delivered at Steinway Hall, Nov. 20, 1871.

"head and front": NYH, Feb. 17, 1871.

"all the branches": WCW, Feb. 24, 1872.

"A party which would": Victoria Woodhull, speech to the Reform Labor League, May 8, 1872, in Madeleine B. Stern, ed., *The Victoria Woodhull Reader* (Weston, MA: M&S Press, 1874), 27.

"the more radical": WCW, May 12, 1871.

"sovereignty of the individual": Victoria C. Woodhull, "And the Truth Shall Make You Free: A Speech on the Principles of Social Freedom," delivered at Steinway Hall, Nov. 20, 1871.

"short cut" and *"hands are unclean"*: Mary Livermore quoted in Susan B. Anthony to Laura DeForce Gordon, Feb. 9, 1871, quoted in Goldsmith, *Other Powers*, 255.

"dirty moral linen": NYH, May 13, 1871.

"as a slander": *Albany (NY) Evening Journal*, May 11, 1871.

WOODHULL'S WOMEN: NYH, May 12, 1871.

"We honor": NYTrib, May 10, 1871.

"If Congress refuse to listen": NYTrib, May 12, 1871. Full speech in supplement to WCW, "The Great Political Issue of Constitutional Equality," Aug. 12, 1871.

"Resolved, That this Convention": NYTrib, May 13, 1871.

"best class of society" and *"terrible earnestness"*: *Washington Patriot*, Jan. 11, 1872, reprinted in WCW, Jan. 27, 1872.

"free love panic": Martha Coffin Wright to Elizabeth Cady Stanton, Mar. 22, 1872, quoted in Goldsmith, *Other Powers*, 304.

"We now propose" through *"conventionalities of red tape"*: *Washington Patriot*, Jan. 11, 1872, reprinted in WCW, Jan. 27, 1872.

"embodying the purposes" through *"a thousand other"*: NYH, Jan. 11, 1872.

"our gracious masters . . . tremble": *Washington Evening Star*, Jan. 11, 1872.

"humbugs": *Washington Evening Star*, Jan. 11, 1872.

"It is this" through *"I was asked if I knew"*: *Washington Patriot*, Jan. 11, 1872, reprinted in WCW, Jan. 27, 1872.

"Mrs. Woodhull's voice": NYH, Jan. 12, 1872.

"work for woman" through *"my whole soul does homage"*: *Washington Patriot*, Jan. 11, 1872, reprinted in WCW, Jan. 27, 1872.

"The signs of the times" through *"Woodhull for President"*: *Washington Chronicle*, reprinted in WCW, Jan. 27, 1872.

Chapter 4

"moonlight excursions": NYH, Sept. 6, 1871.

"I am too weak": NYH, Sept. 6, 1871.

"trunk affair" and *"could clear her skirts"*: NYTrib, Sept. 6, 1871.

"the murder of Alice Bowlsby": NYTrib, Sept. 6, 1871.

"Of late": NYT, Sept. 7, 1871.

"quack doctors": NYH, Sept. 6, 1871.

"committing an abortion" and *"This is worse"*: NYH, Nov. 12, 1870.

"guilty of an attempt": NYH, May 18, 1871.

"I find nothing": NYH, Feb. 11, 1872.

Chapter 5

"little wifey": Broun and Leech, *Anthony Comstock*, 65.

"So bright, so sweet": Broun and Leech, *Anthony Comstock*, 64.

"go to my Father" and *"too cold"*: Broun and Leech, 70.

"Give me a man": Broun and Leech, 69.

"the hydra-headed monster": Anthony Comstock, *Frauds Exposed; or, How the People Are Deceived and Robbed, and Youth Corrupted* (New York: J. Howard Brown, 1880), 389.

"Jesus never would wink": Broun and Leech, *Anthony Comstock*, 72.

"There's the man" through *"the female form divine"*: *New York Sunday Mercury*, Mar. 3, 1872.

"disgusting": NYT, Mar. 4, 1872.

"bawdy": NYH, Mar. 4, 1872.

"all indecent and obscene": Donna Dennis, *Licentious Gotham: Erotic Publishing and Its Prosecution in Nineteenth-Century New York* (Cambridge, MA: Harvard University Press, 2009), 100.

"the curiosity" through *"it hitch[ed]"*: Dennis, *Licentious Gotham*, 127–128.

"print representing a woman": Dennis, 147.

"Strokeall & Company" and *"Ten inches up"*: Dennis, 148.

"extreme penalty": NYT, Mar. 7, 1872.

"Tombs shyster": Anthony Comstock to Robert McBurney, Mar. 23, 1872, in Helen Lefkowitz Horowitz, *Rereading Sex: Battles over Sexual Knowledge and Suppression in Nineteenth-Century America* (New York: Alfred A. Knopf, 2002), 373.

"Get out of the way": Charles Gallaudet Trumbull, *Anthony Comstock, Fighter: Some Impressions of a Lifetime of Adventure in Conflict with the Powers of Evil* (New York: Fleming H. Revell, 1913), 62.

"It is charged by their friends": Broun and Leech, *Anthony Comstock*, 192.

Chapter 6

"Bohemian" through *"as long as a woman's"*: NYT, Mar. 17, 1872.

Chapter 7

"such unembarrassed disporting": NYT, Sept. 17, 1866.

"an exhibition": NYH, May 7, 1872.

"the only full" and *"extraordinary inducements"*: NYTrib, Feb. 17, 1872.

"The play degrades the actor": Pomeroy's Democrat (New York City), May 6, 1872.

"virtuous censors": NYEP, Apr. 23, 1872.

"great nerve": Troy (NY) Weekly, June 8, 1872.

"a worthless and tawdry": NYT, May 11, 1872.

"masculinity" through *"unworthy of a more"*: NYH, Mar. 30, 1872.

"I just want" and *"bettering the world"*: WCW, July 8, 1871.

"to drink your glass": NYT, Aug. 12, 1871.

"magnetic influence": NYH, May 15, 1872.

Chapter 8

"You killed my husband": Trumbull, *Anthony Comstock, Fighter*, 62.

"One of the few": NYT, Oct. 22, 1869.

"home, bright and cheerful" and *"There is not a room"*: Laurence Locke Doggett, *Life of Robert R. McBurney* (Cleveland, OH: F. M. Barton, 1902), 74.

"true Christian manhood": Doggett, *McBurney*, 72.

"agencies of evil": Young Men's Christian Association of the City of New York, *Fourteenth Annual Report of the Young Men's Christian Association* (New York: Published by the association, 1866), 18.

"without charge": Young Men's Christian Association of New York, *A Memorandum Respecting New-York as a Field for Moral and Christian Effort Among Young Men* (New York: Young Men's Christian Association of New York, 1866), 8.

"Feeders of brothels": YMCANY, *Memorandum Respecting New-York*, 6.

"early disappearance": NYT, Apr. 21, 1866.

"indecent and immoral use": NYH, Apr. 23, 1868.

"poor degraded souls": Broun and Leech, *Anthony Comstock*, 71.

"Fear thou not": Trumbull, *Anthony Comstock, Fighter*, 41.

"no obscene book": Horowitz, *Rereading Sex*, 358.

"It is not fair": Trumbull, *Anthony Comstock, Fighter*, 65.

"Expressman dead": Broun and Leech, *Anthony Comstock*, 93.

"Is Mac in?" and *"He's not up"*: Trumbull, *Anthony Comstock, Fighter*, 72.

"dildoes" through *"for reserved females"*: Dennis, *Licentious Gotham*, 251–52.

"Let me glory only in Him": Trumbull, *Anthony Comstock, Fighter*, 81.

Chapter 9

"Vic, Tennie": NYS, June 23, 1871.

MASCULINE COSTUME: NYS, Oct. 3, 1870.

"*My daughters were good*" through "*S'help me god*": *NYH*, May 16, 1871.

"*one of the most*": *NYT*, May 22, 1871.

"*the presidency of the United States*": Gabriel, *Notorious Victoria*, 126.

"*a prominent gentleman*": *Brooklyn Eagle*, May 8, 1871.

"*h'aint no friends of mine*": Goldsmith, *Other Powers*, 273.

HONOR THE MARTYRS: *NYS*, Dec. 18, 1871.

"*frightful hobgoblin*" and "*the silly fables*": *WCW*, Dec. 30, 1871.

"*like herrings*": *NYH*, Feb. 21, 1872.

"*Six hundred millions*" and "*Vanderbilt may sit*": Victoria C. Woodhull, *A Speech on the Impending Revolution* (New York: Woodhull, Claflin, 1872), 9–13.

"*the largest mass of people*" and "*an intolerable bore*": *WCW*, Mar. 2, 1872.

"*Mrs. Victoria C. Woodhull*": *NYT*, Feb. 22, 1872.

BE SAVED BY FREE LOVE: *Harper's Weekly*, Feb. 17, 1872.

"*a fit companion*": *WCW*, Feb. 23, 1872.

"*Vic, oh where is Vic?*": *NYH*, Mar. 15, 1872.

"*Victoria Leagues*": *WCW*, Aug. 12, 1871.

"*ever find a warm*" and "*sincere friends*": *WCW*, Mar. 23, 1872.

"*People's Convention*" through "*Every individual who believes*": *WCW*, Apr. 6, 1872.

MAGNIFICENT BEATS: *WCW*, Apr. 6, 1872.

"*awful and herculean*": *WCW*, June 3, 1871.

"*Have you been deceived*": *WCW*, Apr. 6, 1872.

"*Tit for Tat*": *WCW*, Mar. 1, 1873.

Chapter 10

"*how many blasted*": *NYT*, Aug. 23, 1871.

"*we understand every*": *NYT*, Aug. 23, 1871.

"*This alleged female*": *NYH*, Apr. 3, 1872.

"*25 years' successful practice*": *NYH*, Apr. 4, 1872.

"*a particular judge*": *Charges of the Bar Association of New York Against Hon. George G. Barnard and Hon. Albert Cardozo, and Testimony Thereunder Taken Before the Judiciary Committee of the Assembly of the State of New York*, 1872, 439.

"*quickened*": Clifford Browder, *The Wickedest Woman in New York: Madame Restell, the Abortionist* (Hamden, CT: Archon Books, 1988), 137–138.

ANOTHER WORTHLESS COURT: *NYEP*, Apr. 9, 1872.

Chapter 11

"*defended*": *Jackson (MI) Citizen*, Feb. 6, 1872.

"*run[ning] our craft*" and "*men's spirits*": Ida Husted Harper, *The Life and Work of Susan B. Anthony* (Indianapolis: Hollenbeck, 1898), 1:413.

PEOPLE'S CONVENTION and "*The undersigned citizens*": *WCW*, Apr. 6, 1872.

"*This Liberal Republican movement*": *Cincinnati Daily Times*, Apr. 30, 1872.

"*ragged & torn*": Susan B. Anthony to Martha Coffin Wright, May 22, 1872, in Ann D. Gordon, ed., *The Selected Papers of Elizabeth Cady Stanton and Susan B. Anthony* (New Brunswick, NJ: Rutgers University Press, 2000), 2:496.

"*the sexual liaisons*": Goldsmith, *Other Powers*, 317.

"*Called on Mrs. Phelps*": Susan B. Anthony, diary entry, May 6, 1872, in Stanton and Anthony, *Selected Papers*, 2:492.

"*The eyes of the world*": Underhill, *Woman Who Ran*, 205.

"*The fiasco perfect*": Susan B. Anthony, diary entry, May 10, 1872, in Stanton and Anthony, *Selected Papers*, 2:493.

"*From this convention*" through "*I propose*": *NYH*, May 11, 1872.

"*denunciating*" and "*glorious triumph*": Goldsmith, *Other Powers*, 320.

"party is mindful": "Republican Party Platform of 1872," June 5, 1872, The American Presidency Project (website), Gerhard Peters and John T. Wooley, accessed Sept. 18, 2019, https://www.presidency.ucsb .edu/documents/republican-party-platform-1872.
"swallowing Cincinnati hoofs": Harper, *Susan B. Anthony*, 1:418.
"clutch it as the drowning": Harper, 1:417.

Chapter 12

"spirit of improvement": *NYH*, May 4, 1872.
"You dirty sucker": *NYT*, May 26, 1872.
"as drunk as" and *"May Ames take"*: *NYH*, June 7, 1872.

Chapter 13

"the Free-Lovers' convention": *Day's Doings*, in Amanda Frisken, *Victoria Woodhull's Sexual Revolution: Political Theater and the Popular Press in Nineteenth-Century America* (Philadelphia: University of Pennsylvania Press, 204), 69.
"Women's Rights, Free Love": *Charleston (SC) Daily Courier*, May 13, 1872.
"semi-lunatics" and *"whatever ought to be is"*: *Philadelphia Inquirer*, May 14, 1872, in Frisken, *Sexual Revolution*, 70.
"Mr. Greeley now has": *Rochester (NY) Democrat and Chronicle*, May 13 and 14, 1872, quoted in Frisken, *Sexual Revolution*, 70.
A PIEBALD PRESIDENCY through *"a male brunette"*: *NYH*, May 11, 1872.
"strange combination": *Philadelphia Inquirer*, May 14, 1872.
"Is Woodhull degraded": *Eugene (OR) Guard*, reprinted in *New Northwest* (Portland, OR), May 31, 1872, quoted in Frisken, *Sexual Revolution*, 71.
"Here is a ticket": *New York Evening Telegram*, May 11, 1872, quoted in Frisken, *Sexual Revolution*, 74.
"an outrage by women": *Pomeroy's Democrat*, May 18, 1872.
A FRENZIED NEGRO COACHMAN: *Day's Doings*, June 15, 1872, quoted in Frisken, *Sexual Revolution*, 74.
"dared men": Frisken, *Sexual Revolution*, 23.
"brazen adventuress": *San Francisco Chronicle*, May 14, 1872.
"maggots which vexed the brains": *Washington Daily Critic*, May 14, 1872.
"free-love high priestess": *West Jersey Press* (Camden, NJ), May 15, 1872.
NATIONALIZE LAND through *"Yes, Victoria"*: *NYS*, June 7, 1872.
"a platform which strikes": *NYH*, June 5, 1872.
"workmen with hammers" and *"the dust, dirt"*: *Pomeroy's Democrat*, May 25, 1872.
"stone at first": *WCW*, June 15, 1872.
"The secret of the final": *Woman's Journal*, Aug. 3, 1872.

Chapter 14

"get square": *NYH*, July 2, 1872.
"scrutinized the filthy things": *NYH*, June 29, 1872.
"The Lord's will be done" and *"own precious Lillie"*: Broun and Leech, *Anthony Comstock*, 67.
"Eve" through *"obscene department"*: *NYH*, July 2, 1872.
"What Folly!" and *"Oh, to live"*: Trumbull, *Anthony Comstock, Fighter*, 84.
"Beautiful and rare photographs": *New York Clipper*, June 13, 1872.
"racy books": *New York Clipper*, Aug. 23, 1872.
"Recollect, none of the above" through *"French tickler"*: Dennis, *Licentious Gotham*, 261.
"the great thoroughfare": Comstock, *Frauds Exposed*, 391.
"tribe" and *"inflexible resolution"*: *NYT*, Aug. 28, 1872.
"too indecent": *National Archives Indictment Records, Criminal Docket, Volume 2, US Circuit Court, 1864–1872*, Henry Camp, 374; David Massey, 275; Charles Mackey, 376; Edward Grandin, 377.

Chapter 15

"Filthy as a Digger Indian's cave": *Pomeroy's Democrat*, June 16, 1872.
"Society . . . will have" through *"Isn't he good looking?"*: *NYH*, June 19, 1872.
"whose minds were": *NYH*, June 27, 1872.
"Oyez! Oyez!": *NYH*, July 11, 1872.
"I've got you now": *NYH*, June 28, 1872.
"blood money" and *"the rumble of ambulance"*: *NYH*, July 3, 1872.
"What a change" and *"with a look"*: *NYH*, July 9, 1872.
"Don't fire" [and the remainder of Stokes's testimony]: *NYH*, July 9, 1872.
"said unless" [and the remainder of Mansfield's testimony]: *NYH*, July 9, 1872.
"nature speaking" and *"the imprisoned mind"*: *NYH*, July 14, 1872.
"I understand" through *"I do not care"*: *NYH*, July 15, 1872.
"Sixpence a head": Howe & Hummel, "Autobiographical," *Danger! A True History of a Great City's Wiles and Temptations* (Buffalo, NY: Courier, 1886).
"My God": Edgar Salinger, letter to the editor, *New Yorker*, Dec. 28, 1946.

Chapter 16

"Ladies' Physician": *NYH*, Aug. 14, 1872.
"ante-natal murderesses" through *"relief from trouble"*: Anthony Comstock, *Traps for the Young* (New York: Funk & Wagnulls, 1883), 154.

Chapter 17

"skillful and grotesque" and *"Worth a hot night"*: *CA*, Aug. 13, 1872.
"Adultery served": *NYT*, Aug. 1, 1872.
"so gloomy": *NYT*, Aug. 25, 1872.
"We have our doubts": *NYEP*, Aug. 5, 1872.
"to brighten the stage" and *"brilliantly inaugurated"*: *NYH*, Aug. 27, 1872.

Chapter 18

"Give me war": Debby Applegate, *The Most Famous Man in America* (New York: Tree Leaves Press, Doubleday, 2006), 327.
"I need some little" and *"My Darling Queen"*: Victoria Woodhull to Isabella Beecher Hooker, quoted in Goldsmith, *Other Powers*, 267, 271.
"A Citizen in Hartford": *Hartford (CT) Daily Courant*, Nov. 14, 1871.
"terrible wash of dirty linen": Harriett Beecher Stowe, *My Wife and I: or, Harry Henderson's History* (New York: Houghton, Mifflin, 1871), 266.
"Remember, Victoria Woodull": *WCW*, May 17, 1873.
"personal and social magnetism" through *"I do not seem to think"*: Milton Allan Rugoff, *The Beechers: An American Family in the Nineteenth Century* (New York: Harper & Row, 1981), 369–372.
"I came to love": Goldsmith, *Other Powers*, 90.
"Have you come to see me?" through *"I felt that I ought not"*: *WCW*, Nov. 2, 1872.
"That that damned lecherous": *WCW*, Nov. 2, 1872.
"No woman shall stand": Elizabeth Cady Stanton, interview in the *Brooklyn Argus*, July 26, 1873, in *The Great Brooklyn Romance: All the Documents in the Famous Beecher-Tilton Case, Unabridged* (New York: P. H. Paxon, 1874), 34–35, https://ia802909.us.archive.org/35/items/greatbrooklynrom00newy/greatbrooklynrom00newy.pdf.
"I do not intend" through *"I believe in public justice"*: *NYT*, May 22, 1871.
"Whom do" and *"I mean you"*: *WCW*, Nov. 2, 1872.
"opiates": Rugoff, *Beechers*, 380.
"Some day you" through *"Mr. Beecher, if I am compelled"*: *WCW*, Nov. 2, 1872.

"Yes, I am": Victoria C. Woodhull, "And the Truth Shall Make You Free: A Speech on the Principles of Social Freedom," delivered at Steinway Hall, Nov. 20, 1871.

"The lecture in itself": *Pomeroy's Democrat*, Nov. 25, 1871.

"though its thunders" and *"braying Ass"*: *WCW*, Dec. 9, 1871.

"one of the dirtiest": *Independent*, Nov. 23, 1871, quoted in Gabriel, *Notorious Victoria*, 150.

"Will you lend": Victoria Woodhull to Henry Ward Beecher, June 3, 1872, reprinted in *NYH*, Aug. 22, 1874.

"And please drop me a line": Henry Ward Beecher to Frank Moulton, June 3, 1872, reprinted in *NYH*, Aug. 22, 1874.

"trooly loil" through *"the proud daughters"*: *Memphis Sunday Appeal*, Nov. 17, 1872.

"a disgraceful tirade": *Springfield (MA) Republican*, Oct. 1, 1872.

"vile vituperation": *Boston Herald*, Sept. 11, 1872.

"never equaled in vulgarity": *Boston Herald*, Sept. 30, 1872.

"obscene calumnies": *Hartford (CT) Courant*, Sept. 21, 1872.

Chapter 19

"as refreshing" and *"jubilant joy"*: J. E. P. Doyle, comp., *Plymouth Church and Its Pastor, or Henry Ward Beecher and His Accusers* (St. Louis: Bryan, Brand, 1875), 214.

"There is nothing secret": *WCW*, Dec. 28, 1872.

To the Public: *WCW*, Nov. 2, 1872.

"spring chickens" and *"the red trophy"*: The Philosophy of Modern Hypocrisy, *WCW*, Nov. 2, 1872.

The Beecher-Tilton Scandal through *"If an omelet has to be made"*: *WCW*, Nov. 2, 1872.

"Eloquent and Thrilling": *Chicago Post*, Oct. 22, 1872.

"animated and dashing" and *"a new, simple"*: *Chicago Times*, Oct. 28, 1872, reprinted in *Cincinnati Commercial Tribune*, Oct. 31, 1872.

"Weekly with the Beecher scandal": *WCW*, Dec. 28, 1872.

"last and most desperate": *Springfield (MA) Republican*, Oct. 30, 1872.

"If there is any": *Portland (ME) Daily*, Oct. 30, 1872.

Chapter 20

"obscene book, pamphlet": Coverage of 1865 federal obscenity statute in Dennis, *Licentious Gotham*, 254.

"They are arrested on a charge" through *"The idea of the government vindicating"*: *NYH*, Nov. 3, 1872.

"Fifth Avenue" and *"citizen's bedroom"*: *NYH*, Nov. 3, 1872.

"the seed from which": *NYH*, Nov. 4, 1872.

"I tell you, Nettie" [and other comments at Plymouth Church choir practice]: *Sunday Mercury*, Nov. 3, 1872.

"For it is God": *Brooklyn Eagle*, Nov. 4, 1872.

Chapter 21

"Let no Republican": *NYT*, Nov. 5, 1872.

"the great Presidential battle" and *"dreadful note of preparation"*: *NYH*, Nov. 4, 1872.

"Let the Best Men Win": *NYH*, Nov. 5, 1872.

"Old Kaintuck": *NYT*, Nov. 6, 1872.

Horace Gone West and His Hangers-on: *NYT*, Nov. 6, 1872.

"There was nothing purchasable": *NYT*, Nov. 7, 1872.

"destitute of principle" and *"as much open"*: *NYT*, Nov. 8, 1872.

"confine its attentions": *NYT*, Nov. 7, 1872.

"He is not the worst beaten individual": *Illinois State Register*, Nov. 19, 1872.

Today's Breakfast Table: *NYT*, Nov. 5, 1872.

"Do you swear that you will fully" and *"Do you swear that you are"*: Election Laws of the United States and the New York State Registry Laws, Relating to Registration and Elections in the Incorporated Cities of the State, (New York and Brooklyn Excepted,) and in Incorporated Villages of the State Containing

over Ten Thousand Inhabitants together with Forms and Instructions for the Guidance of Supervisors and Inspectors of Election (Issued under the Direction of Charles M. Dennison, Chief Supervisor of Elections, N. D. of N. Y., 1876, 21–22).

"ladies at Rochester": NYT, Nov. 6, 1872.

Chapter 22

"in the name": NYH, Nov. 9, 1872.
"for a thousand years" and *"a spiritual glow"*: Sunday Mercury, Nov. 10, 1872.
"She is the individual" through *"Your Honor, when I represent"*: NYH, Nov. 10, 1872.
"Do you know a Mr. Cutler" [and the remainder of Challis's testimony]: NYH, Nov. 10, 1872.
"spring chickens" [and the remainder of Woodhull's testimony]: NYH, Nov. 10, 1872.
"very familiarly" and *"Good evening, Mother"*: NYH, Nov. 10, 1872.
"Did you ever hear" and *"the red trophy of her virginity"*: NYH, Nov. 10, 1872.
"words that were imputed": NYH, Nov. 10, 1872.
"Mr. Beecher, this thing" and *"Entirely"*: Jamestown (NY) Journal, Nov. 22, 1872.
"red hot" and *"Their next"*: Sunday Mercury, Nov. 10, 1872.

Chapter 23

"How do you like it here?" through *"Justice! I'm damn sorry"*: NYS, Jan. 31, 1872.
"an error": NYH, Nov. 23, 1872.

Chapter 24

How a Gross Scandal and *"two women of bad reputation"*: Brooklyn Eagle, Nov. 15, 1872.
"cannot too soon": Brooklyn Eagle, Nov. 19, 1872.
"ranged itself" and *"ranged himself"*: Brooklyn Eagle, Nov. 23, 1872.
"publishers, manufacturers": NYT, Mar. 15, 1873.
"the exterminator": Chicago Post, Nov. 28, 1872.

Chapter 25

"Moral Cowardice": WCW, Dec. 28, 1872.
"The Distinguished Lady Bankers": Boston Journal, Dec. 16, 1872, and Boston Traveler, Dec. 17, 1872.
"We have bad women enough": WCW, Jan. 25, 1873.
"Stop their press": Springfield (MA) Republican, Dec. 21, 1872.

Chapter 26

"Is this your usual method": Harper, Susan B. Anthony, 1:426.
"without having a lawful right": Enforcement Act of 1870, section 19, excerpted in Ann D. Gordon, The Trial of Susan B. Anthony (Federal Judicial Center, Federal Judicial History Office, 2005), 52.
"Not a particle": Harper, Susan B. Anthony, 1:427.
"the indispensable ingredient": Gordon, Trial of Susan B. Anthony, 3.
"If the former": Harper, Susan B. Anthony, 1:429.

Chapter 27

"paradise for murderers": Pomeroy's Democrat, Nov. 16, 1872.
"Down with the Assassins": CA, Nov. 19, 1872.
"Reign of Murder": NYH, Nov. 20, 1872.
"Is hanging for murder": NYTrib, Nov. 20, 1872.

"As God shall judge me": *New York World*, Dec. 19, 1872, reprinted in *Albany (NY) Argus*, Dec. 20, 1872.
"Gentlemen, have you agreed" through *"Guilty of murder in the first degree"*: NYH, Jan. 5, 1873.
"upon that day": NYH, Jan. 7, 1873.

Chapter 28

"What can I do" and *"Mr. Beecher, I am not a Christian"*: Frank Moulton Statement to the Public, Aug. 24, 1874, in *Great Brooklyn Romance*, 253.
"tripartite covenant" and *"all causes of offense"*: The Tripartite Convention, Apr. 2, 1872, in *Great Brooklyn Romance*, 41–42.
"unguarded enthusiasm" and *"utterly untrue"*: *Theodore Tilton vs. Henry Ward Beecher, Action for Crim. Con. Tried in the City Court of Brooklyn, Chief Justice Joseph Neilson, Presiding, Verbatim Report by the Official Stenographer* (New York: McDivitt, Campbell, 1875), 1:422.
"Confide to me": Isabella Beecher Hooker to Henry Ward Beecher, Nov. 1, 1872, in *Great Brooklyn Romance*, 262.
"Do not fail me": Isabella Beecher Hooker to Henry Ward Beecher, Nov. 27, 1872, in *Great Brooklyn Romance*, 266–267.
"What is to be done?" and *"Give me the letters"*: *Theodore Tilton vs. Henry Ward Beecher*, 1:424.
"to the pillory": Goldsmith, *Other Powers*, 357.
"The people were fooled": *Detroit Weekly Tribune*, Nov. 29, 1872.
"in the embraces": *Pomeroy's Democrat*, Dec. 7, 1872.
"Well, we always": *Theodore Tilton vs. Henry Ward Beecher*, 1:426.
"True Story": *Theodore Tilton vs. Henry Ward Beecher*, 1:429.
"A Complaining Friend" and *"You urge"*: Theodore Tilton to the *Brooklyn Eagle*, Dec. 27, 1872, in *Great Brooklyn Romance*, 360–361.
"vague, fast and loose letter": *Brooklyn Eagle* editorial, quoted in *Charleston (SC) Daily News*, Jan. 14, 1873.
"blow after blow": Elizabeth Tilton to Theodore Tilton, Dec. 28, 1872, in *Great Brooklyn Romance*, 361.

Chapter 29

"something for Jesus": Broun and Leech, *Anthony Comstock*, 116.
"Present Situation": WCW, Dec. 28, 1872.
"The Naked Truth": NYH, Jan. 4, 1873.
"In my heart": Broun and Leech, *Anthony Comstock*, 117.
"lily-livered loons" through *"the personification"*: WCW, Feb. 8, 1873.
"Yes, I am here": CA, Jan. 10, 1873.
"You are filling": WCW, Feb. 8, 1873.
"male prostitute": NYH, Jan. 14, 1873.
"malignancy unprecedented": CA, Jan. 10, 1873.
"the point of a bayonet": CA, Jan. 22, 1873.
"The Fearless": *Daily Albany (NY) Argus*, Apr. 18, 1873.
"took a scalpel": WCW, Feb. 22, 1873.
"a bouquet of advertisements" through *"Modest and Delicate"*: WCW, Feb. 15, 1873.

Chapter 30

"Blessed are they": Anthony Comstock, diary entry, Feb. 1873, in Broun and Leech, *Anthony Comstock*, 120–121.
"my bill": Trumbull, *Anthony Comstock, Fighter*, 90.
"I am an employee": D. M. Bennett, *Anthony Comstock: His Career of Cruelty and Crime* (New York: Liberal and Scientific Publishing House, 1878), 1,028–1,029.
"Special Agent": Anthony Comstock, diary entry, Feb. 17, 1873, in Broun and Leech, *Anthony Comstock*, 136.

"subvert the people" through *"to put the United States Mail Service"*: WCW, Feb. 22, 1873.
"cheerless leaving": Anthony Comstock, diary entry, Feb. 1873, in Broun and Leech, *Anthony Comstock*, 137.
Comstock's Christianity: NYH, Feb. 24, 1873.
"The exhibitions of today": Anthony Comstock, diary entry, Feb. 1873, in Broun and Leech, *Anthony Comstock*, 138–139.
"Remember the Sabbath day" through *"Thy will be done"*: Trumbull, *Anthony Comstock, Fighter*, 95–99.

Chapter 31

I am a Polander: NYT, Feb. 14, 1873.
"all acts and parts of acts": Laws of the State of New York Passed at the Ninety-fifth Session of the Legislature, Begun January Second, and Ended May Fourteenth, 1872, in the City of Albany (Albany: V. W. M. Brown, 1872), 1:509–510.
"broadside" and *"counsel more familiar"*: CA, Feb. 10, 1873.

Chapter 32

"with regret": NYT, Feb. 16, 1873.
"Poor fellow": NYH, Mar. 1, 1873.
"the awful toilet": NYH, Mar. 22, 1873.
"It's too long": NYH, Mar. 22, 1873.
"Stokes downcast?": NYH, May 5, 1873.

Chapter 33

"assailed by a nameless animal": *Albany (NY) Argus*, Dec. 3, 1872.
Beecher vs. Bowen: *Brooklyn Eagle*, Apr. 15, 1873.
The Bowen-Beecher Scandal: *Brooklyn Eagle*, Apr. 21, 1873.
"benefit his health": *Brooklyn Eagle*, May 31, 1873.
"From every stormy": *Brooklyn Eagle*, May 31, 1873.
"This I will not": *Theodore Tilton vs. Henry Ward Beecher*, 1:54.
"I will die": Henry Ward Beecher to Frank Moulton, Jan. 1, 1871 [known as "Letter of Contrition"], in *Great Brooklyn Romance*, 255.
"For two years": Henry Ward Beecher, draft of unsent resignation letter, May 31, 1873, in *Theodore Tilton vs. Henry Ward Beecher*, 1:43.
"If he publishes": *Theodore Tilton vs. Henry Ward Beecher*, 1:44.
"as befits one" through *"Your loving H.W.B."*: Henry Ward Beecher to Frank Moulton, June 1, 1873, in *Great Brooklyn Romance*, 178.
"For the Former" and *"Today is a good day"*: *Brooklyn Eagle*, June 2, 1873.
"It would be simply reported": Frank Moulton, statement to the public, Sept. 11, 1874, in *Great Brooklyn Romance*, 342.
"I don't believe": *Brooklyn Eagle*, June 2, 1873.
"Have you seen" through *"I can bear anything"*: *Theodore Tilton vs. Henry Ward Beecher*, 1:45.
"Mr. Tilton's course": *Brooklyn Eagle*, June 2, 1873.
"Go down to your church": Emma Moulton, testimony, in *Theodore Tilton vs. Henry Ward Beecher*, 1:721.
"I am a little heart-hungry": Henry Ward Beecher to Frank Moulton, July 14, 1873, in *Great Brooklyn Romance*, 338.

Chapter 34

"You must not speak" and Victoria Woodhull Dying: NYS, June 7, 1873.
"Well . . . if she wants to be willful": NYTrib, June 13, 1873.

"Is It a Crime": Harper, *Susan B. Anthony*, 1:436.

"At that time": An Account of the Proceedings on the Trial of Susan B. Anthony, on the Charge of Illegal Voting, at the Presidential Election in Nov., 1872, and on the Trial of Beverly W. Jones, Edwin T. Marsh and William B. Hall, the Inspectors of Election by Whom Her Vote Was Received (Rochester, NY: Daily Democrat and Chronicle Book Print, 1874), 6.

"She is not competent": *Proceedings on the Trial*, 14.

"It is for the jury" through *"Gentlemen of the jury"*: *Proceedings on the Trial*, 66.

"Has the prisoner" and *"Yes, your honor"*: *Proceedings on the Trial*, 81–84.

"The sentence is" and *"May it please your honor"*: *Proceedings on the Trial*, 84–85.

"I am feeling": *Brooklyn Eagle*, June 26, 1873.

"Stick to the case": *NYS*, June 27, 1873.

"I want to get": *NYS*, June 28, 1873.

"We want a verdict" through *"the court room was as empty"*: *NYH*, June 28, 1873.

"And thus ends the most" through *"No sane person"*: *WCW*, July 12, 1873.

"several month's intimacy": *WCW*, July 12, 1873.

Chapter 35

"That gentleman" and *"In shape and gesture"*: *NYH*, Aug. 7, 1873.

"Law good enough to satisfy": *NYH*, June 11, 1873.

"wretch Rosenzweig": *NYH*, Aug. 7, 1873.

"pet case" through *"In this Summer weather"*: *NYH*, July 8, 1873.

"In rendering": *NYEP*, Oct. 30, 1873.

"Guilty of manslaughter" through *"Anybody else think that?"*: *Pomeroy's Democrat*, Nov. 8, 1873.

"misery": *NYH*, Nov. 2, 1873.

"a manifest miscarriage": Howe & Hummel, *Danger*, chapter 16.

Chapter 36

"to avoid any manner": *Brooklyn Eagle*, Oct. 4, 1873.

"God is a present help": *Brooklyn Eagle*, Nov. 1, 1873.

"charges": *NYS*, Oct. 27, 1873.

"dropped from the rolls": *Brooklyn Eagle*, Nov. 1, 1873.

"if I have slandered him" through *"Are we to understand"*: *Brooklyn Eagle*, Nov. 1, 1873.

Chapter 37

"Reformation or Revolution": *NYH*, Oct. 18, 1873.

"For heaven's sake": *WCW*, Oct. 18, 1873.

"Go in, old gal" and *"Wet your whistle"*: *NYH*, Oct. 18, 1873.

"mad terror": *Nation*, Sept. 25, 1873.

"We are on the verge" [and the remainder of Woodhull's speech]: Victoria C. Woodhull, *Reformation or Revolution, Which? Or, Behind the Political Scenes* (New York: Woodhull & Claflin, 1873).

"Black Crook": *NYH*, Oct. 18, 1873.

"the crowd began to swarm": *St. Paul Daily Press*, Feb. 12, 1874, reprinted in *WCW*, Mar. 7, 1874.

"members of the senate": *Atlanta Constitution*, Feb. 10, 1876.

"ladies who were": *Cincinnati Daily Enquirer*, Nov. 7, 1875.

"hear exactly how": *Atlanta Constitution*, Feb. 10, 1876.

"the scalpel of her oratory": *Reading Times*, Oct. 22, 1874.

"the diseases that": *The Standard* (Northfield, MN), Feb. 12, 1874, reprinted in *WCW*, Mar. 7, 1874.

"in impressing the most": *Waterton Daily Times*, Sept. 1, 1875.

"That she tells much truth": *Monroe County Republican*, reprinted in *WCW*, Mar. 7, 1874.

"If you want to put": *St. Paul Pioneer*, Feb. 13, 1874, reprinted in *WCW*, Mar. 7, 1874.

"one of the two or three": *Waterton Daily Times*, Sept. 1, 1875.

"seems to speak": *Monroe County Republican*, reprinted in *WCW*, Mar. 7, 1874.

"launch[ing] forth": *Leavenworth Daily Times*, Jan. 11, 1874.

"They do say as how": *San Francisco Chronicle*, July 4, 1874.

"People's ideas now": *Cincinnati Daily Enquirer*, Nov. 7, 1875.

"masterpiece" through "and if she lives": *Waterton Dispatch*, Sept. 1, 1875, reprinted in *WCW*, Sept. 18, 1875.

"the best known woman": *Cincinnati Daily Enquirer*, Nov. 7, 1875.

"the most remarkable woman": *Waterton Dispatch*, Sept. 1, 1875, reprinted in *WCW*, Sept. 18, 1875.

"more talked and written about": *Elmira (NY) Daily Advertiser*, Sept. 14, 1875, quoted in Frisken, *Sexual Revolution*, 143.

"Victoria came; Victoria conquered": *Quincy (IL) Daily Whig*, Jan. 30, 1874.

Epilogue

"the rumors, insinuations": Henry Ward Beecher to Examining Committee of Plymouth Church, June 27, 1874, in *NYT*, July 11, 1874.

"contriving and willfully intending": *Theodore Tilton vs. Henry Ward Beecher*, 1:3.

"thrust her affections": *Theodore Tilton vs. Henry Ward Beecher*, 2:49.

"Gentlemen, you have seen": *Theodore Tilton vs. Henry Ward Beecher*, 2:85.

"It is a miracle" and "produce sufficient evidence": *Theodore Tilton vs. Henry Ward Beecher*, 3:842.

"No voice uttered": *Alexandria (VA) Gazette*, July 3, 1875.

"the old scandal": Henry Ward Beecher to a friend, Feb. 16, 1877, in Joseph Howard, *Life of Henry Ward Beecher* (Philadelphia: Hubbard Brothers, 1887), 547–548.

"the grandest woman in the world": Underhill, *Woman Who Ran*, 273.

"I wish to leave": Underhill, 273.

"I was charmed": Gabriel, *Notorious Victoria*, 247.

"She was more alive": Gabriel, 251.

"The happiest year": Underhill, *Woman Who Ran*, 286–287.

"It will be": Underhill, 301.

"We hope that you will find": Trumbull, *Anthony Comstock, Fighter*, 238.

"distinctly and disgustingly obscene" and "Not at all libidinous": *New York Evening World*, Aug. 5, 1893.

"the world's standing joke": Broun and Leech, *Anthony Comstock*, 229–230.

"It is indeed": *NYT*, Sept. 11, 1915.

BIBLIOGRAPHY

Abbot, Lyman. *Henry Ward Beecher*. New York: Houghton, Mifflin, 1903.

———. *Henry Ward Beecher: A Sketch of His Career*. New York: Funk & Wagnalls, 1883.

Abelson, Elaine S. *When Ladies Go A-thieving: Middle-Class Shoplifters in the Victorian Department Store*. New York: Oxford University Press, 1989.

An Account of the Proceedings on the Trial of Susan B. Anthony, on the Charge of Illegal Voting, at the Presidential Election in Nov., 1872, and on the Trial of Beverly W. Jones, Edwin T. Marsh and William B. Hall, the Inspectors of Election by Whom Her Vote Was Received. Rochester, NY: Daily Democrat and Chronicle Book Print, 1874.

Allen, Irving Lewis. *The City in Slang: New York Life and Popular Speech*. New York: Oxford University Press, 1993.

Anon. *The Youthful Days of Josephine Mansfield, The Beautiful Boston Girl*. New York, 1872.

Applegate, Debby. *The Most Famous Man in America: The Biography of Henry Ward Beecher*. New York: Doubleday, 2006.

Ashbee, Henry Spencer, ed. *Catena Librorum Tacendorum: Being Notes Bio- Biblio- Icono- Graphical and Critical, on Curious and Uncommon Books, by Pisanus Fraxi*. Original privately printed in London, 1885.

———, ed. *Index Librorum Prohibitorum: Being Notes Bio- Biblio- Icono- Graphical and Critical, on Curious and Uncommon Books, by Pisanus Fraxi*. Original privately printed in London, 1877.

Ashbee, Herbert. *The Gangs of New York: An Informal History of the Underworld*. Garden City, NY: Garden City Publishing, 1927.

Barclay, George Lippard. *Life, Adventures, Strange Career and Assassination of Col. James Fisk, Jr*. Philadelphia: Barclay, 1872.

Bates, Ann Louise. *Weeder in the Garden of the Lord: Anthony Comstock's Life and Career*. New York: University Press of America, 1995.

The Beecher-Tilton Scandal: A Complete History of the Case from November, 1872, to the Present Time, with Mrs. Woodhull's Statement, as Published in Woodhull & Claflin's Weekly, November 2d, 1872. New York: F. A. Bancker, 1874.

The Beecher-Tilton War: Theodore Tilton's Full Statement of the Great Preacher's Guilt; What Frank Moulton Had to Say; the Documents and Letters from Both Sides. New York: A Book of Reference, 1874.

Beisel, Nicola. *Imperiled Innocents: Anthony Comstock and Family Reproduction in Victorian America*. Princeton, NJ: Princeton University Press, 1997.

Bellesiles, Michael A. *1877: America's Year of Living Violently*. New York: New Press, 2010.

Bennett, D. M. *Anthony Comstock: His Career of Cruelty and Crime*. New York: Liberal and Scientific Publishing House, 1878.

Blake, Katherine Devereux. *Champion of Women: The Life of Lillie Devereux Blake*. New York: Fleming H. Revell, 1943.

Brands, H. W. *The Murder of Jim Fisk for the Love of Josie Mansfield: A Tragedy of the Gilded Age*. New York: Anchor Books, 2011.

Brian, Denis. *Sing Sing: The Inside Story of a Notorious Prison*. New York: Prometheus Books, 2005.

Broun, Heywood, and Margaret Leech. *Anthony Comstock: Roundsman of the Lord*. New York: Albert & Charles Boni, 1927.

Browder, Clifford. *The Wickedest Woman in New York: Madame Restell, the Abortionist*. Hamden, CT: Archon Books, 1988.

Brown, T. Allston. *A History of the New York Stage: From the First Performance in 1732 to 1901*. New York: Dodd, Mead, 1903.

Brown, William Adams. *Morris Ketchum Jesup: A Character Sketch*. New York: Charles Scribner's Sons, 1910.

Browne, Junius Henri. *The Great Metropolis: A Mirror of New York*. Hartford, CT: American Publishing, 1869.

Byrnes, Thomas. *Professional Criminals of America*. New York: Cassell, 1886.

Cheli, Guy. *Sing Sing Prison*. Images of America. Charleston, SC: Arcadia, 2003.

Clews, Henry. *Fifty Years in Wall Street*. New York: Irving, 1908.

Comstock, Anthony. *Frauds Exposed; or, How the People Are Deceived and Robbed, and Youth Corrupted*. New York: J. Howard Brown, 1880.

———. *Traps for the Young*. New York: Funk & Wagnalls, 1883.

Croffut, W. A. *The Vanderbilts and the Story of Their Fortune*. New York: Belford, Clarke, 1886.

Darwin, M. F. *One Moral Standard for All: Extracts from the Lives of Victoria Claflin Woodhull and Tennessee Claflin*. New York: Caulon, undated.

Dennis, Donna. *Licentious Gotham: Erotic Publishing and Its Prosecution in Nineteenth-Century New York*. Cambridge, MA: Harvard University Press, 2009.

Doggett, Laurence Locke. *Life of Robert R. McBurney*. Cleveland, OH: F. M. Barton, 1902.

Doyle, J. E. P., comp. *Plymouth Church and Its Pastor, or Henry Ward Beecher and His Accusers*. St. Louis: Bryan, Brand, 1875.

Ellington, George. *The Women of New York, or Social Life in the Great City*. New York: New York Book Company, 1870.

Foote, Edward B. *Medical Common Sense: Applied to the Causes, Prevention and Cure of Chronic Diseases and Unhappiness in Marriage*. Published by the author, 1864.

Fox, Richard Wightman. *Trials of Intimacy: Love and Loss in the Beecher-Tilton Scandal*. Chicago: University of Chicago Press, 1999.

Frisken, Amanda. *Victoria Woodhull's Sexual Revolution: Political Theater and the Popular Press in Nineteenth-Century America*. Philadelphia: University of Pennsylvania Press, 2004.

Gabriel, Mary. *Notorious Victoria: The Uncensored Life of Victoria Woodhull—Visionary, Suffragist, and First Woman to Run for President*. Chapel Hill, NC: Algonquin Books of Chapel Hill, 1998.

Gilfoyle, Timothy J. *City of Eros: New York City, Prostitution, and the Commercialization of Sex, 1790–1920*. New York: W. W. Norton, 1992.

Goldsmith, Barbara. *Other Powers: The Age of Suffrage, Spiritualism, and the Scandalous Victoria Woodhull*. London: Granta Books, 1998.

Goodspeed, J. W. *The Life of Col. James Fisk, Jr., "The Prince of Erie," of Miss Helen Josephine Mansfield, "The Erie Princess," of Edward L. Stokes, the Assassin, and of Hon. Wm. M. Tweed, of New York, the Notorious Leader of the Infamous Tammany Ring*. New York: H. S. Goodspeed, 1872.

Gordon, Ann D. *The Trial of Susan B. Anthony*. Federal Judicial Center, Federal Judicial History Office, 2005.

The Great Brooklyn Romance: All the Documents in the Famous Beecher-Tilton Case, Unabridged. New York: J. H. Paxon, 1874.

Harper, Ida Husted. *The Life and Work of Susan B. Anthony*. Vol 1. Indianapolis: Hollenbeck, 1898.

Hawley, Elizabeth Haven. "American Publishers of Indecent Books, 1840–1890." PhD diss., Georgia Institute of Technology, 2005.

Heywood, E. H. *Cupid's Yokes: or, The Binding Forces of Conjugal Life*. Princeton, MA: Co-operative Publishing, 1878.

Horowitz, Helen Lefkowitz. *Rereading Sex: Battles over Sexual Knowledge and Suppression in Nineteenth-Century America*. New York: Alfred A. Knopf, 2002.

Howard, Joseph. *Life of Henry Ward Beecher*. Philadelphia: Hubbard Brothers, 1887.

Howe & Hummel. *Danger! A True History of a Great City's Wiles and Temptations*. Buffalo, NY: Courier, 1886.

Huntington, Rev. Bishop. *Restel's Secret Life: A True History of Her from Birth to Her Awful Death by Her Own Wicked Hands*. Philadelphia: Old Franklin Publishing House, 1897.

Jones, Willoughby. *The Life of James Fisk, Jr., Including the Great Frauds of the Tammany Ring*. Philadelphia: Union, 1872.

Keller, Allan. *Scandalous Lady: The Life and Times of Madame Restell, New York's Most Notorious Abortionist*. New York: Atheneum, 1981.

Knox, Thomas Wallace. *Life and Work of Henry Ward Beecher*. Hartford, CT: Park, 1887.

Lane, Frederick S. *The Decency Wars: The Campaign to Cleanse American Culture.* New York: Prometheus Books, 2006.

Lening, Gustav. *The Dark Side of New York Life and Its Criminal Classes from Fifth Avenue down to the Five Points: A Complete Narrative of the Mysteries of New York.* New York: Fred'k Gerhard, Ag't., 1873.

Lerner, Renée Lettow. "Thomas Nast's Crusading Legal Cartoons." *Green Bag Almanac,* 2011.

Macrae, David. *The Americans at Home: Pen-and-Ink Sketches of American Men, Manners, and Institutions.* Edinburgh: Edmonston and Douglas, 1870.

Marshall, Charles F. *The True History of the Brooklyn Scandal.* Philadelphia: National Publishing, 1874.

Martin, Edward Winslow. *Behind the Scenes in Washington.* Continental Publishing, 1873.

———. *The Secrets of the Great City: A Work Descriptive of the Virtues and the Vices, the Mysteries, Miseries and Crimes of New York City.* Philadelphia, PA: Jones, Brother, 1868.

McAllister, Ward. *Society as I Have Found It.* New York: Cassell, 1890.

McAlpine, R. W. *The Life and Times of Col. James Fisk, Jr.* New York: New York Book Company, 1872.

McCabe, James D., Jr. *Lights and Shadows of New York Life; or, The Sights and Sensations of the Great City.* Philadelphia: National Publishing, 1872.

Morris, Lloyd. *Incredible New York: High Life and Low Life from 1850 to 1950.* New York: Syracuse University Press, 1951.

Morum, Speculator. *Bibliotheca Arcana, Catalogus Librorum Penetralium: Being Brief Notices of Books That Have Been Secretly Printed, Prohibited by Law, Seized, Anathematized, Burnt or Bowdlerised.* London: George Redway, 1885.

Moss, Frank. *The American Metropolis: From Knickerbocker Days to the Present Time; New York City in All Its Various Phases.* London: The Authors' Syndicate, 1897.

Murphy, Cait. *Scoundrels in Law: The Trials of Howe and Hummel, Lawyers to the Gangsters, Cops, Starlets, and Rakes Who Made the Gilded Age.* New York: HarperCollins, 2010.

National Association for the Amendment of the Constitution. *Constitution and Addresses of the National Association of the Constitution of the United States.* Published by the association, 1864.

Oliver, Leon. *The Great Sensation.* Chicago: Beverly Company, 1873.

Paine, Albert Bigelow. *Th. Nast: His Period and His Pictures.* New York: Macmillan, 1904.

Pictorial History of the Beecher-Tilton Scandal: Its Origin, Progress and Trial, Illustrated with Fifty Engravings from Accurate Sketches. New York: Frank Leslie, 1875.

Pirok, Alena R. "Mrs. Satan's Penance: The New History of Victoria Woodhull." *Legacy* 11, no. 1 (2011): 34–50.

Pratt, Frank. "Sketch of Life of Anthony Comstock, Taken Down Stenographically, from His Own Words on Friday Evening, December 17, 1886, at the Massasoit House, Springfield, Massachusetts." Typescript, in Comstock biographical file, Kautz Family YMCA Archives.

Rovere, Richard H. *Howe & Hummel: Their True and Scandalous History.* New York: Farrar, Straus and Giroux, 1947.

Rugoff, Milton Allan. *The Beechers: An American Family in the Nineteenth Century.* New York: Harper & Row, 1981.

Sachs, Emanie. *The Terrible Siren: Victoria Woodhull.* New York: Harper & Brothers, 1928.

Sante, Luc. *Low Life: Lures and Snares of Old New York.* New York: Farrar, Straus and Giroux, 1991.

Searle, W. S. "Beecher's Personality." *North American Review* (May 1, 1887): 487–497.

Shaplen, Robert. *Free Love and Heavenly Sinners: The Story of the Great Henry Ward Beecher Scandal.* New York: Alfred A. Knopf, 1954.

Smith, Matthew Hale. *Bulls and Bears of New York: With the Crisis of 1873, and the Cause.* Hartford, CT: J. B. Burr, 1875.

———. *Sunshine and Shadow in New York.* Hartford, CT: J. B. Burr, 1868.

———. *Twenty Years Among the Bulls and Bears of Wall Street.* Hartford, CT: J. B. Burr, 1871.

Stafford, Marshall P. *The Life of James Fisk, Jr.: Being a Full and Accurate Narrative of All the Enterprises in Which He Has Been Engaged, Together with an Account of His Tragic Death.* Published by the author, 1872.

Stanton, Elizabeth Cady, and Susan B. Anthony. *The Selected Papers of Elizabeth Cady Stanton and Susan B. Anthony.* Edited by Ann D. Gordon. Vol. 2, *Against an Aristocracy of Sex, 1866 to 1873.* New Brunswick, NJ: Rutgers University Press, 2000.

Stanton, Elizabeth Cady, Susan B. Anthony, and Matilda Joslyn Gage. *A History of Woman Suffrage*. Rochester, NY: Charles Mann, 1887.

Stern, Madeleine B. *The Pantarch: A Biography of Stephen Pearl Andrews*. Austin: University of Texas Press, 1968.

———, ed. *The Victoria Woodhull Reader*. Weston, MA: M&S Press, 1874.

Stone, William L. *History of New York City: From the Discovery to the Present Day*. New York: E. Cleave, 1868.

Stowe, Harriet Beecher. *My Wife and I: or, Harry Henderson's History*. New York: Houghton, Mifflin, 1871.

Strong, Theron G. *Landmarks of a Lawyer's Lifetime*. New York: Dodd, Mead, 1914.

Sutton, Charles. *The New York Tombs: Its Secrets and Its Mysteries; Being a History of Noted Criminals, with Narratives of Their Crimes*. San Francisco: A. Roman, 1874.

Swanberg, W. A. *Jim Fisk: The Career of an Improbable Rascal*. New York: Charles Scribner's Sons, 1959.

Theodore Tilton vs. Henry Ward Beecher, Action for Crim. Con. Tried in the City Court of Brooklyn, Chief Justice Joseph Neilson, Presiding, Verbatim Report by the Official Stenographer. 3 vols. New York: McDivitt, Campbell, 1875.

Thompson, Noyes L. *The History of Plymouth Church*. New York: G. W. Carleton, 1873.

Tilton, Theodore. *Victoria C. Woodhull: A Biographical Sketch*. New York: Golden Age, 1871.

Todd, John. *Serpents in the Doves' Nest*. Boston: Lee and Shepard, 1867.

Tone, Andrea. *Devices & Desires: A History of Contraceptives in America*. New York: Hill and Wang, 2001.

Tracy, Benjamin F. *The Case of Henry Ward Beecher: Opening Address by Benjamin F. Tracy, of Counsel for the Defendant*. New York: George W. Smith, 1875.

Train, Arthur. *Courts and Criminals*. New York: McKinlay Stone & MacKenzie, 1912.

———. *True Stories of Crime from the District Attorney's Office*. New York: Charles Scribner's Sons, 1912.

Trumbull, Charles Gallaudet. *Anthony Comstock, Fighter: Some Impressions of a Lifetime of Adventure in Conflict with the Powers of Evil*. New York: Fleming H. Revell, 1913.

Twain, Mark. *Mark Twain's Letters*. Vol. 5, *1872–1873*, edited by Lin Salamo and Harriet E. Smith. Oakland: University of California Press, 1997.

Underhill, Lois. *The Woman Who Ran for President: The Many Lives of Victoria Woodhull*. Bridgehampton, NY: Bridge Works, 1995.

Walker, Edwin C. *Who Is the Enemy: Anthony Comstock or You?* New York: Published by the author, 1903.

Waller, Altina. *Reverend Beecher and Mrs. Tilton: Sex and Class in Victorian America*. Amherst: University of Massachusetts Press, 1982.

Werbel, Amy. *Lust: Censorship and the Rise of American Obscenity in the Age of Comstock*. New York: Columbia University Press, 2018.

White, Bouck. *The Book of Daniel Drew: A Glimpse of the Fisk-Gould-Tweed Régime from the Inside*. New York: Doubleday, Page, 1910.

Woodhull, Victoria. *Selected Writings of Victoria Woodhull: Suffrage, Free Love, and Eugenics*. Edited by Cari M. Carpenter. Lincoln: University of Nebraska Press, 2010.

———. *A Speech on the Impending Revolution*. New York: Woodhull, Claflin, 1872.

Young Men's Christian Association of the City of New York. *Annual Reports, 1865–1874*.

———. *A Memorandum Respecting New-York as a Field for Moral and Christian Effort Among Young Men*. New York: Young Men's Christian Association of New York, 1866.

INDEX

Page numbers in italics refer to images.